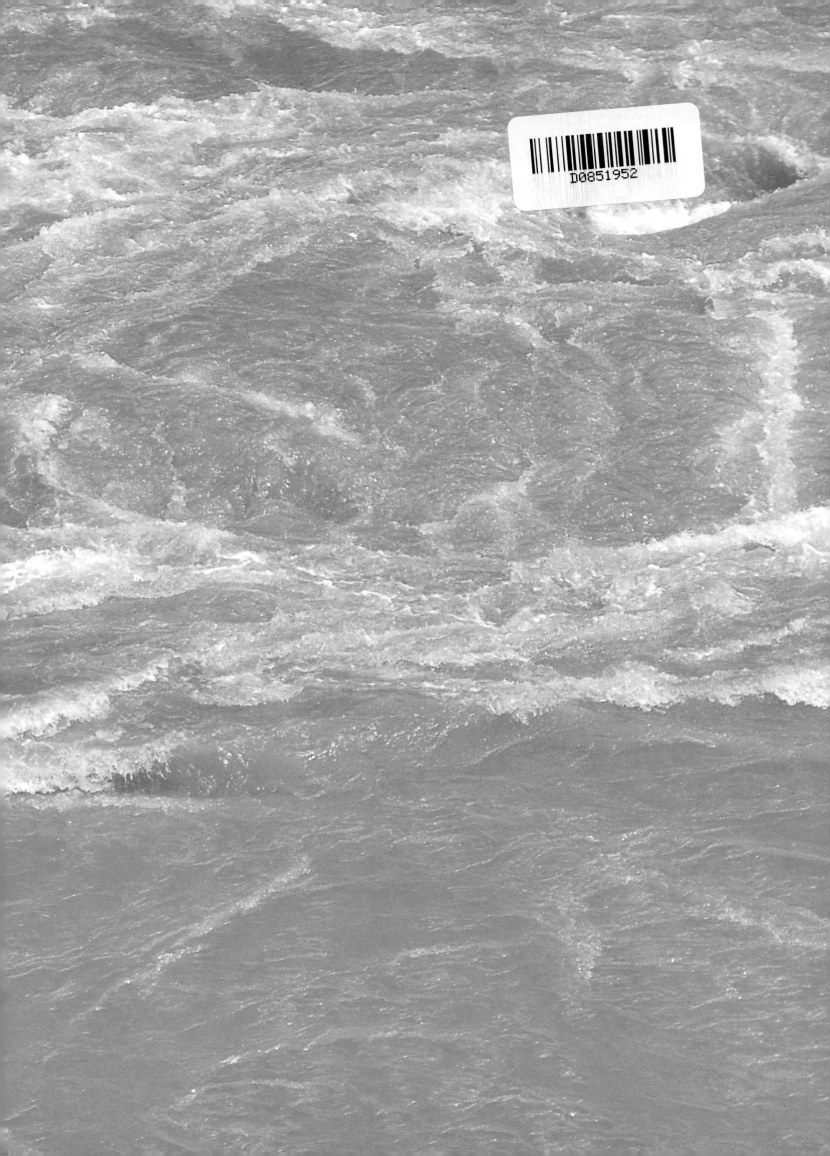

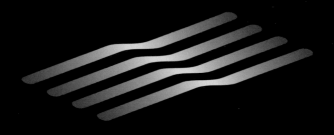

THE FRASER RIVER

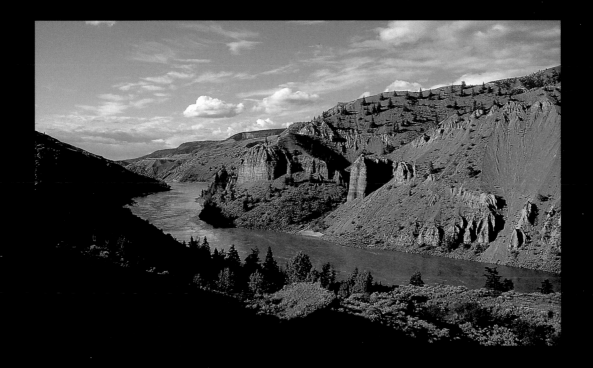

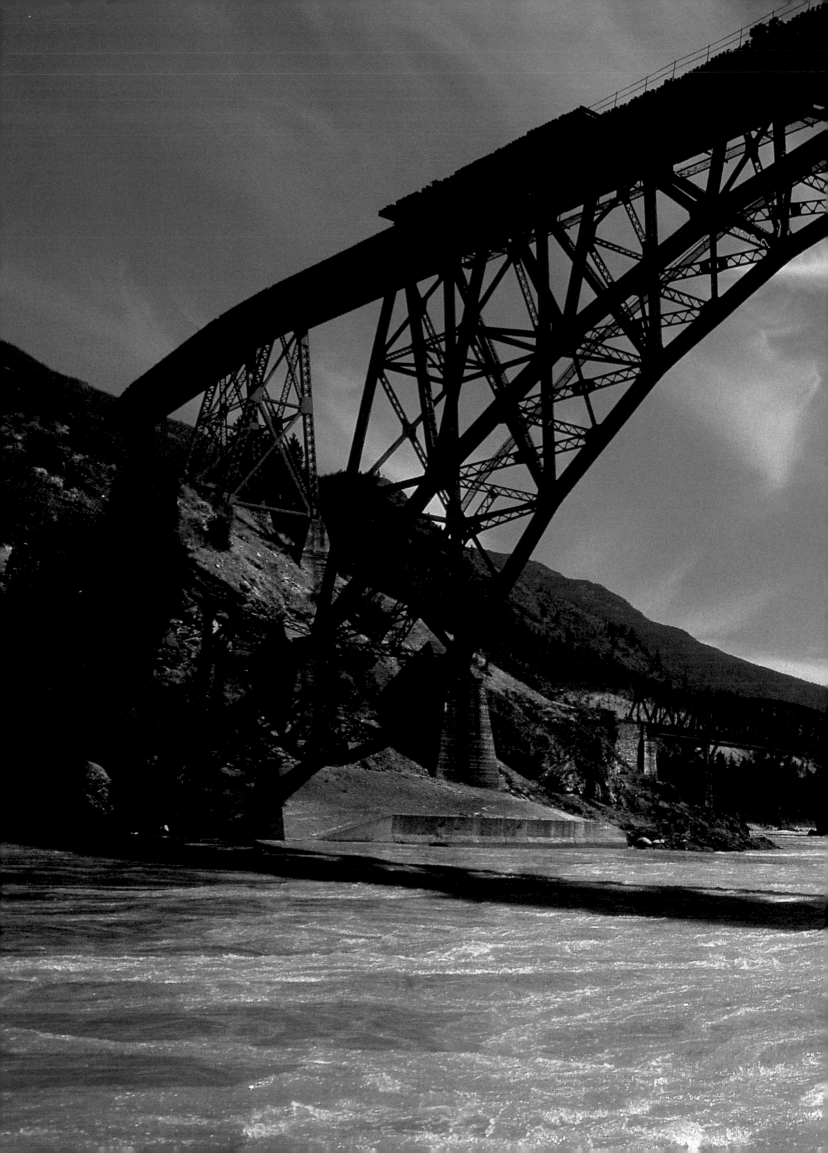

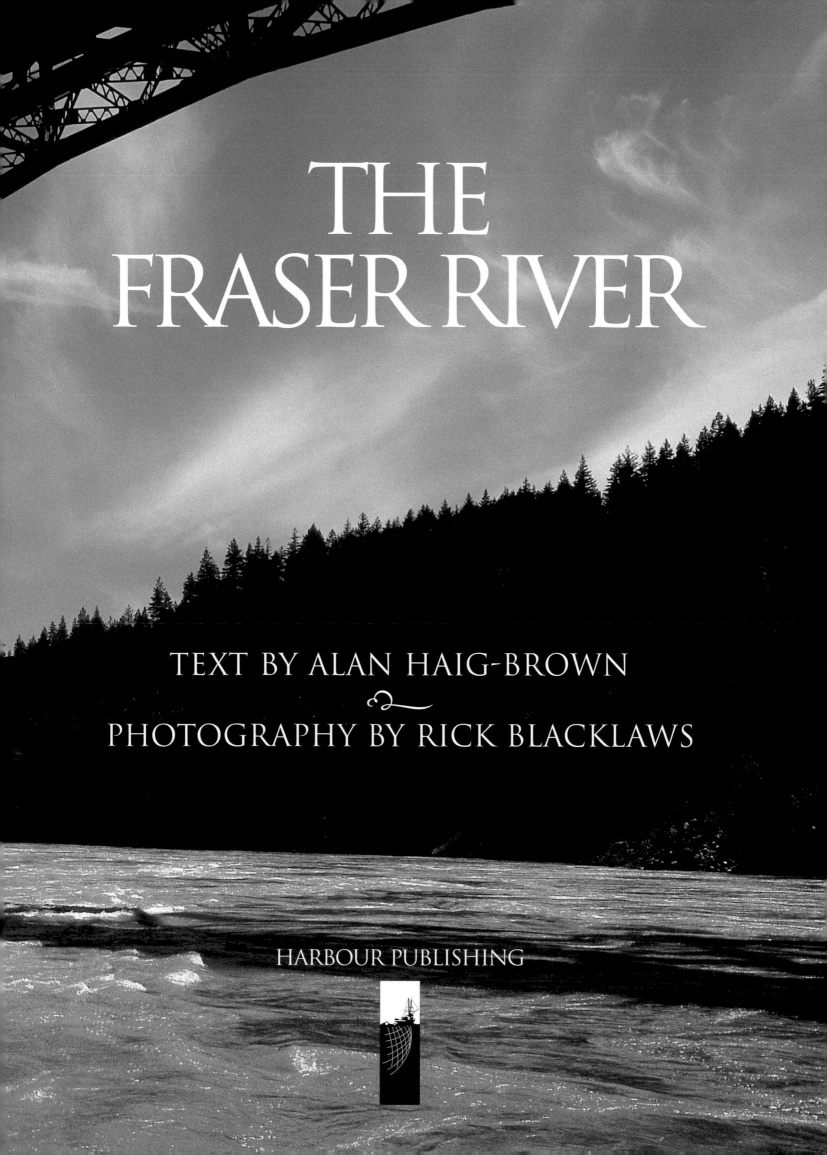

THE FRASER RIVER

TEXT BY ALAN HAIG-BROWN

PHOTOGRAPHY BY RICK BLACKLAWS

HARBOUR PUBLISHING

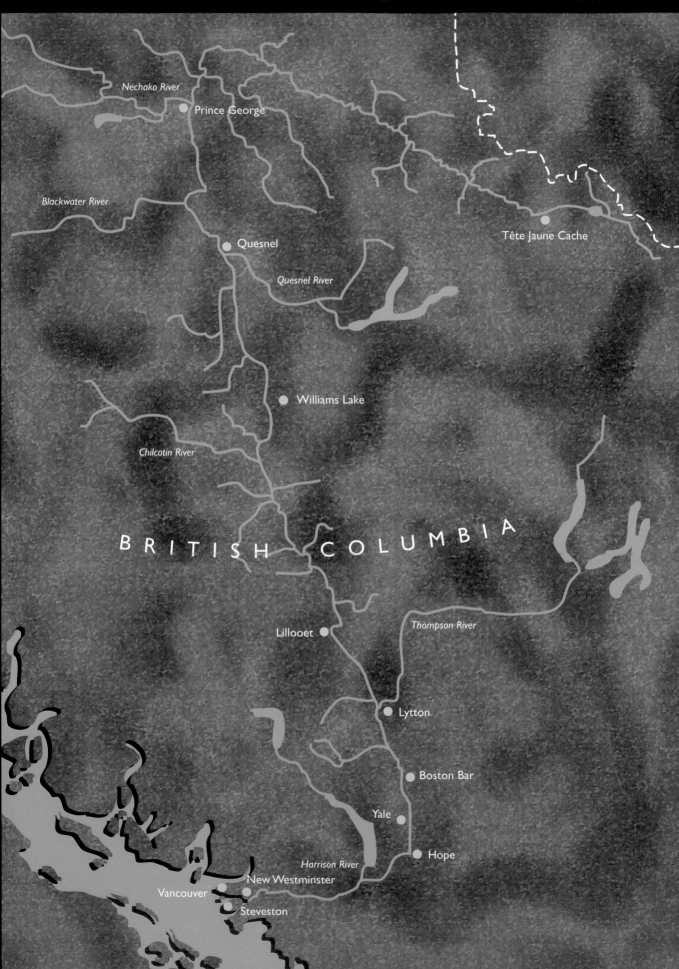

Nechako River

Prince George

Blackwater River

Quesnel

Quesnel River

Tête Jaune Cache

Williams Lake

Chilcotin River

B R I T I S H   C O L U M B I A

Lillooet

Thompson River

Lytton

Boston Bar

Yale

Hope

Harrison River

New Westminster

Vancouver

Steveston

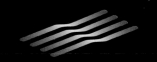

CONTENTS

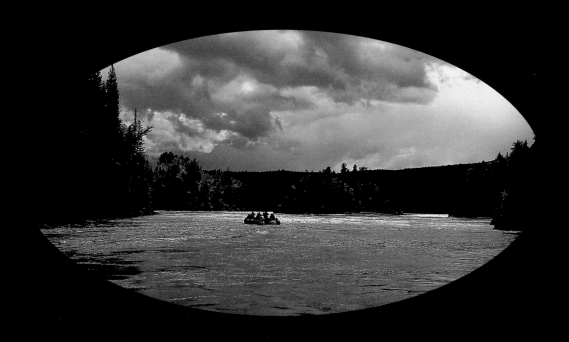

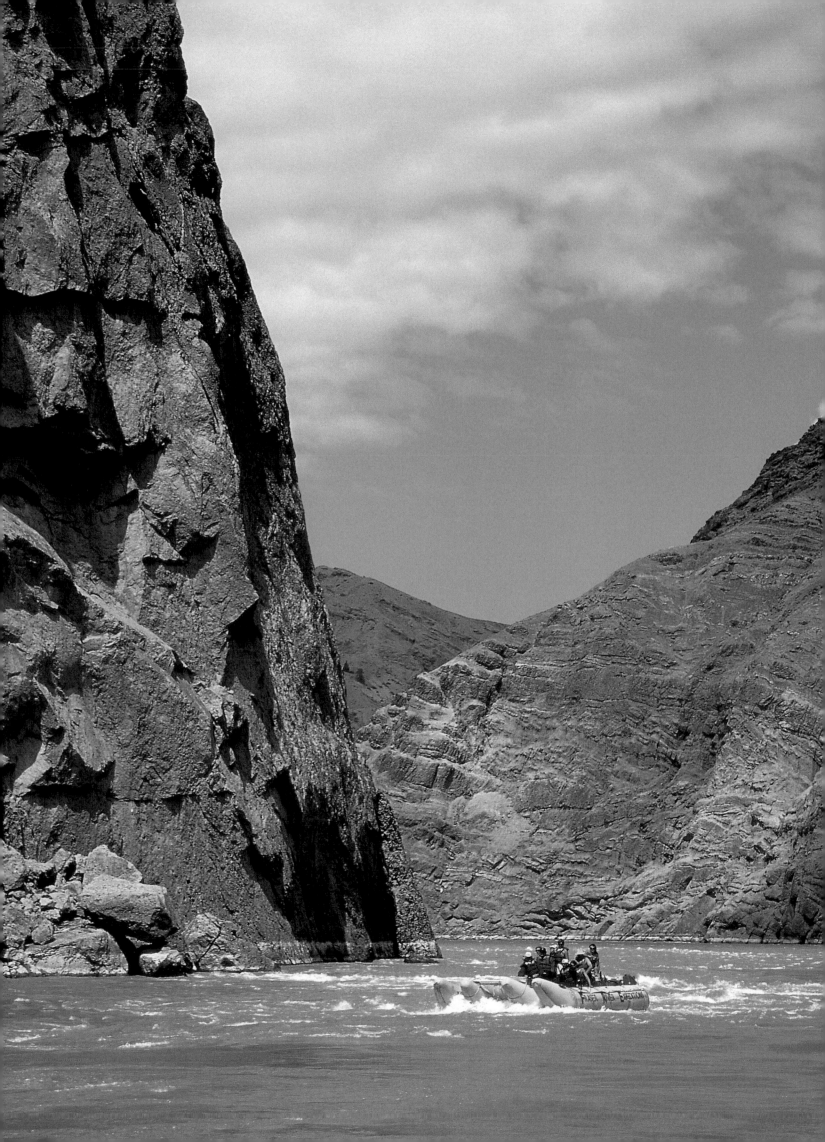

1

THE SPIRIT OF SALMON BOY

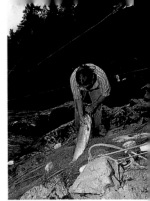

*T*he Fraser River is one of the world's great rivers. From its beginnings in a stream-soaked hillside 3660' above sea level, in the Fraser Pass of the continental divide, the river stretches 820 miles (1368 km) to the sea and drains one-fourth the area of British Columbia. By the time the river reaches the town of Hope, its flow ranges from a winter low of 700 cubic metres to 10,000 cubic metres per second during spring freshet. The river seems placid and majestic as it moves along its last 75 miles to the sea, but its force is such that when it empties into the Gulf of Georgia, it tosses its golden-brown plume of silt 30 miles out into the salt water. Geologically the Fraser Canyon dates from the Miocene period, some 20 million years ago, while the Fraser Valley and the river deltas have been laid down in the 10,000 years since the last ice age. The river is building a delta out into the Gulf of Georgia of some 28 feet per year in areas of moderate depth, and parts of it have grown 840 feet in the past thirty years. By any standards, this is a big river.

Beyond the impressive numbers and facts, the Fraser has great dimensions in time and place, in lives and cultures. To imagine the river is to conjure up not one image but many images, all of them different. Snow from Mount Robson melting in summer sun to feed the sturdy little mountain stream above Tête Jaune Cache; a Tsilhqot'in family dipnetting sockeye from sagebrush-dotted benches in the dry belt of the Plateau, awestruck tourists perched over the sheer cliffs of Hells Gate watching the whitewater torrent churning below, a couple of skookum tugboats guiding a deep-sea ship to the docks for a load of lumber to be carried to Japan, myriad birds swooping up from the rich marsh grasses of the estuary—these are only a few of the many faces, moods and seasons of the Fraser.

Like most British Columbians, I have collected my own images of the river from its bridges—more than one of them called by the generic "the Fraser bridge." From the big bridges in the Lower Mainland I catch glimpses of the working river as I drive into town— from the Alex Fraser I'll look for barges and deep-sea ships bound for the Fraser Surrey Dock; from the Port Mann I'll watch for swooping sea gulls to tell me that the oolichans are in. From the iron railway bridge at Mission I look to see if the Department of Fisheries boat is out counting migrating salmon; from Gang Ranch I glance down to see if a miner has returned to work the bar there in search of gold; at Prince George I watch spring come in as the floating pans of ice pile

French Bar Canyon is home to the first white water downriver from Fort George Canyon. The names by which we know the Fraser River bars today were given in the nineteenth century, for geographical features, for the miners who worked the bars or for the ethnic background of those miners. The river has been walked many times by the newcomers of the last century, as well as the First Nations people for millennia before that.

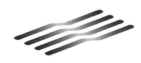

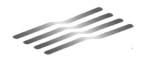

up against the bridge's supporting pylons.

I have also been lucky enough to run a fishing boat down the Fraser from Queensborough to Steveston and out along the jetty, feeling the sea swell of a summer westerly as the boat rounds the lightship at the edge of the delta, and I have ridden the river's currents on towboats, jet boats and river rafts. With each new experience I learn something new about the innumerable personalities of the river, and I am taken more deeply into its overwhelming beauty.

Some 2.4 million British Columbians live in the Fraser River Basin—the area drained by the river and its tributaries—but the life of the river reaches still further. The economy of present-day BC was built on the products of the river, first the furs taken from Cariboo beaver swamps and gold from the Fraser bars, and later the massive salmon runs, riverside wood products industry and agricultural harvests from rich delta soil. Immense shipping and transportation facilities have been built up around the estuary, and the recreation trade on the Fraser alone generates $1 billion per year.

The Fraser River has paid a high price for our comfort and prosperity: its health

The job of yarding tugs is to move the thousands of cubic yards of logs, lumber and wood chips that are the currency of the lower Fraser River. Rick Blacklaws took this photograph from New Westminster, in the calm of very early morning. The three bridges in the background, which link the Fraser Valley with the Lower Mainland, are (nearest to farthest away) a railway bridge, the Pattullo Bridge (for automobile traffic) and the SkyTrain bridge (for light rapid transit).

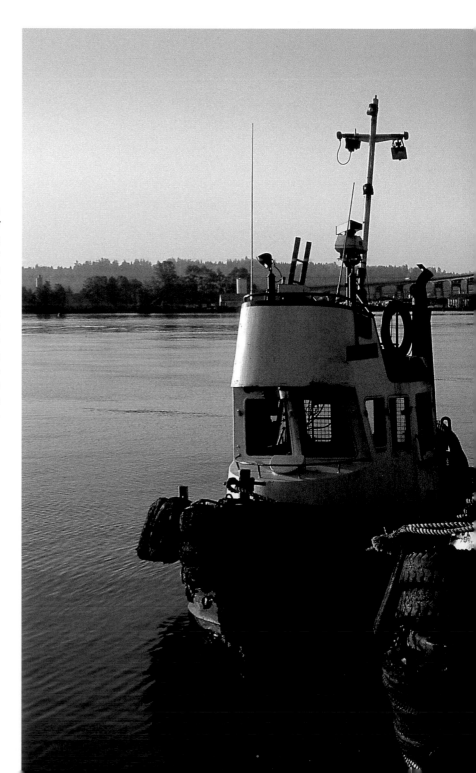

is in serious danger. We have poured into it mill effluents and other industrial waste, chemicals and super-nutrients from huge farms, and poorly treated sewage and chemical street runoff from towns and cities. We have contaminated the river's groundwater, throttled streams and tributaries with dams, choked waterways and fishways with waste from logging, and harmed the very surface of the river with air pollution.

Fortunately, it is not too late to save the Fraser. A river system, like a living organism, is every bit as capable of healing its wounds as it is liable to succumb to infection—if we give it some help.

To restore the river to health, we first have to comprehend it. According to cartographers, the Fraser scribes a huge letter *S* on the lower half of the map of BC, but to describe the river as a one-way line running from a complex of streams in the shadow of Mount Robson to the salt water of the Gulf of Georgia, is akin to describing the human nervous system by drawing a solid line from the feet to the brain. The river is not a single moving band of water, but a wonderfully complex network which has lately come to be called the Fraser River Basin. As the human body has arms and legs, the Fraser has its major

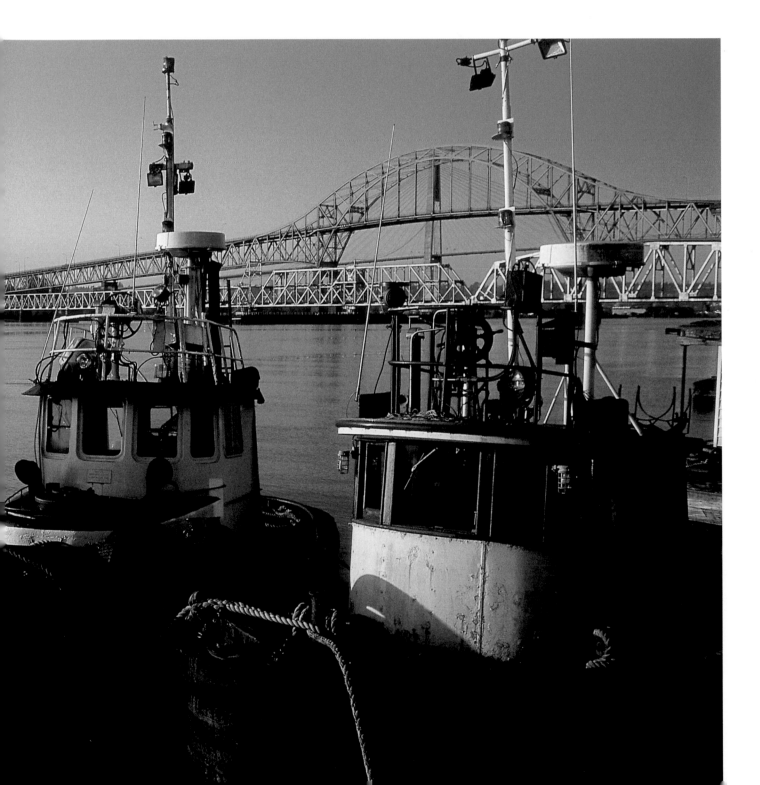

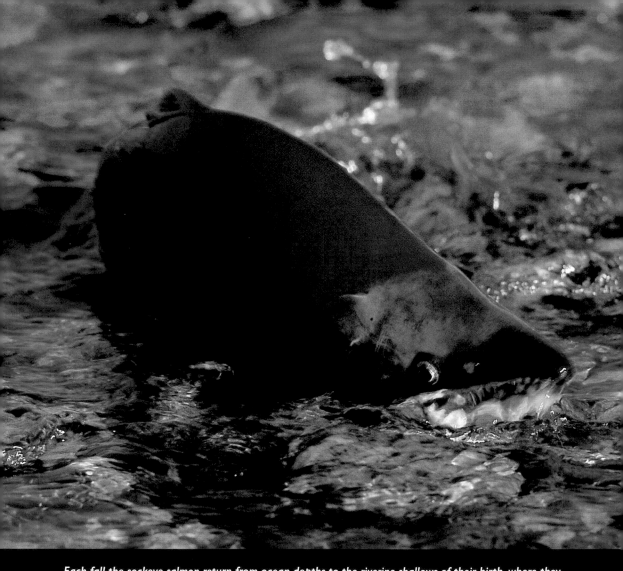

Each fall the sockeye salmon return from ocean depths to the riverine shallows of their birth, where they spawn and die. Their bodies in turn fertilize the lakes where their offspring will rear. This salmon shows the distinctive hump and red colour of the spawning male—characteristics he must display if he is to compete with other males to fertilize the female's eggs.

tributaries, the Thompson, Quesnel, Nechako, Blackwater (West Road), Chilcotin and Harrison rivers, each of which is also a basin with its own network of tributaries. Every waterway in the Fraser Basin, from the largest tributary river to the smallest feeder creek, is connected to every other waterway and plays a part in the life of the whole basin. The river system is the water held in the trunk of a tree and in the lobe of a cactus. It is the water that the plants give to the air and the water that the dry dirt of a bank draws out of the air. It is the clear bubbling mountain brook and the little Cariboo pothole lake, white-rimmed with alkali. The system includes living creatures from the microscopic organisms buried in the riverbed, to the birds and insects that need its deltas and marshes, to the land-dwelling mammals living along its banks. Most especially, the river is the fish that swim through its waters.

If the network of Fraser basin waterways resembles the nervous system of a living organism, so the anadromous fish—those that are born in the river and return to die there—resemble nervous impulses, travelling up and down the system bearing intelligence of its overall state of being. Throughout the human history of the river, when people have thought about it as an interconnected system, it is usually because fish have carried that message to them.

When I was a boy growing up in Campbell River, more than a hundred miles upcoast from the Fraser, two of the finest boats moored at the fishermen's dock in front of the local courthouse were the *Chilko Lake* and the *Quesnel Lake*. The commercial fishers who worked those boats talked with reverential anticipation about the Chilko and Quesnel sockeye, whose peak runs, like those of the Stuart and Adams rivers, passed through our fishing grounds in Johnstone Straits every four years.

Some years later, I heard the story of the salmon boy from a Tsilhqot'in (Chilcotin) elder. A boy was playing on the ice along the edge of the river when he was swept hundreds of miles away down the Chilcotin and Fraser rivers. When he arrived at the sea coast, he was taken in by an old woman of the coastal people. She offered him great kindness, but recognizing that he must return to his own people, she showed him how to turn himself into a salmon and swim back upriver. He did this, and some weeks later when he was taken out of the family net, he was accepted by his sister. The boy grew into a man and eventually travelled to the sun in search of a wife. Having learned something of the river, he was ready to reach the sky.

In its proper telling, the story of the salmon boy is long and complex with the texture of old wood, of canyons and time. It evokes the very roots of our land and human beings' historic dependence on rivers and fish. In my own story, which is quite a bit shorter, I grew up on a salmon river, travelled out to sea as a commercial fisherman, went on to live a large part of my life among the river people of the interior plateau, and now find myself drawn back to the rivers.

Much of my thinking about the Fraser system crystallized when I met Rick Blacklaws, who was in the advanced stages of his own complicated voyage of discovery of the river. Rick is an archaeologist, professional photographer and fanatic riverman who has been probing the Fraser mystery on many fronts for many years. He has directed archaeological digs along its banks, he has organized educational expeditions throughout its length, he has pioneered the first program of Fraser Studies at a BC college (Langara), and for over ten years he has assiduously recorded his discoveries on film.

It was Rick who first took me out on a raft through the Fraser Canyon. In honour of Rivers Day one year, he arranged for us to ride a raft through Hells Gate with a handful of river people and Vicki Gabereau, host of the national CBC Radio program. The trip, and the wonderful radio program that was aired a month later, were typical of Rick's continuing commitment to bring people to the river, and bring the river to people. He is not only a walking compendium of Fraser arcana, but also one of the Fraser's most fervent and articulate advocates. The doubling up of our river manias made this book inevitable.

We offer it as much as possible in the spirit of the story of the salmon boy, in the hope it will evoke some of the richness of the physical river as well as something of its captivating majesty.

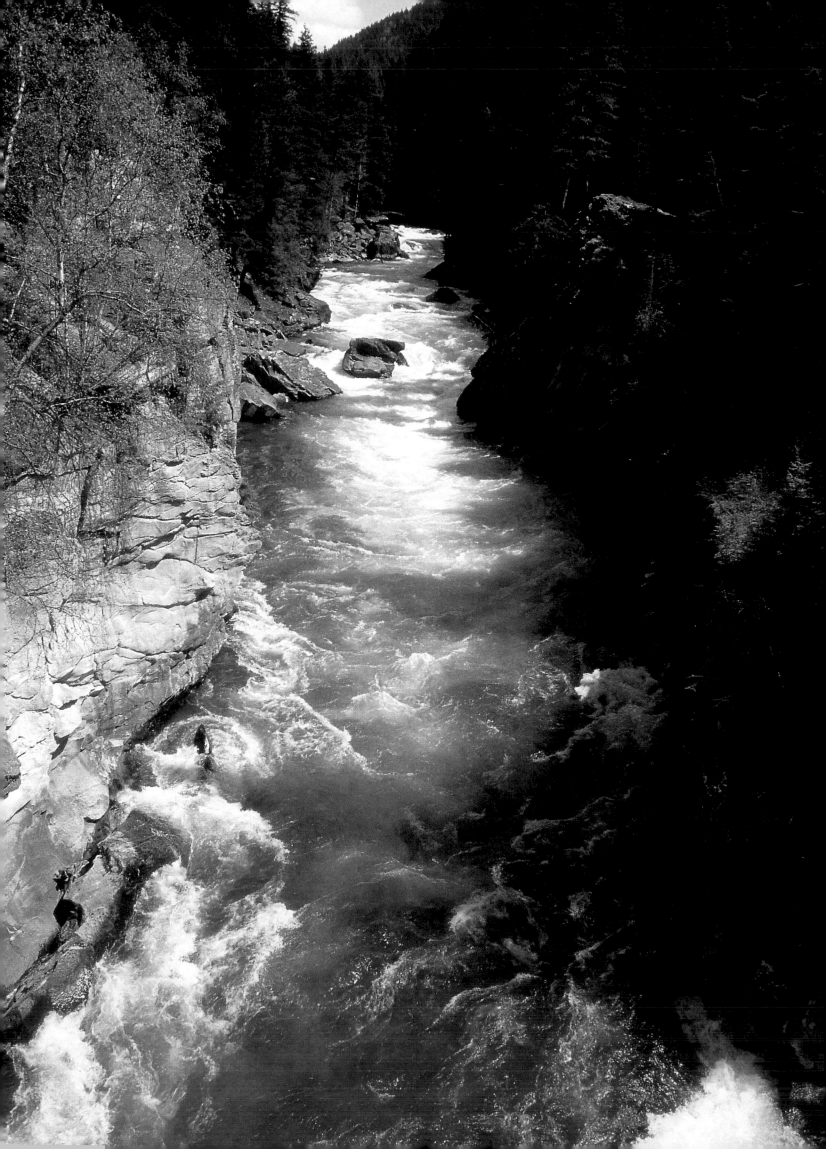

UPPER REACHES

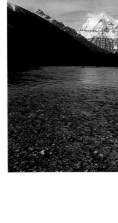

*T*he gentleman explorers of nineteenth-century Europe took great delight in venturing up the world's great rivers, on a quest for the source. We all have seen dusty old books with titles like *To the Source of the Nile* or *Up the Mighty Amazon*, chronicling the exciting (and expensive) pastimes of book-writing adventurers like Stanley and Livingstone. Chuckle as we might over such excesses and the public appetite for stories in which men triumph over nature, many of us retain a fascination with tracing a river to its source.

A century later, it is an easy drive up the Yellowhead Highway to a point in Mount Robson Provincial Park, just inside British Columbia from the Alberta border, where a bridge crosses a sturdy young mountain stream and a nondescript sign announces that the source of the Fraser lies only 30 miles (50 km) away, in the alpine tundra of the Fraser Pass. Both the Columbia and the Thompson rivers have their origins near this area as well.

According to Wayne VanVelzen, manager of Mount Robson Park, the Fraser comes not from one point on the slope, "but from a wide variety of rivulets from two distinct drainages. Even in the driest years after the snows have melted, the whole sidehill remains wet with springs."

In this rugged mountainous area, rich with mountain caribou and grizzly bears, the network of streams and the meltwater of the Fraser Pass course through the alpine wildflowers, gathering volume as they flow down to a tiny unnamed lake and then northwest through spruce and pine forests. By the time it reaches the highway bridge, the stream is already large enough to deserve the designation "river." It flows fast and clear, and judging from its rocky banks, it is capable of rising dramatically when the snow melts.

In the first few miles downriver from the bridge, the Fraser is braided into streams by willow-covered gravel bars, and this part of the river still has a new look and feel—as if it were still actively cutting and scouring its way into the earth's crust.

A few more miles downriver is Moose Lake, which has the distinction of being the only lake on the main stem of the Fraser. The lake is just over 6 miles (10 km) long. Carved out by the scouring force of a glacier, it is slowly being filled in with gravel washed down by the river.

Overlander Falls, about 2 miles (3 km) downriver from Moose Lake, is named for the hardy group of Ontario migrants who

Until it reaches Tête Jaune Cache, the Fraser is a kookum little stream made turbulent by the confines of the Rocky Mountains. Just downriver from the spot where this photograph was taken, near Tête Jaune, the river reaches the broad Rocky Mountain trench and becomes much calmer as it flows through the broad fault valley. There are hundreds of these wild mountain streams in the headwaters of the Fraser, each one churning along its course toward the sea and joining all the others to become part of the Fraser River.

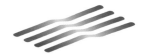

in 1862 set out for the Cariboo gold fields, crossed the Rockies by packhorse, and rafted down the Fraser and Thompson rivers to their destination. Both parties encountered terrible hardships. One adventurer, a man named Carpenter, was drowned when his canoe capsized in the Grand Canyon near Prince George. His diary was found after his death and its last entry read: "Arrived at the Grand Canyon; ran the canyon, and was drowned." But in spite of the gruelling voyage, only six of the Overlanders died and many went on to successful lives in BC, including the only woman Overlander, Catherine O'Hare Schubert, who gave birth to her fourth child only hours after arriving at Kamloops in October.

This part of the Fraser, and the next 8 miles (13 km) to Rearguard Falls, are dominated by the majesty of Mount Robson, at 13,048 feet (3954 m) the highest point in the Canadian Rockies. In popular belief the Fraser has its origins in this mountain—a more dramatic story than the truth of the river's beginnings on a boggy hillside almost 60 miles (100 km) to the southeast. But Mount Robson's massive glacier does make a major contribution to the river as it passes by. Long after the last of the snow has melted from the lower lands, the glacier goes on slowly releasing much-needed summer meltwater, some of which finds its way to the river. In the heat of summer, Rearguard Falls explodes in cool whiteness.

At the top of a steep footpath down to Rearguard Falls, a sign informs the visitor that this is the farthest point, 768 miles (1280 km) from the sea, that chinook salmon attain on the river. But local observers know that in recent years, several hundred of the big fish have struggled up through the 30-foot (9-m) drop of the falls to spawn even farther up the main river and into Robson Creek.

The bulk of this stock of chinook, 2,000 to 3,000 fish, spawn in the 3 miles (5 km) downriver from Rearguard to Tête Jaune Cache. The river alters its flow slightly at this point. A massive slide occurred recently in a mountain draw several miles up a small local feeder creek, and a bit of gravel from that slide has found its way into the Fraser. This is one of the great miracles of a wild and healthy salmon river. In a process of

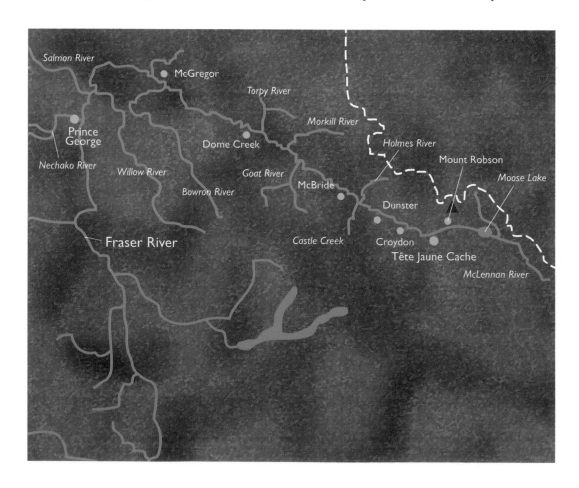

continual rejuvenation, gravel from slides such as this replace the spawning gravels that are regularly washed out by spring freshets. Where streams and tributaries have been dammed, these gravels settle out in artificial lakes, and the gravel in downstream spawning grounds is never replenished.

The little community of Tête Jaune Cache, like the surrounding Yellowhead country, was named for the yellow-haired Iroquois trapper who first brought Hudson's Bay Company men to this spot, a strategic point along a major fur-trading route. Indeed, the river flat below Tête Jaune is a maze of gravel bars, islands and swamp, all of it prime trapping territory. The boom years for Tête Jaune occurred years later, but they were brief. Photos from around 1911, when the Grand Trunk Pacific Railway was being built through the Yellowhead Pass and along the Fraser and Nechako rivers to the Pacific coast, show English dandies in a log-and-tent town that is today no more than a tangle of willow bush along the river. But if the new village is a little smaller, it is a good deal more stable.

As the river system has worked over the millennia to shape the valley of the upper river, so has it shaped the lives of Gene and Linda Blackman, who live near Tête Jaune. The Blackmans' modern log house is built on a spot that has been an auspicious location for centuries. The ground outside their home still bears a depression where an ancient semi-subterranean Native winter dwelling once stood. Down the riverbank from this site is the reason for its existence—a gravel bar marked from top to bottom with barely submerged chinook spawning redds. These are the furrows that the adult chinook build with their tails and with the aid of the river current. They lay their eggs up to 18" (45 cm) deep, then move upstream to dig new redds. As they dislodge gravel from each new redd, the ones below are filled.

Gene Blackman spent his childhood in the bush near Tête Jaune, working along the riverbank and in trappers' canoes and river boats to help bring home beaver,

Moose Lake, in Mount Robson Provincial Park, is the only lake on the Fraser's main stem. This accounts for the muddy texture of the river over much of its length—lakes provide slack water where rivers move slowly and sediments are dropped from the water column.

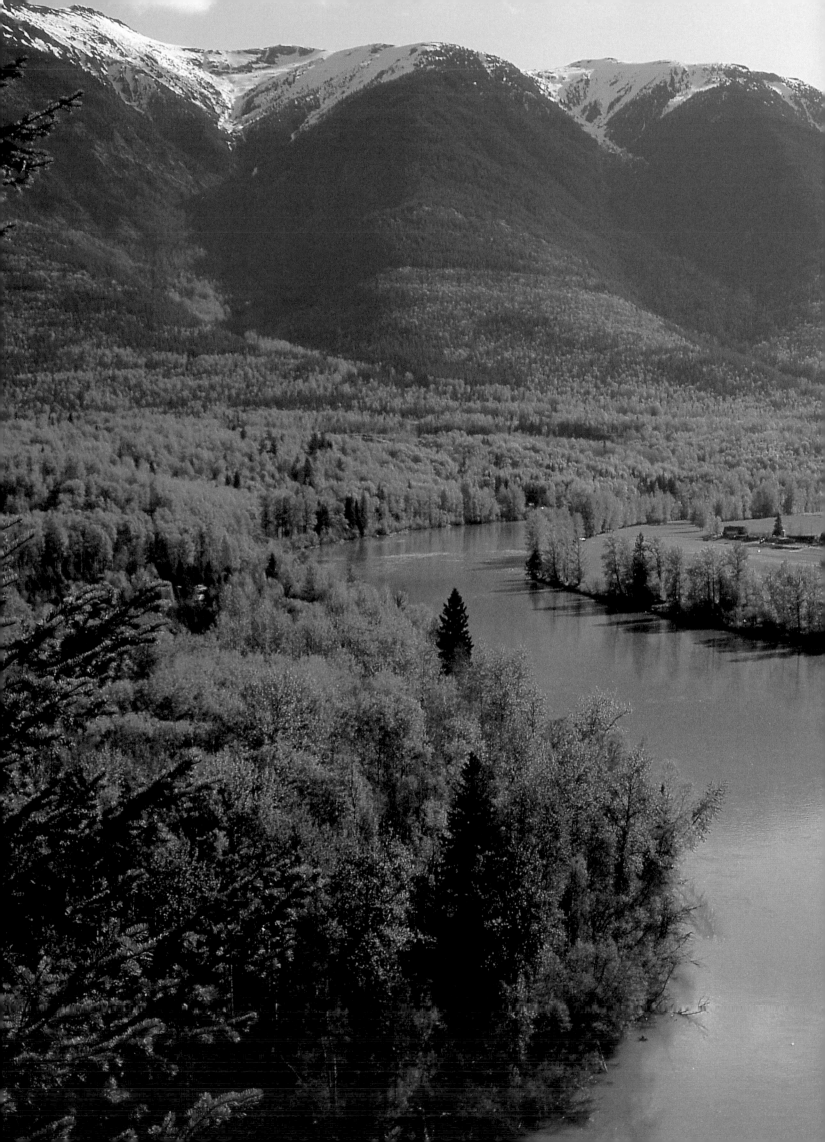

Below Tête Jaune Cache, the Fraser enters the great fault line valley known as the Rocky Mountain trench. The river is too small at this point to fill the great valley, so it meanders from side to side across the soft sediments laid down by an ancient glacial lake. Where there is a meandering river, there is a rhythm of high and low water which redistributes fertile soils and makes good farmland. It is on these rich sediments that the Culp family works their farm, which is shaped by the path of the river.

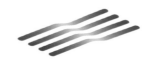

lynx and other furs. In the 1970s, when hunting was still permitted in the Tête Jaune area, it was not unusual for him and his friends to take a canoe to Moose Lake and work their way down through the bars and willows to bag a moose for the winter larder. Linda Blackman grew up on the shores of Moose Lake in the 1950s and early 1960s, when her dad was the station agent for the little railway town of Red Pass, named for its bright red rocks, at the lake's outlet. Nothing is left of the community today except the rail bridge Linda and the other kids fished from.

Now, after spending a couple of decades away, the Blackmans have come back. "I've been told when I was young that once you drink the waters of the Fraser, you will always return," Gene says.

Downriver from Tête Jaune, the river slows and takes a northwest course, making its meandering way through a valley that runs along the base of the Rocky Mountains. The plate that forms the southern side of the fault valley, the Columbia Mountains, moves ever so slowly north in relation to the Rockies. This valley is called the Rocky Mountain trench, and according to June Ryder, a geomorphologist with J. M. Ryder & Associates Terrain Analysis, it is "controlled by geological structures, big fault lines that separate the two mountain ranges." The trench filled with glaciers in the ice age, and when they melted and retreated, they dumped glacial moraine—sediments and gravel—onto the valley floor. Around the time the glaciers were melting back, this area and much of the northern reaches of the Fraser were covered by a huge interior lake, which deposited more sediment. The result of this glacial activity is the fertile benchlands of the river valley bottom, and homesteaders living along this part of the river have cleared fields among the curls and bends of the placid stream.

At this point the Fraser, too small to cover the width of this great trench, winds from side to side, cutting slowly into the ancient lake silt. The undulation is typical river behaviour: unless it is confined by resistant rock, a young river generally sets itself a meandering course, even if it has to spend hundreds of years cutting loops out of the countryside.

Crystal clear above Tête Jaune, the Fraser is soon joined by the McLennan River from the south, and begins to take on a silty colour. By now the river is carrying its own genetic marker. According to Ray Cox, a geologist at Kwantlen College in Surrey, BC, an outcropping of white mica near Tête Jaune is constantly being eroded by the river waters, so that tiny flakes of this distinctive mica are scattered down the length of the Fraser, all the way to the sands of the estuary some 800 miles (1300 km) away. The river becomes what it passes through, each mineral vein and clay bank making its contribution to the darkening mixture.

By the time the Fraser has wandered along the valley to McBride, some 36 miles (60 km) northwest of Tête Jaune, it is a smooth, quiet river curving its way past farmers' meadows and the sand bars and cutbanks that border them. McBride was established as a station for the Grand Trunk Pacific Railway in the early years of the century. As soon as the tracks went through, railway officials encouraged settlement throughout the area. But people were slow to move to this northern valley, and in the 1950s the Canadian National Railway, having taken over the line from the Grand Trunk soon after its construction, was still sending out colonization agents to recruit potential farmers.

One of those agents found Floyd Caywood farming a too-small place down in Oregon in the 1950s, and gave him a great price on moving his farm equipment to the upper Fraser. Caywood bought a farm at Dunster, a few miles from McBride, and he is still there. His land almost never needs irrigation, and "our wells are filled by seepage from the river, so if you were to irrigate, it's best to dig a well and not worry about them damn bureaucrats and water rights." The broad sweep of river around the farm is much more than

Counting Spawners

Curtis Culp of Dunster, BC supplements his farm income by "working-out." For a couple of months in summer, he counts chinook salmon for the Department of Fisheries and Oceans, a job that has grown into a passion, especially as public awareness increases. "When I started in 1978," he says, "there would be two or three guys in the river trying to kill the spawning fish with others on the bank encouraging them. Now they would be telling them to get out."

At the same time, more and more fish are returning to spawn in this part of the Fraser between late July and early September. Curtis counts fish on ten tributary rivers between the foot of Mount Robson and Goat River, about 20 miles (32 km) below McBride, and the chinook runs on all of them have grown despite continuing habitat degradation from clearcut logging on the hillsides. In 1979 Curtis counted only 289 returning chinook in Swift Creek. Over the most recent five-year cycle, he has never counted fewer than 800, and one year the creek had 1,300 spawners. He has even seen 100 wandering sockeye in the Holmes River at McBride.

Curtis knows the health of the fish is a yardstick for the health of the river, and he is pleased about the increases. He is concerned that the government is now permitting an aquaculture company to come and kill about 30 chinook each year for their eggs. In the process of catching the fish, selecting them and holding them in cages, the company runs a high-speed jet boat up and down over the spawning beds. Many people living along the Fraser believe jet boats disturb the habitat of fish and other living creatures in the river, and they think the jet boats should be banned.

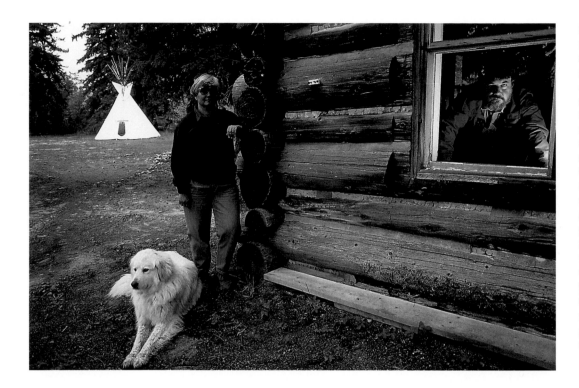

Linda and Gene Blackman both grew up around the Upper Reaches of the Fraser, and now they have returned to live here. Gene's dad was a trapper and guide and Linda's dad was a station agent, but now the Blackmans work in tourism. The huge teepee in the background will become part of a bed-and-breakfast; from here visitors can enjoy vistas that sweep from icy mountain-tops miles away to chinook spawning grounds virtually in the front yard.

a serenely beautiful adjunct to the property. In 1972, the freshet flooded the lower pasture to within a foot of the barn. "That is good," says Caywood's son-in-law, Curtis Culp, "because the field gets a good soaking and comes up all nice and green. But at the same time, we know that there is enough snow on those mountains to flood a foot over the house if it all came down at once."

The smaller, clearer upper river is more user-friendly than the brown giant of the lower reaches. Caywood's grandchildren cool off during haying time by swinging out over the river on a rope with a baseball bat tied onto it. The drop into the always-cold river would refresh even the sweatiest haying hand. Then there was the time Floyd drafted the kids to help him launch his little sailboat and they sailed through a baptism ceremony being held just down from the farm. The river freezes in November, and later they clear the snow to make a skating rink. When the ice begins to thaw in spring, long crystals form that are perfect for making ice cream at home. In early spring and late fall, sandbars emerge from the shallowing river, producing what Caywood's daughter Bonnie jokingly calls a "poor man's beach." For a time the family had a sauna down

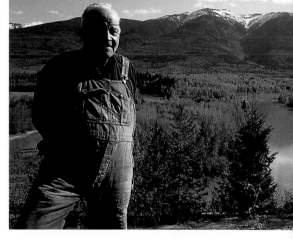

by the riverbank, where the kids liked to hang out before jumping straight into the water. Once when three sheep fell in the river, Bonnie had to kick everybody out of the sauna so she could use it to warm up the sheep.

To this day the land bordering the stretch of the Fraser between its headwaters and Prince George has not attracted large communities of people. To a railway company this may seem a misfortune, but for the river it is a blessing. It is no coincidence that this stretch of the Fraser has both the smallest human population density and the least polluted water on the main stem.

In 1995, at age eighty-three, Floyd Caywood was still cutting 13 cords of wood each year. He has farmed his diamond-shaped piece of riverside land at Dunster, near McBride, since 1958 when a Canadian National Railway agent found him working a small Oregon farm and talked him into moving to northern BC.

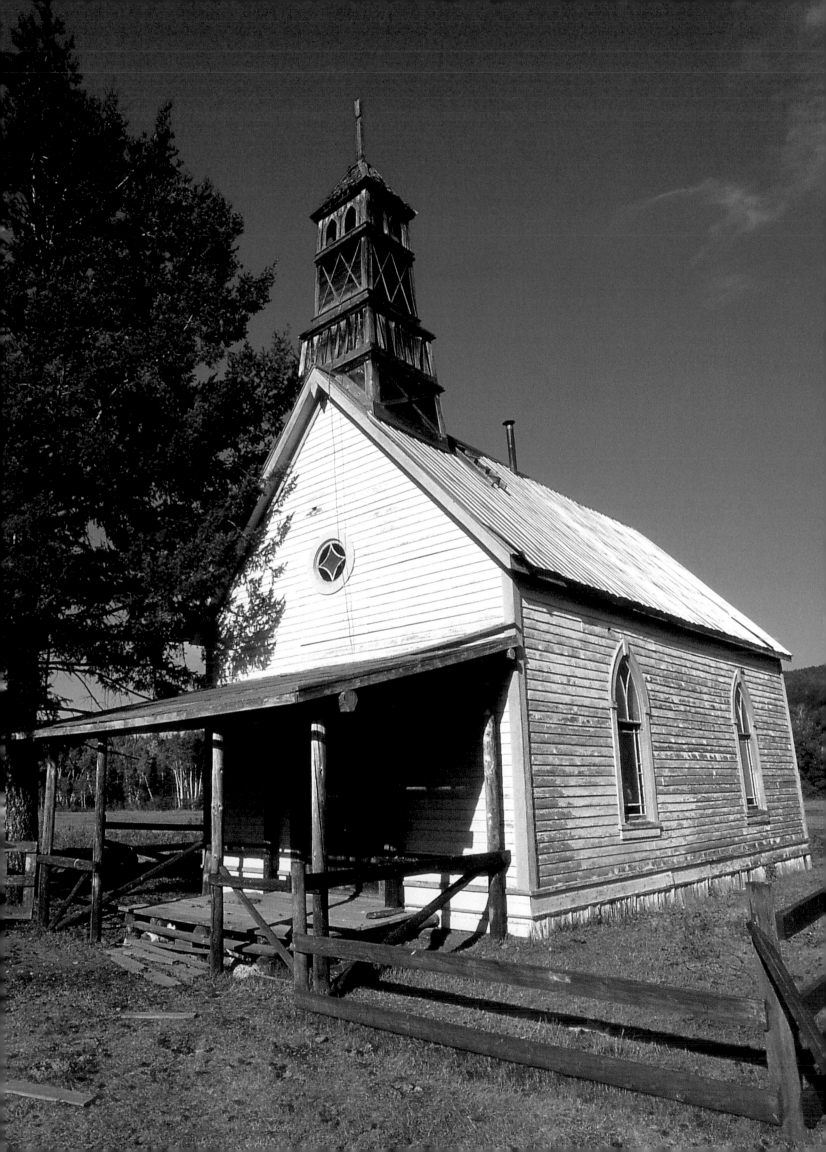

3

CARIBOO

A few miles short of Summit Lake and the Arctic watershed, the Fraser River leaves the fault line valley that is the Rocky Mountain trench and swings southward toward Prince George. This whole area was covered by a vast lake during the last ice age, some 10,000–15,000 years ago. Geographers call it Glacial Lake Prince George because its mass was centred in the area where the city of Prince George now stands. The lake allowed fish to move from one watershed to another, and it deposited silt on what are now the slopes across the river. In places river gravel has washed up on top of the glacial silt. The glacier retreated north from this part of the Fraser Basin, which we know because the drumlins—streamlined glaciated hills—near Prince George are oriented to the north. Later the lake flooded up over some of the drumlins, draping them in a mantle of lake sediments.

The Fraser has barely begun its new course when it is joined by the Nechako River from the west, and the land at the confluence of these two large rivers has been a major centre of human settlement for centuries.

Oral history tells of a group of Nechako River people travelling down the Fraser River to avenge the massacre of their people at Chunlac on the banks of the Nechako. Having no quarrel with the Lheit-Lit'en (Fort George) people, the Dakelh (Carrier) nation living at what is today Prince George, but not wanting to raise an alarm, they slipped by the riverbank village under cover of darkness. More recently the growing city of Prince George has become the nerve centre of northern BC, the hub of industry, commerce, government and academia in the area.

The first European settlement at the junction of the Fraser and Nechako rivers was named Fort George, after the reigning British monarch George III. Simon Fraser established the fort for the North West Company in the fall of 1807, after founding Fort McLeod just to the north in 1805 and Fort St. James and Fort Fraser in the summer of 1806. Fort George, on the site of today's Prince George, survived as a Hudson's Bay Company post for over a century until it was closed in 1915, although it was less important to the company than Fort St. James. At the time of its founding, Simon Fraser and the North West Company still hoped that the big river would turn out to be the Columbia and a good supply route to the west coast.

Neither proved to be the case, and it wasn't until the Grand Trunk Pacific Railway was built through the area in 1914 that the Fort George site came into its own. The rail link to Vancouver via the

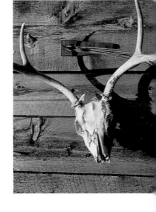

At Alexandria a tidy little Catholic church stands in memory of the era of European colonization. Christian missionaries established headquarters in First Nations communities throughout the northern reaches of the Fraser Basin, and tried hard to erase the ancient river cultures and the power of their memories. Instead, First Nations cultures have absorbed the acceptable aspects of Christianity and maintained their deep river traditions.

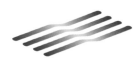

Pacific Great Eastern took still longer—another thirty-eight years. By the 1950s, the railway and improved highways were in place and the river became much less important for transportation. But its water and drainage were natural assets for a forest industry city as the age of pulp mills swept in. Tiny rural towns throughout the province lost their bush mills and their populations to centralized urban workplaces through the 1960s and '70s, while Prince George grew quickly in importance.

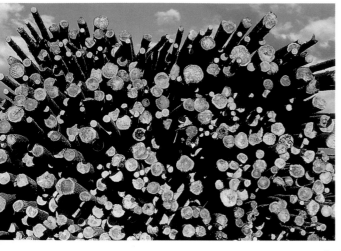

Prince George is one of those British Columbia cities that looks as if it were designed by people who no longer, or perhaps never, lived there. The skyline is dominated by mills with red and white striped smokestacks and huge piles of wood chips waiting to be turned into pulp. The downtown core is a dusty mix of shops that serve the locals and fine hotels where government and corporate bureaucrats park their rental cars after flying in from outside. There are suburbs filled with nuclear families, many of whom have built their lives around jobs at the local mill or in the service industries, from bars to universities, that serve the core population of forest workers. And there are transients, single people and families who move from town to town following a job or a dream.

In Fort George Park down by the river, an excellent museum receives visitors, and a fenced-in acre contains all that remains of the original Lheit-Lit'en village—the gravestones. The stones have been moved into a circle where they commemorate, in English and missionary-developed syllabics, the lives of people with the famous name Quaw who died in 1898, a seven-year-old named Francis Tuppage who died in 1889, and a half dozen others. In the early years of the century the living were moved to reserves north of town, well away from any participation in the city's development.

The forests of the Fraser River Basin slow snowmelt and hold the waters, which are then released through the long dry summer months. This part of the Basin is prime logging country, and the mills along this stretch of the river handle a huge volume of lumber. The forestry industry is essential to the province's economy, but logging and processing practices have a direct effect on the Fraser Basin, particularly the sensitive feeder creeks and salmon streams.

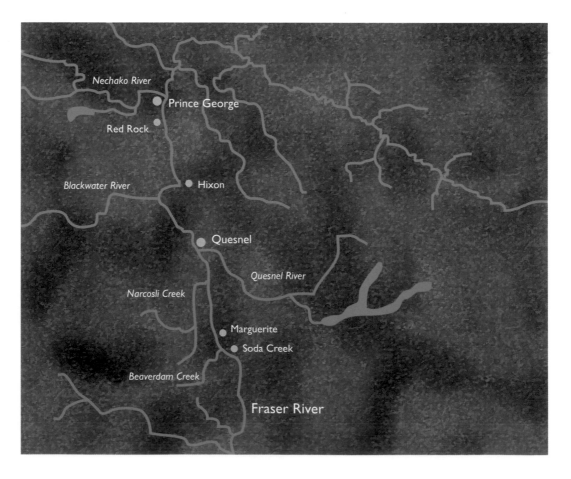

Looking south toward Prince George, you can see the Nechako River on its way to join the Fraser.
The Kenny dam on the Nechako, a̶̶̶ ̶200 km upriver (to the right) of the area shown here, ̶̶̶̶had a severe
impact on salmon stocks. Yet in 1987, two levels of government allowed Aluminum Company of Canada
(Alcan) to divert the river further. Dam expansion has now been stopped, but the existing dam
continues to threaten the sensitive stocks.

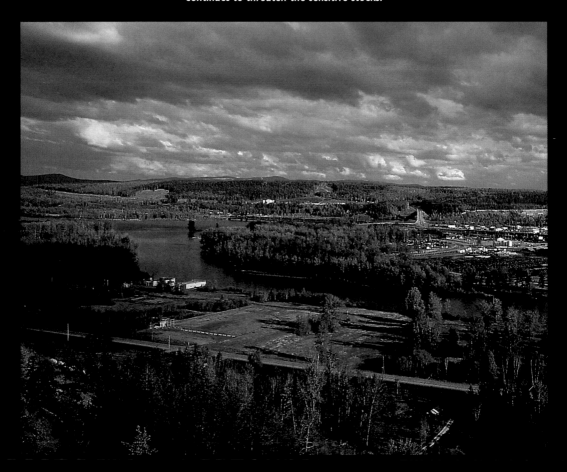

The Leg-Hold Trap on the Nechako

One of the Fraser's proudest claims is that its main stem remains unharnessed by dams, from its source in the Rocky Mountains to the sea. Three of its major tributaries, the Thompson, Quesnel and Chilcotin rivers, have also remained free of major dams, largely in deference to the salmon.

The one tragic exception is the Nechako River. If we think of the Fraser's main tributaries as the limbs of a human body, then the Nechako is caught in the jaws of a leg-hold trap.

In the late 1940s, the government of the day granted extensive water rights to the Aluminum Company of Canada (Alcan) to dam the Nechako and divert some of the water through a tunnel in the coast mountains to a hydroelectric plant at Kemano. The deal included an option to raise the dam at a future date to divert even more

water. In 1952 Alcan built the Kenny dam on the Nechako, and for the next four years the river was virtually starved of water while the reservoir filled. Even after a more normal flow was restored, natural cycles were ignored and flows were irregular. There was no longer a spring freshet to wash silt from the spawning beds, or a steady summer flow to cool exhausted salmon at the end of their migration up through the Fraser from the sea. At any time of year, when the fry were in the river, sudden shifts in water levels could leave them stranded in small pools, susceptible to predation and rising temperatures. In the cold of winter, even a brief draw-down of the river level could leave salmon redds and their precious eggs exposed to freezing temperatures.

In 1987, in spite of evidence that the existing dam had damaged salmon stocks, the governments of BC and Canada signed a further agreement with Alcan allowing the diversion to be expanded. At that time,

in one of the greatest co-ordinated efforts of diverse groups of British Columbians who care about the rivers, the Rivers Defence Coalition was formed. Commercial and sport fishers, environmentalists, scientists, academics, First Nations people and other concerned British Columbians joined forces and fought the good fight, while Alcan proceeded with a half-billion-dollar start on the project.

The expansion project was halted in 1994 by order of Premier Mike Harcourt's provincial government and the jaws of the leg-hold trap on the Nechako were loosened. The defence coalition managed to prevent the destruction of the Nechako, but only with the herculean efforts of volunteers. The power of those who would despoil the rivers often seems as limitless as the river itself. More than one person has said that the developer need win the attack only once, while the environmentalist must defend the river every day.

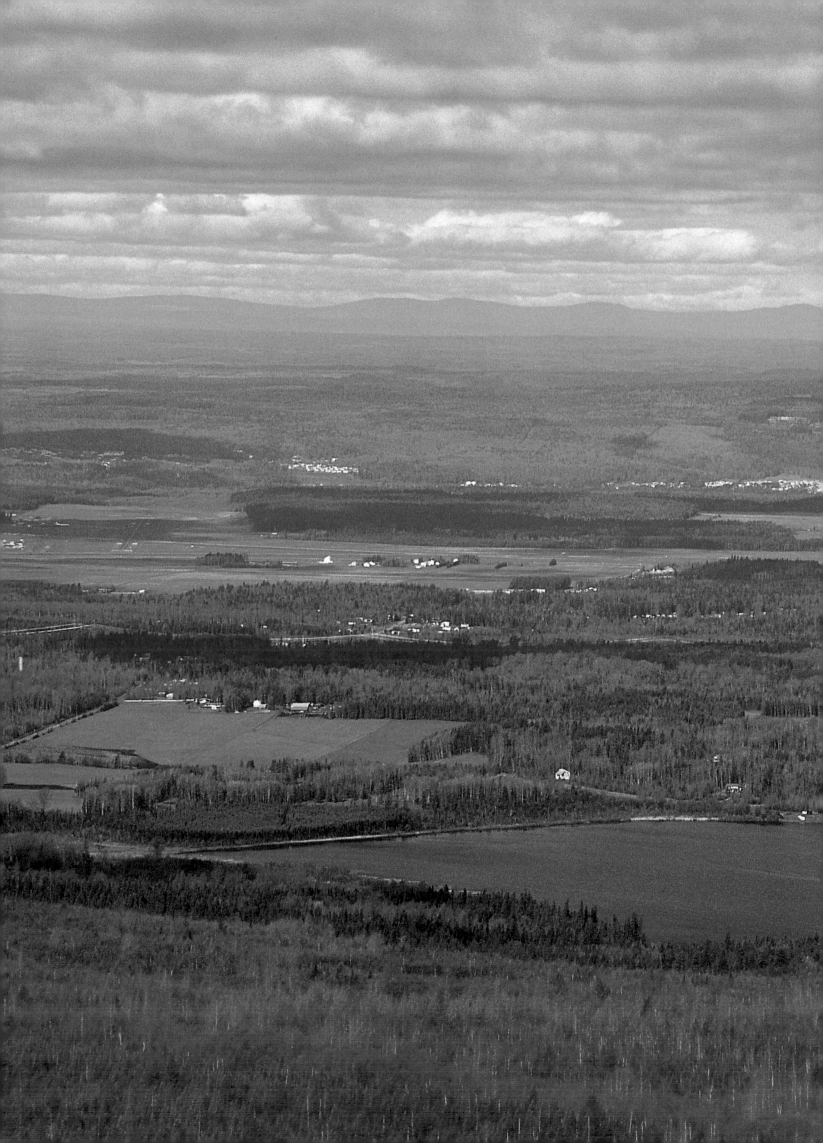

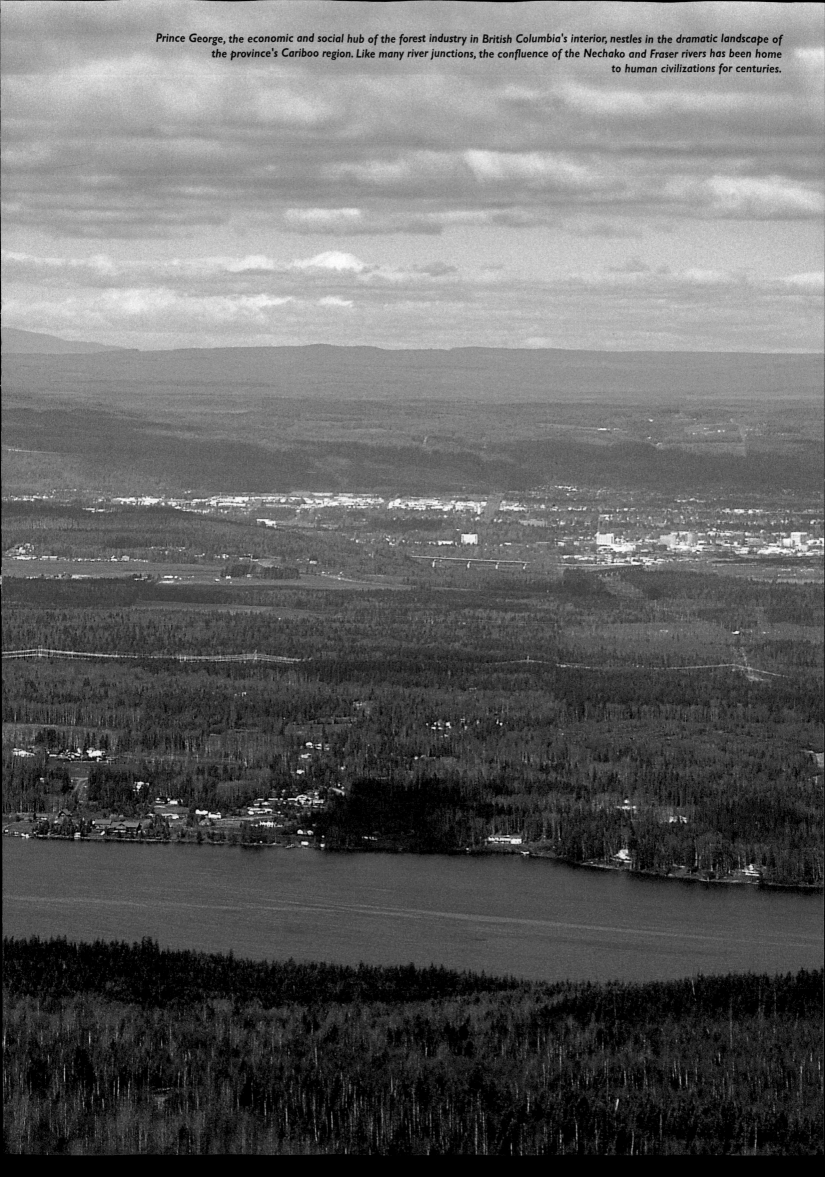

Prince George, the economic and social hub of the forest industry in British Columbia's interior, nestles in the dramatic landscape of the province's Cariboo region. Like many river junctions, the confluence of the Nechako and Fraser rivers has been home to human civilizations for centuries.

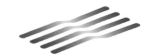

You can walk from the park to the confluence of the Fraser and Nechako rivers on a path that runs along the south shore of the Fraser. Just at the point where the two rivers become one, a rail bridge of stern industrial design and steel construction employs a dozen small spans to stretch across the broad flat of the newly enlarged Fraser. A drawbridge is built into one of the spans to accommodate the paddle wheelers that were still a feature of the river when the bridge was built in 1914. Downriver, a broad, flat modern highway bridge needs only half as many spans to reach across the water. But it too shows its respect for the power of the river ice, with steel cladding on the upriver sides of each column.

A river walk winds upstream from the Fort George park to Cottonwood Park, just into the mouth of the Nechako. That's where I met Clianh Hoeppner and Jason Buckley, two

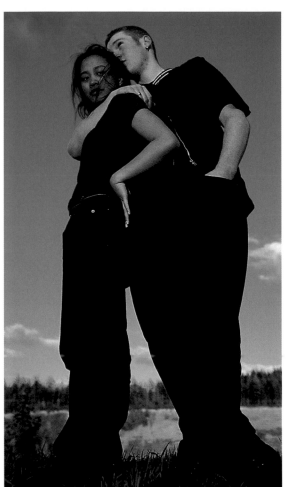

From a human perspective, there can be no greater argument for looking after the Fraser River Basin than to respect the right of our young people to live in a healthy environment. Clianh Hoeppner and Jason Buckley have grown up along the river. Now, as young adults, they begin to define themselves in its life.

teenagers who had driven their car out onto the gravel beach to look at the river and each other. When I asked them what the river meant to them, Clianh said, "It's beautiful," and Jason said, "It's polluted." They pointed out a small island, near the south shore between the two bridges, with a small forest of cottonwoods on its downstream end and a grassy meadow at the upstream end where the floodwaters peak. "I've heard that some people get married on that island," Clianh said. "Yah," Jason added, "when the river is low, people drive their four-by-four trucks out there and have beer parties."

Like many cities and towns along the Fraser, Prince George is beginning to recognize that the river is one of its greatest resources, not just a place to dump waste or a barrier to be crossed. More and more space is being made for people along the shores. Deserted industrial sites are being cleaned up and fenced so that wide paths can be laid around the shore, bringing the people closer to the river than they have been since paddle wheeler times. In March, when the ice is just breaking up in the river and beginning to float away in great pans, the river can mesmerize an observer on the Prince George river walk. For residents who have endured the dreary month of February when it seems winter will never end, this is a place where spring literally opens as they watch.

These changes are good for the Fraser, if they signal a growing awareness of the river as a living body of water. During the post-World War Two years, when logging activity in northern BC mushroomed and Prince George exploded with shipping, sawmilling, and pulp and paper production, the Fraser was profoundly injured as a result. Now Prince George has grown to the point where it no longer accepts pollution as an inevitable part of progress. People live here because they like living here. They like the neighbours, the slower pace, the hockey rink, the blues club downtown, the lakes in the surrounding countryside. These are people who see a future for Prince George as something more than a good-paying resource job.

One of them is Dr. Robert Dykes, who moved to Prince George and opened a family practice in the late 1960s. It was a time when the pulp mills were expanding and the city was booming, and Dykes soon had to start asking questions about the mills' effect on his patients' health. In 1984 he and a small group of concerned citizens founded the Nechako Environmental Coalition. They tackled the issue of air pollution, then turned their attention to the Fraser, asking for and getting occupational water testing to check dioxin levels.

Dioxins and their chemical cousins, furans, are trace compounds found in effluent from the chlorine bleaching process that most BC pulp mills used until the 1990s. These chemicals were targetted by environmentalists because dioxins were found to be highly carcinogenic to rats, and to have properties that allow them to linger for years in the environment, growing more concentrated as they work their way up the food chain. A study found that sturgeon living at Stone Creek, about 15 miles (25 km) downstream from Prince George, had the largest concentration of dioxins in the area. "It was far enough down for the dioxins to settle out of the current," Dykes explains. "The Department of Fisheries declared resident fish inedible and many First Nations even swore off salmon."

Alternate bleaching processes using chlorine compounds or oxygen have allowed mills to reduce or eliminate their output of dioxins and furans. When the mills converted to a hydrogen peroxide process, says Dykes, the number of rail cars carrying chlorine into Prince George dropped from one per day to one per month, and that is good for the river. In fact, the Coalition is optimistic: dioxins have a half life of seven years, so the river could be relatively free of them in twenty years. The 1996 report of the Fraser Basin Management Program notes that dioxin and furan discharges in liquid effluent decreased by 96 and 97 percent respectively between 1990 and 1994, and in 1994 the provincial Medical Health Officer removed the consumption advisory for mountain whitefish. But the mills need much more cleaning up. Every year they discharge tons of other pollutants into the river. The effect of these substances on river ecosystems has not been measured, and some of the contaminants have not even been identified, yet releasing them into the river is perfectly legal.

The mills are not the only polluters. In the Prince George area, urban growth increasingly jeopardizes the health of the river. Individual water consumption is down and certain industrial pollutants of air and water have been reduced, but groundwater is highly vulnerable here, and problems of organic and chemical household wastes, meltwater from snow removal, and proliferation of cars and trucks have barely been touched.

The forest industry is taking a particularly heavy toll on the watershed in this area. The over-harvest of Crown lands has driven down the annual allowable cut, and timber-hungry forest companies are paying high prices for trees from private lands, which cover a significant area in the ranching country of central BC. Logging causes massive runoffs of topsoil into tributaries, Dykes explains, "which causes siltation of the salmon spawning grounds. Before the logging, the forest cover slowed the melting of the snow so that the run-off came more evenly over the spring and summer."

The problem cannot be solved without putting limits on the harvest of trees on privately owned land—a sensitive issue to raise in a town where nearly everyone is directly or indirectly dependent on the forest industry. But a growing number of citizens are raising the issue anyway. They know the health of the forests is inseparable from the health of the river, and that both resources must be provided for in the long term.

The creatures at the bottom of the food chain in the Fraser River, and the first to show the effects of pollution there, are the benthonic organisms, the abundant tiny animals that dwell in the mud of the river bottom. Environment Canada's National Hydrology Research Institute has begun to study these organisms by gathering them with plankton nets in shallow waters, and taking samples above and below Prince George to gain base-line information. In 1996 two young researchers on the river told me they would think twice before eating a fish caught from this part of the Fraser.

Fort George Canyon, 14 miles (24 km) downriver from Prince George, is the traditional fishing grounds of the Lheit-Lit'en (Fort George) nation. In addition to the usual net fishery, this group has revived a bit of ancient technology—the fish wheel, a delightfully simple, self-propelled device which has the great advantage of allowing fishers to release nontargetted species.

This spot also has some of the most treacherous rapids on the river. In 1793 Alexander Mackenzie wrote of this stretch of the Fraser: "The great body of water, at the same time tumbling in successive cascades ... rolls through this narrow passage in a very turbid current, and full of whirlpools." The canyon is also starkly beautiful. A series of small islands thrust their sheer rock walls up twenty or thirty feet from the river bottom, but the river ignores them, twisting and turning its way among the rocks and islands and flowing from the bottom of the canyon with renewed vigour.

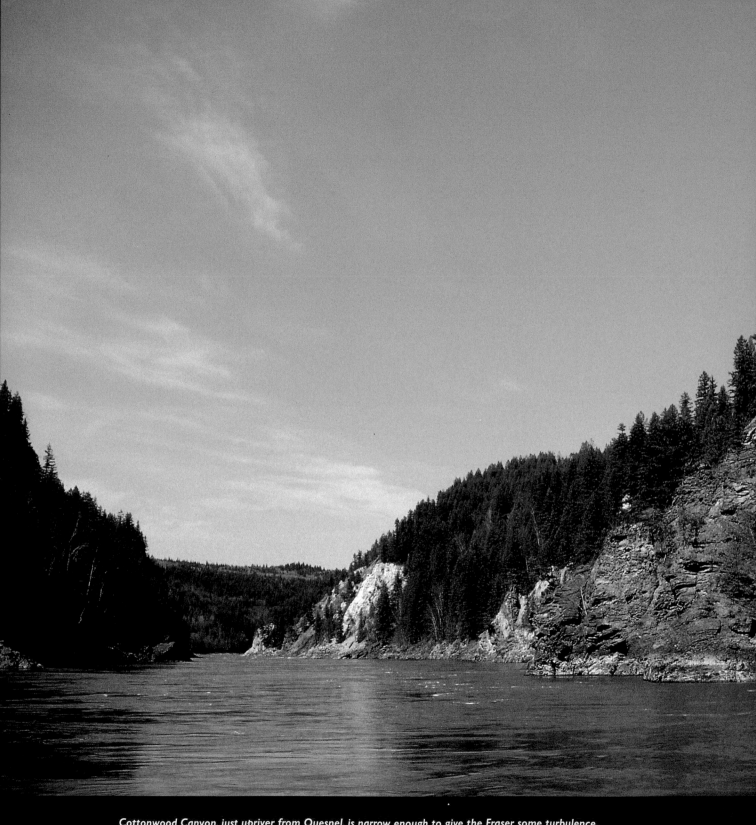

Cottonwood Canyon, just upriver from Quesnel, is narrow enough to give the Fraser some turbulence. But it is a relatively minor barrier to river traffic, and provided more excitement than danger for early steamboat passengers.

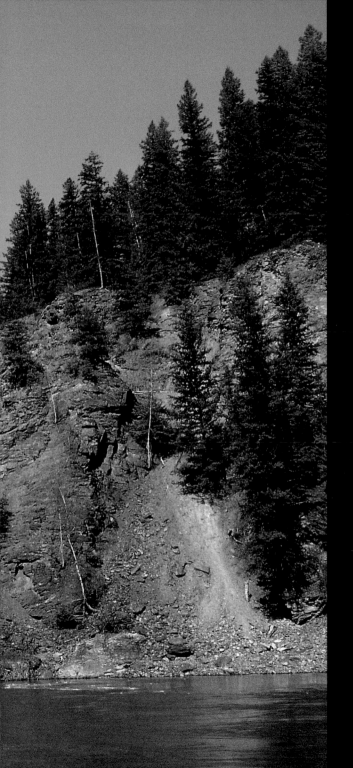
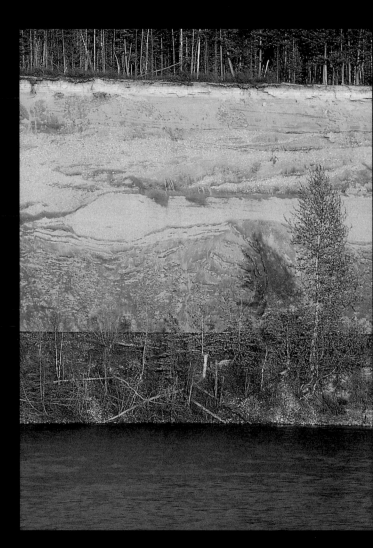

A fine sandy silt gives this riverbank, along the northern Fraser River, its distinctive golden colour. The sediment was deposited thousands of years ago when this area was covered by the massive Glacial Lake Prince George.

Except for Fort George Canyon and the turbulent Cottonwood Canyon lower down, the Fraser is quite placid between Prince George and Soda Creek. It was this 120-mile (200-km) piece of river that saw the heyday of steamboat travel in the late nineteenth and early twentieth centuries. For many decades, the huge steam-driven paddle wheelers were the best way to move people and freight north and south through the central interior. But this part of the Fraser also has a wide valley with good low benches, perfect for carrying both railway and highway along most of the east side of the river to Prince George. With the construction of those arteries in the early 1900s, river traffic on the Fraser River all but disappeared.

Downriver 35 miles (56 km) from Fort George Canyon, the Blackwater (West Road) River joins the Fraser at its west bank. This is the river that the First Nations advised Alexander Mackenzie to take in 1793, when he was on his way to the Pacific Ocean. It runs along part of an ancient trade route that brought coastal products like dried seaweed, oolichan grease and dentalia shells into the interior, in exchange for dried soapalallie and buckskin. Obsidian, a black volcanic glass mined from Anahim Peak near Ulkatcho just west of the headwaters of the Blackwater, was traded in both directions on that route. In his determination to make the mouth of the Fraser, Mackenzie went right past the confluence of the Blackwater, but later decided to retrace his steps.

Junctions of major trade routes become important centres of commerce all over the world, and the confluence of the Blackwater and Fraser rivers was no exception. A large Dakelh (Carrier) village was located there, but little is known about it. Its use as a sorting ground for a logging operation has destroyed much of what could have been an important archaeological site.

About 15 miles (25 km) downriver from the Blackwater confluence, the Fraser funnels energetically though Cottonwood Canyon before accepting the gold-bearing waters of the Cottonwood River. This is the stream that brought so much gold down to the Fraser from Williams Creek and the Barkerville area and, between 1858 and 1862, drew crowds of gold seekers in search of the mother lode. In the process they ripped up the creek and river gravels, founded Barkerville and took out millions in gold, and then most of them left. But the area still supports a few people, said to have incurable gold fever, who keep searching for shiny flecks in their pans and rocker boxes. A graph showing the rise and fall of the stock market and the price of gold through the twentieth century would probably be a mirror image of the population of gold miners living on the Fraser. In the depression years of the 1930s, hundreds of men stayed out of the labour camps by turning to the Fraser River and undertaking the gruelling work of panning its gravel bars.

A few miles below the mouth of the Cottonwood, the Fraser goes into three convolutions reminiscent of an angry boa. In a hay field hundreds of feet above the first big bend in the river, the water's work is having its effect. The river is eroding the base of the bank as relentlessly as an acid-bearing tide eating away the foot of the Colossus, and the top of the bank is responding by slumping its way downhill. Like a row of books tipped on the shelf, the field, complete with willow trees and fences, drops in steps that lean back on each other as they succumb. In early spring, the winter ice of the river grinds at the banks, sending billows of delta-bound mud into the water. The waters rise in freshet in May and June, and the currents tear away still more of the soil—soil that has lain in this place for thousands of years since settling out of Glacial Lake Prince George. In summer, winds will blow down the river, drying the muddy banks and lifting still more of the fine, rich dirt into the water. Then in winter, the springs that feed underground streams in the hillside will freeze as they are exposed to the cold air. The freezing will lift tons of soil and hold it ready to cascade down the slope with the spring thaw. These natural forces, repeated thousands of times over as many years, can move a mountain of soil to the river. The river will move it into the gravel bars, and then lose it to the sea.

Downstream from these great slouching banks, the Fraser has twisted away from the base of the hills, leaving behind a broad, flat peninsula. Through some quirk of hydrology, the river hasn't cut this great bend into an island but has wrapped the edges of the peninsula with a mile or two of gravel bar.

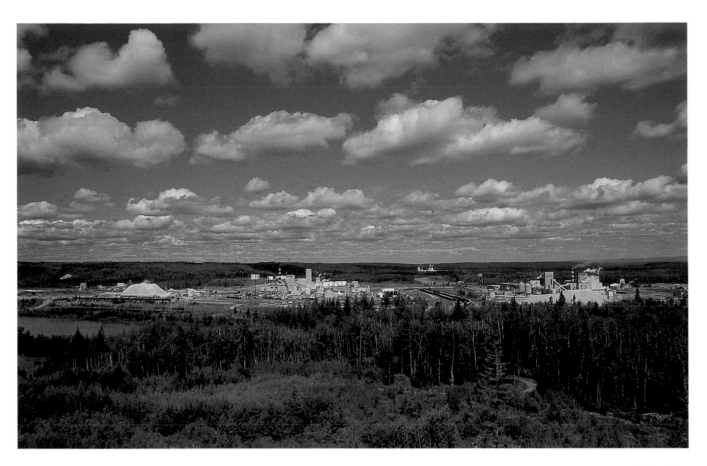

Just downriver, at the Fraser's confluence with the Quesnel River, is the city of Quesnel, centre of administration for three Dakelh nations and another interior BC town that grew up around the forest industry. Several lumber and pulp mills have been built on the narrow strip of land that runs between the rivers before they finally join forces. Here, as in all pulp mill communities, the mills create both employment and pollution, and concerned residents debate the balance of benefits. Individuals and groups in the area are devoting attention to air and noise pollution and to their greatest concern, contamination of the river. One mill, Cariboo Pulp and Paper, has been working with the municipality of Quesnel since 1986, sharing a treatment plant where mill effluent is processed before it is dumped into the river. Some 130,000 cubic yards (100,000 m³) of treated waste is piped across town and into the Fraser, although the Quesnel River is closer, because of the "greater dilution" power of the larger river. By this time the Fraser has already received effluent from another pulp mill just upstream and three mills in Prince George. "The ideal solution would be to not dump any of it into any river," says John Morrison, a supervisor at the mill, "but what are you going to do with it?"

Dr. Eric Hall and others at the University of British Columbia are working on the answer to Morrison's question. Dr. Hall is a member of the Department of Civil Engineering and an associate professor with the Chair in Forest Products Waste Management. He explains that there are two types of pulp mill. The mechanical mill, a less common type, needs 5,200 gallons (20,000 L) to make one ton of pulp. Most mills on the Fraser are the other type—chemical mills, or kraft mills, which require 15,600–20,800 gallons (60,000–80,000 L) of water to make one ton of pulp. Clearly the best thing for the river is for the mills to re-use as much of that water as possible, or "close the loop." "The industry has set up long-term goals toward closed-loop mills," Hall says. "They currently practise progressive systems closure, so that every time money is spent to solve a production problem, the reduction of water use is also addressed."

A closed-loop mill is designed to clean pollutants from the water it uses in making

Prince George pulp mills, like those at Quesnel, have dramatically reduced their discharge of some pollutants into the Fraser. But plenty of other mill wastes are just beginning to be identified and measured, and their effects tracked. The "closed loop" technology, which allows mills to reuse their waste water, may be the only effective way to protect our rivers from industrial effluents. If waste water is not clean enough to be reused in a mill, it is definitely not clean enough to be dumped into the Fraser Basin or any river.

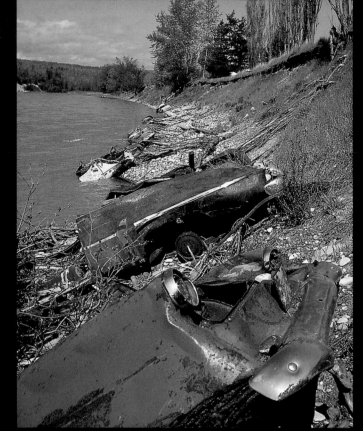

Installing riprap is a time-honoured method of strengthening riverbanks to keep them from eroding, but the usual material is stone or broken rock. This boneyard of old cars along the river at Quesnel demonstrates a practical but short-sighted attempt to control the river in the 1950s and 1960s.

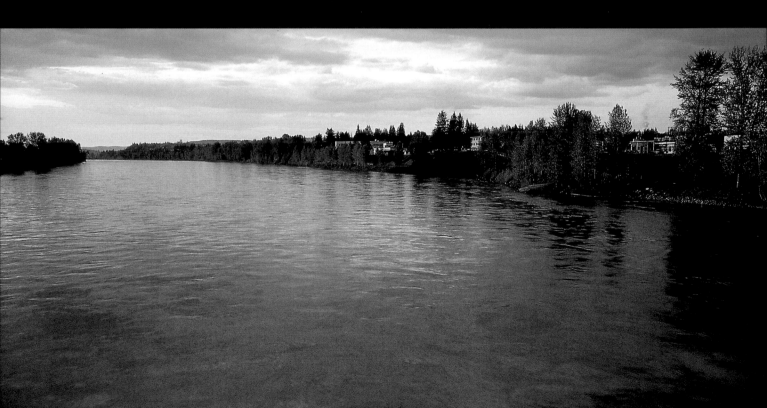

paper so that the water can be used again. New water is brought in only to replace small amounts lost through steam. Two of these mills have been built in Canada: one in Meadow Lake, Saskatchewan, where there was a shortage of water, and a second built by Louisiana Pacific in Chetwynd, BC. Introducing the closed loop to a chemical mill is difficult because of the volume of water required, but one or two closed-loop chemical mills have been built in Scandinavian countries. "The technology exists," Hall says, "but the cost of retrofitting a mill would be out of this world." BC mills are using less chlorine, but kraft mills still produce the largest volume of waste water in the Fraser Basin—and the most dangerous. We cannot afford not to close the loop on the pulp mills. We want our paper, but we also want our river.

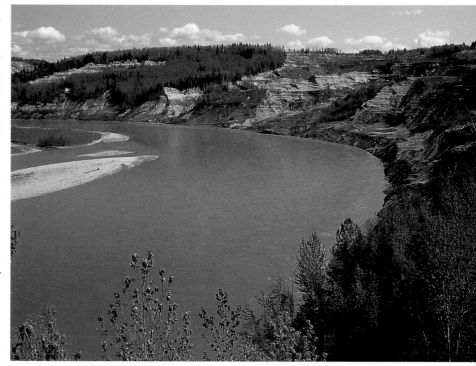

Just upriver from Quesnel, the Fraser's erosive power can be seen in an area of great slumping banks, made of sandy, unstable sediment left by Glacial Lake Prince George. As the water eats away at the outside bank and groundwater seepage erodes it further, the top responds by succumbing in layers. Eventually the river will wear down this land and cut straight through the bend.

The people of Quesnel acknowledge their indebtedness to the river that gave their town birth, most obviously in a special walk that extends along the Fraser and Quesnel riverfronts. Interpretive signs along the way mark important points in the town's history. Among these are the Fraser River gold rush, which reached a peak at Quesnel in 1859 when 10,000 miners arrived from downriver. The street that runs along the river is still lined with hotels waiting for guests to come up from the paddle wheelers, but these great vessels exist now only as ghosts, made material by a pair of rusted relics from the SS *Enterprise*. The *Enterprise* was the first paddle wheeler on the upper Fraser, built at Alexandria in 1863 from lumber whip-sawn at the site. The very boilerplates, engines, paddle axle and other ironwork that rest on their concrete pad along the river walk, were carried 300 miles (480 km) on pack mules from Port Douglas at the head of Harrison Lake, after being brought that far by steamboat from the lower Fraser. Other artifacts and signs along the river tell of the Fraser's role in hydraulic mining, a process in which huge pumps employed the massive force of river water to dislodge gravel and sediments from hillsides, then to wash it down through sluices to remove the gold. This highly destructive form of mining is no longer permitted in BC.

At another stop along the river walk, the visitor learns a well-hidden fact of BC history, that in the 1870s and 1890s half the people living in this area were Chinese. F. W. Howay reports in *British Columbia*, his 1914 history of BC, that white miners on the Fraser gravel bars worked with both ears open to tales of better-paying bars upriver, and gradually left the lower bars until only the more diligent Chinese miners were left.

But no sign tells the tourists and joggers who enjoy the riverside walk that much of the land on which it is built is an important graveyard of the First Nations. Numerous bones were unearthed in the construction of the hospital at the upstream end of the park, but archaeologists and oral historians agree that still more graves lie under the lawns and paths. Among them are the graves of five members of the Tsilhqot'in nation who were hanged following the Chilcotin War in 1864. In an example of British justice being applied to First Nations, British forces asked the Tsilhqot'in leaders to a peace meeting, then took them captive. Colonial Judge Matthew Baillie Begbie ordered them to be hanged. It is said the men stood together singing as the gallows was tipped. Their voices still haunt the Quesnel waterfront.

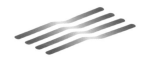

Between Quesnel and Soda Creek the river flows steadily and evenly between low banks that give to hay-growing benchlands. This is a fertile land, with ranches stretching along both shores of the river—not the manicured, white rail-fenced parcels of wealthy owners, but solid barbed wire and Russell-fenced working ranches. Logging trucks in the yards testify to the ranchers' need for extra work in the long months between cattle sales. For some of them, the river became even more important when the electrical service was improved. That's when it became economical to pump water up the relatively low riverbanks to the hay lands.

It was this easygoing stretch of river that in 1793 led Alexander Mackenzie to ignore the expert advice of local Natives and continue down the Fraser. Only when he arrived at the place that now bears his name, Alexandria, and saw that the hills would soon close in and the river's personality would be transformed, did Mackenzie change his mind. This spot was a major cultural and linguistic crossroads of the Athapaskan-speaking Dakelh people and the Salishan-speaking Secwepemc (Shuswap), and a crucial trade intersection. The fur trading fort that was founded at Alexandria is gone, from its original site on the west bank where it could serve the Tsilhqot'in Nation and from its later site on the east bank of the river. The Hudson's Bay Company, recognizing that the produce of gold miners could soon overtake that of fur trappers, and that the Tsilhqot'in could not be controlled, moved their operations to Quesnel in 1867.

At 'Estilagh, the Fraser River splits the lands of the Alexandria Band of the Tsilhqot'in Nation. From spring to early fall, a reaction ferry at Marguerite connects the two sides. The ferry is a safe and modern vessel, composed of two hulls with a deck similar to that of a bridge and a small operator's cabin on the upstream side. Cables from the upstream side of each hull are attached to pulley blocks on a main line stretched across the river. By making slight adjustments to the length of the attaching cables, the ferry operator changes the angle of the

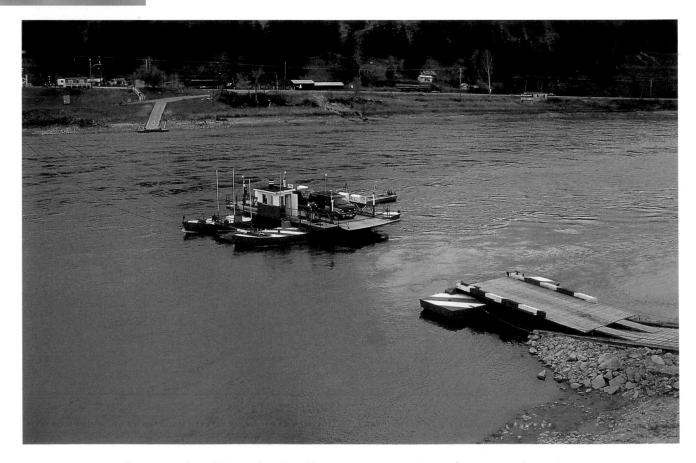

The reaction ferry ("friction ferry") at Marguerite works with the river's energy in a harmonious, nondestructive way. The vessel runs on cables. It is carried silently back and forth on the downstream current, with just a slight shift in the angle of the hull as necessary to adjust to the movement of the river.

hulls in relation to the river current. The current pushes on the side of the hulls and moves the ferry on its pulleys across the river. A second wire is stretched across the river just downstream of the ferry, and a tail wire extends from the downstream end of the ferry hulls to this wire. In the past there were several of these ferries at various points on the river, but now there are only three: at Marguerite, Big Bar and Lytton.

Soda Creek, a few miles downriver, marks the lower limit of steamboat navigation on the upper Fraser. Just downriver from here, the Soda Creek rapids and steep, riverbanks served to prevent, or at least discourage, the passage of paddle wheelers, and in winter this area is also the locus of some spectacular ice jams. The riverbanks grow steep and frequent tributary streams cut deep furrows into the sides, so that scores of trestles and steep grades would be needed for railway or highway construction. Thoroughfares that otherwise follow the Fraser leave the river at this point and take an easier route, as they have done since the first rails and roads were built.

Using a ship's wheel, Brenda Cowlin adjusts the angle of the reaction ferry to the river current.

Today the community of Soda Creek is a small collection of houses on a bench just above high water. But in the years following 1863 when it became the northern terminus of the Cariboo Wagon Road, constructed to take thousands of prospectors and adventurers up the river, Soda Creek was a booming little port. Wagon and pack trains would arrive here after the 170-mile (283-km) haul on the wagon road, then transfer their northbound cargo to the paddle wheelers for the final leg to Quesnel or on to Fort George. More recently, the Soda Creek ferry crossed the river at this point. The ferry served the growing number of ranchers and trappers working out on the Chilcotin plateau and up along the west side of the Fraser, until the 1970s when road access was improved and the ferry was discontinued in favour of the one at Marguerite.

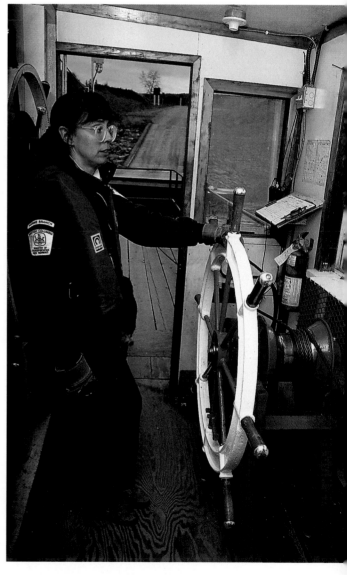

Before rail and highway transportation, the Fraser River between Prince George and Soda Creek was a thoroughfare for canoes and then steamboats. It was the most efficient means of moving freight, so it had great economic value, of which a huge, white-painted, black-smoke-belching paddle wheeler was the most visible symbol. Today the river is many times more valuable than it was in the paddle wheeler days, for it is still the route for salmon headed north to their spawning grounds near Stuart Lake, Quesnel Lake and Rearguard Falls, and it is the avenue by which infant salmon find their way to the rich growing grounds of the Pacific Ocean.

But mixed with the ocean-bound salmon fry are the embarrassing results of modern life along the Fraser. If we imagine the river functioning something like a human body, we cannot expect it to stay healthy when it has to digest tons of toxins every year. People who live in cities with mill-based economies, like Prince George and Quesnel, are becoming more aware of the mills' effect on the river, but we are only just developing baseline information with which we can measure pollutants and their effects.

Cities and towns along this part of the river, from Prince George to Soda Creek, are true river towns. Their earliest definitions grew out of canoe and steamboat travel, out of river gold and river people. Their future, too, depends on the Fraser—the delicate life source that flows by their riverfront streets.

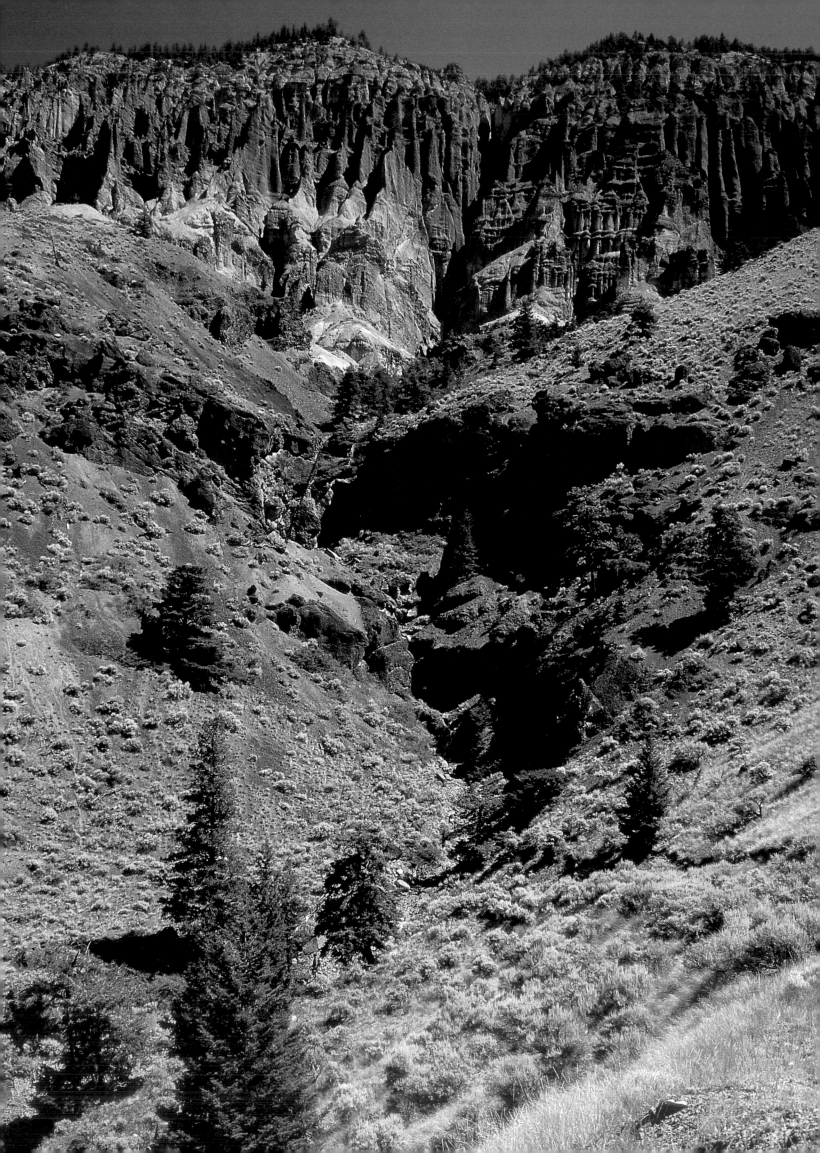

4

PLATEAU

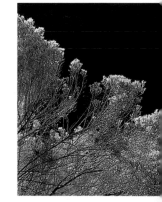

Downriver from Soda Creek, the vegetation along the Fraser River is a mix of bunchgrass and sage, with lodgepole pine on the drier ridges, fir on the shaded northern-exposed slopes, and aspen where snowmelt collects in the gullies. Where the sidehills are forested, their very steepness has spared them from most logging. Like most of the land between Prince George and Soda Creek, this is Cariboo ranch country, a place where subtle variations in temperature and rainfall give more grass here or more sage there. The southern-exposed benches of river gravel, with their thin layers of soil, are often covered with small cactus. Much of the higher land has a climate that tolerates little more than root crops, but the area right around Soda Creek is noted throughout the Cariboo for its special microclimate, with enough frost-free days to grow the vegetables that early European miners and settlers missed in the new land.

The old basin of Glacial Lake Prince George narrows significantly at this point, and the river enters the plateau region. The river walls are made of silt, interspersed with beds or layers of much coarser material laid down when streams entered the lake, or when smaller ice dams formed and broke on the tributary streams, causing glacial outburst floods which carried gravel and boulders into the lake. In glacial times, a large ice blockage stood in this area for thousands of years, creating the glacial lake to the north and laying down the plateau.

The Fraser has incised itself into this plateau, so that the hills, which have been set back from the river, now crowd in close, forcing the river far below the edges of the landscape. From the water it is impossible to see the flat land up on the plateau, and except for a few vantages, the river cannot be seen from the land. Many years ago, when my wife and I hitchhiked to the Soda Creek reserve to visit friends, we got out of a car on the road high above the little village, just at dusk. It was a mile walk down the switchbacks of the road, and by the time we got to our friends' house it was dark. In the light of the following morning I was amazed on walking over to the edge of the plateau to find that we were still hundreds of feet above the Fraser River. Later in the day we went farther down the road and stood on a bench that was still nearly a hundred feet above the water. I felt a long way from my home on the gentle banks of the Campbell River.

Since then I have visited some of the less turbulent rivers of eastern North America and gained some understanding of what it

e Cathedrals—turrets,
nacles and a myriad other
ricate shapes—have been
rved by wind, rain and dust
the face of this hillside
ar Lone Cabin Creek in the
d-Plateau.

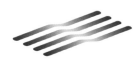

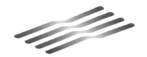

must have been like for Simon Fraser when he entered the netherworld of the Fraser below Soda Creek in the summer of 1808. Born in Vermont, Fraser would have been accustomed to rapids, but not the combination of wilderness, rapid and canyon that he was to find as he continued down the Fraser. In his journal, he agrees with the people he called Atnah that this part of the river is "a dreadful chain of difficulties apparently insurmountable . . ."

Fraser made his voyage in fragile bark canoes that were heavily laden with supplies, and a crew that included two clerks, two Native guides and nineteen French Canadian voyageurs. In April 1996 a group of friends and I took the same route, but we travelled in a neoprene raft, and in place of a bunch of voyageurs we had a 40-hp outboard. The raft is made with a wood and metal compartment suspended between a pair of 30-foot (9 m) tubes, and gains additional support and stability from two more 23-foot (7 m) tubes lashed to the outside of the larger tubes. These tubes were first built by the US military to support floating bridges, so they are extremely rugged and buoyant.

Like Fraser, I spent most of the trip sitting in the middle of the raft and letting the guide do the work. But our guide, Darwin Baerg, unlike Fraser's local guides who normally stayed on the shore, had made the trip several times before and knew what to expect around each bend in the river.

I spent more than twenty years living in the Cariboo and Chilcotin, on the east side of the Fraser at Williams Lake and Alkali Lake, and on the west side at Stoney. Yet the greater part of the river from Soda Creek to Lillooet remained nearly as unfamiliar to me as it had been to Simon Fraser. The river was a powerful brown presence swelling along almost silently while I passed high over it on the Sheep Creek Bridge that joins Bella Coola and the Chilcotin to the main highway at Williams Lake. I had seen the river from bridges upstream and downstream of the Sheep Creek. I had seen it at the Alkali Lake Band's fishing place and a couple of other spots where you get to glimpse the river from a road that hugs the high shoulder of the steep valley. But like most Cariboo residents, I had in my mind only these snapshots of this part of the Fraser. Darwin and his raft would give me the full movie.

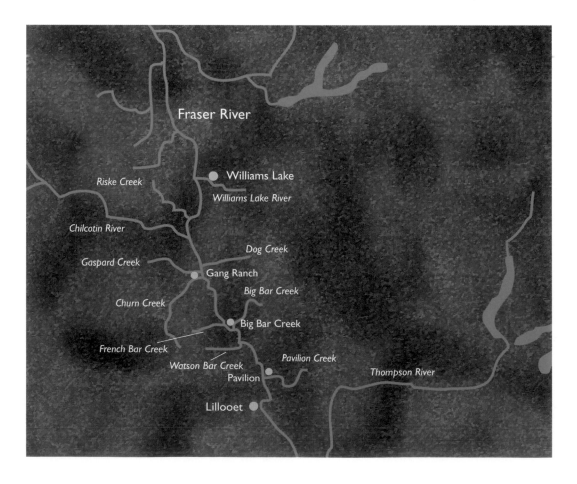

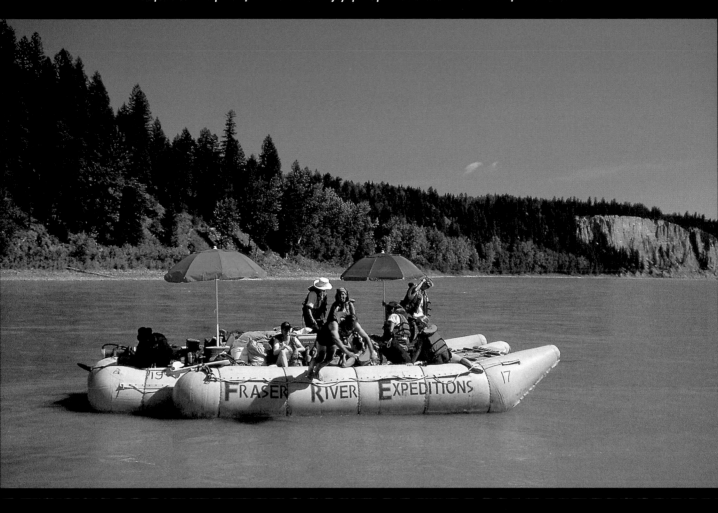

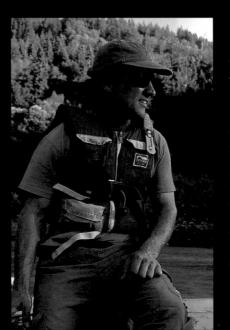

Senior guide Darwin Baerg grew up in the Fraser Valley, and since then has expanded his love and knowledge of the Fraser's waters, rocks and currents, from Tête Jaune's cold green water to the brackish tidal waters of the coast. He and his wife Susan arrange river rafting trips from one day to three weeks in duration. For the Baergs, introducing people to the experience of the river has grown from a business to a dedication.

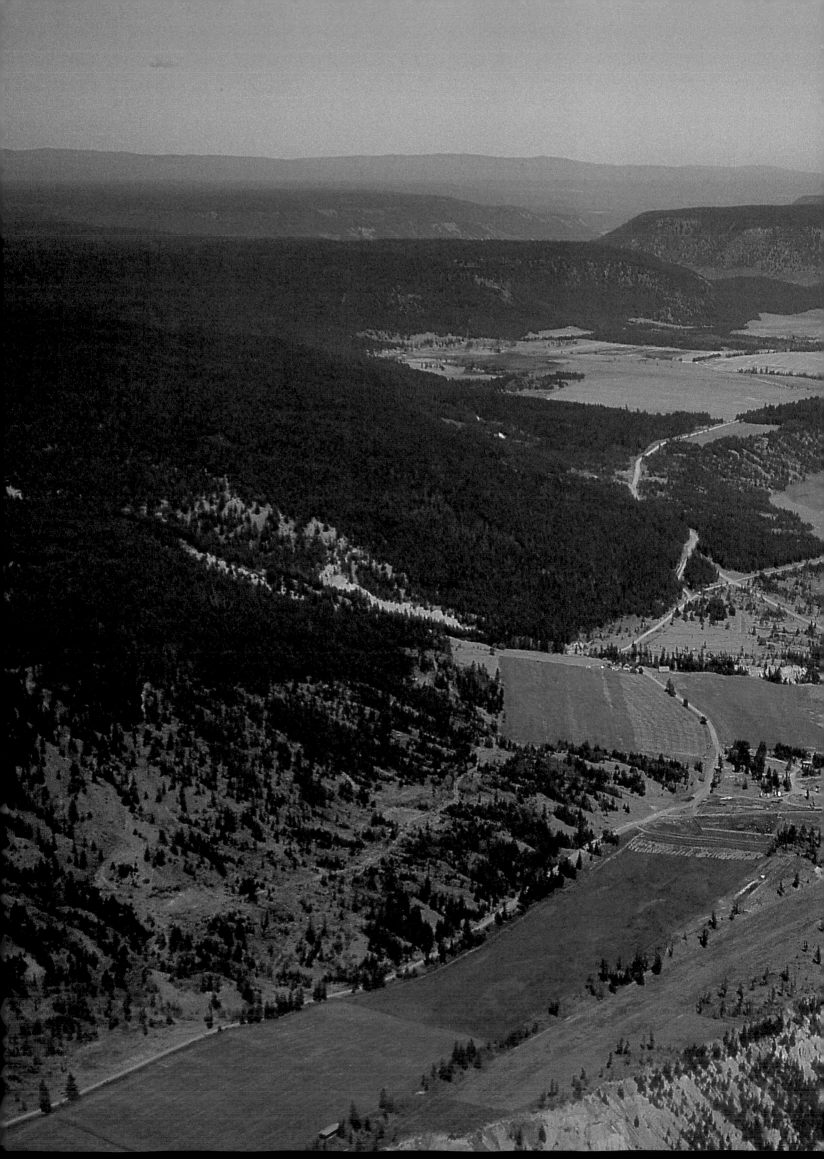

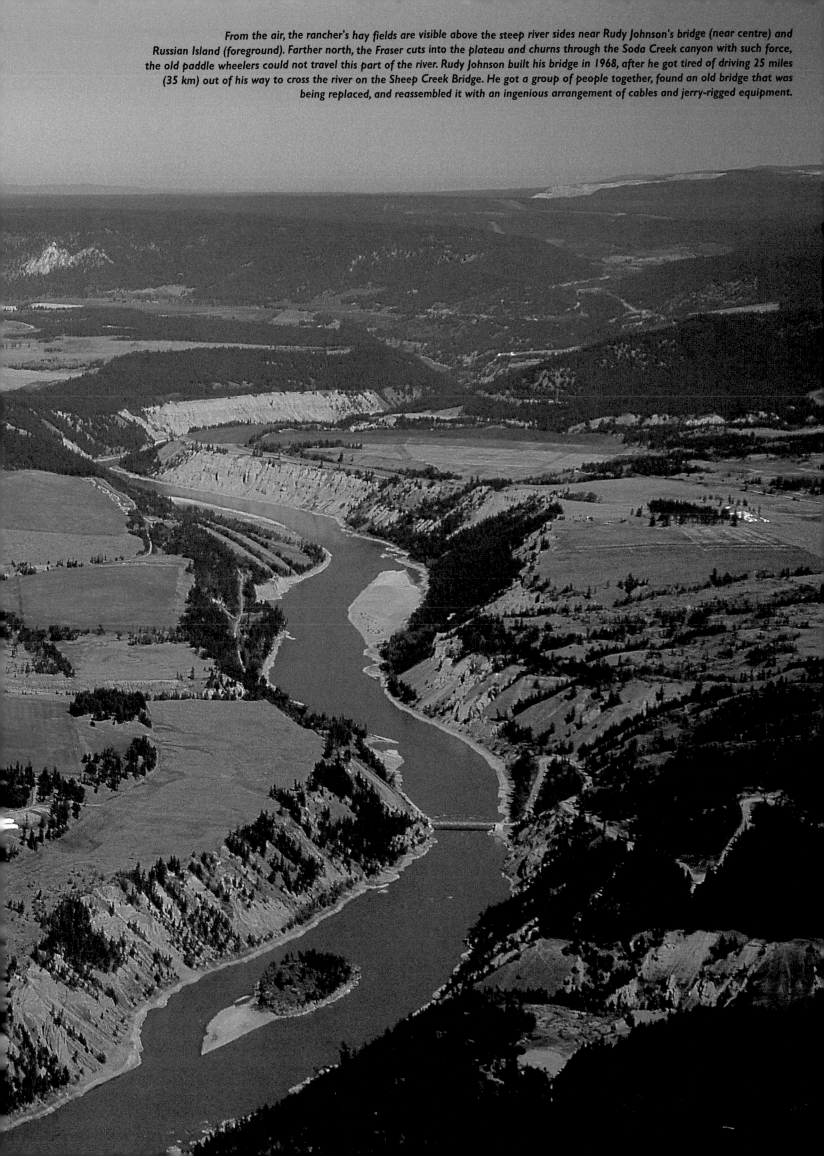

From the air, the rancher's hay fields are visible above the steep river sides near Rudy Johnson's bridge (near centre) and Russian Island (foreground). Farther north, the Fraser cuts into the plateau and churns through the Soda Creek canyon with such force, the old paddle wheelers could not travel this part of the river. Rudy Johnson built his bridge in 1968, after he got tired of driving 25 miles (35 km) out of his way to cross the river on the Sheep Creek Bridge. He got a group of people together, found an old bridge that was being replaced, and reassembled it with an ingenious arrangement of cables and jerry-rigged equipment.

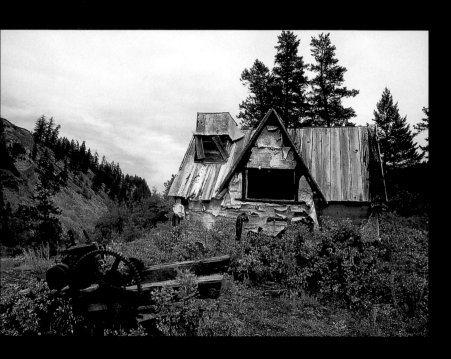

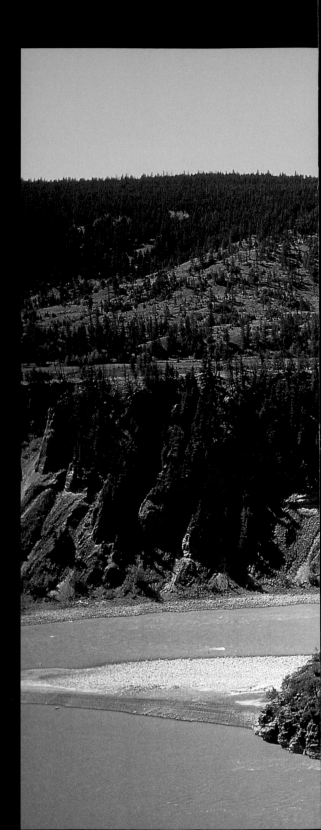

According to local stories, the home and mining operation on Russian Island were built by a Russian immigrant who came here to mine gold. What equipment has been left behind indicates both placer and hard rock mining were undertaken here, and the house itself is very well built. The island was accessible only by aerial tram (built by the same man) during the summer or across the ice in winter, so all materials for the house and outbuilding had to be hauled great distances by hand. The island was abandoned in the 1950s or 1960s, and today it is inhabited only in the summer—by several pairs of nesting geese.

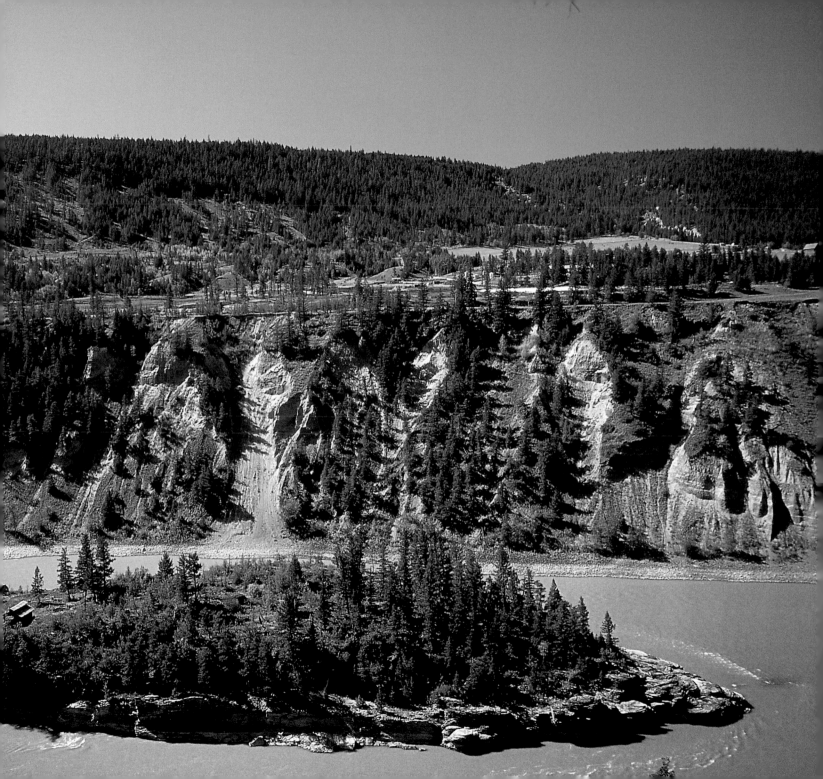

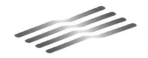

As Darwin eased the raft downriver toward the Soda Creek canyon, we passed by the rocky promontory where I had stood above the Fraser on that first trip thirty-five years before. There a group of workers from the reserve were raising a circle of prairie-style teepees. They stopped and waved, and as we drifted by on the raft, we felt that wonderful detachment from the world of the landbound. Then we were into the dreaded Soda Creek canyon, ready to be battered by the elements, but the big tubes rode the rapids with only a hint of splashing. Darwin told us the passage isn't always so smooth—at lower water levels, with less river to ease the raft over the rocks, the ride would have been rougher.

Below the rapids the Fraser is heavy and brown, and it settles into its deep power mode. Even when our motor was stopped the river bore us along at a steady 4 or 5 miles per hour (7–8 km/h), the current a throbbing hiss along the shore gravel. When the edge of a back eddy caught us, the boat turned a full circle in the stream as we gazed up at the hugely steep gravel banks. In some places they rise a hundred yards or more above the river, and we saw no more people, or any sign that they existed on those high banks, until we reached Rudy Johnson's bridge 10 miles (16 km) downriver from the canyon.

Land status maps along this part of the Fraser show that the east shore of the river has been neatly subdivided into 5- to 10-acre (2- to 4-hectare) lots. They were developed for returning World War One veterans, but few were taken up. There weren't many employment opportunities here, and even more discouraging, most of the lots were located on very steep hillside. Clearly whoever authorized the plan could not read a topographical map. To this day, only one or two of these privately owned lots are occupied.

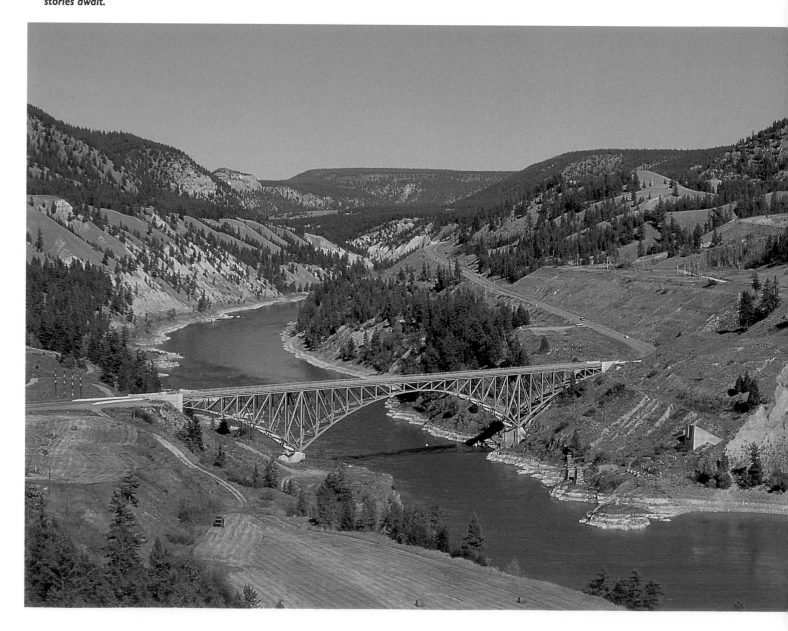

On one of them, down a dirt road that winds down from the old highway and through the steep land along the river, is Norrie Overton's 300-acre (120-hectare) sidehill ranch and her trailer home clinging to the hill. "Mom and I first came down to look at the place in 1971," she says. "Charlie Browse from the 150 Mile had used it as spring turnout for his cattle, and we bought it from him for $11,000."

Ranchers make good use of the privately owned sidehills along this part of the river. They are not allowed to put their cattle out onto the government range until mid-May, to prevent damage to the fragile grasses, but the hillsides get more sunlight and "green up" faster, so cattle can be held there until turnout.

"I love the river," Norrie says. "My mom was a rock hound and I do lapidary with jade and Chilcotin agate. Right now I have two sluice boxes working in the runoff from our road. I get my husband to gravel it, then when the snow melts I wash the gravel for gold." She led me outside to see a 300-pound (135-kg) boulder of rare tremolite white jade that her dad found in the river. "He couldn't get it up here and he was worried that someone else would find it, so he kept covering it with gravel until we finally got it with the front-end loader."

Norrie and her mom may have been the first people to actually live on this steep river sidehill since it was "taken up" in 1902. Rather like her trailer home, Norrie seems to have become a part of the sidehill and part of the river.

All along the Fraser for the next 95 miles (150 km) or so, ranches sit up on the benches, some of which are a few yards wide, some of which stretch back 800 yards (725 m) or more. Occasionally the river-rafter can peer up at the lip of a high bench and make

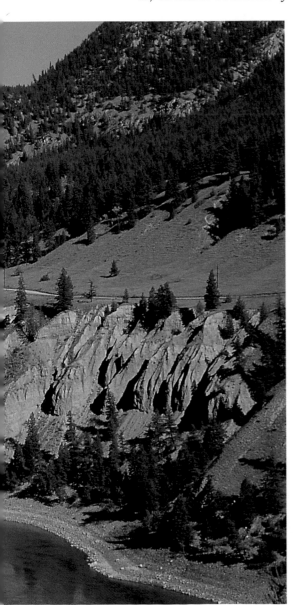

out just a hint of a line of aluminum irrigation sprinklers on a rancher's field. But these sprinklers are not fed by the river: they draw from mountain streams that gravity has brought to them, the same streams that go on to join the Fraser.

As the raft took us past the point where the waters from Williams Lake Creek enter the Fraser, I remembered walking in the deep valley that comes down a few miles away. Through that valley runs a huge pipeline bearing the partially treated sewage of Williams Lake, a town of more than 10,000 people. As in other municipalities on the Fraser watershed, the debate on sewage treatment and water quality is a lively one here, but solutions are slow in coming. Meanwhile, the town continues to grow while the ability of the river to carry away its waste does not.

Below Williams Lake Creek, the river took our raft past more steep banks whose surfaces ranged from fine riverine pea gravel, to rounded boulders, back to fine layered sediments. All of it was laid down ten or fifteen thousand years ago as the great glacial ice sheets retreated from the land. About 6 miles (10 km) along we passed the outlet of little Chimney Creek, and after another few miles I saw the familiar green steel arch of the "new" (built in 1962) Sheep Creek Bridge. On the east bank, just below the arch of the new bridge, are the remains of the stone pylons that held up the old wooden suspension bridge, built in 1904.

Shortly after we drifted under the bridge, we saw the first house we had seen since passing by Rudy Johnson's bridge. In the 1970s a young woman lived at that ranch who became a champion barrel racer. I used to go and watch, partly to see the young women guiding powerful quarter-horses around drums in intricate manoeuvres, but mostly because it was an excuse to drive just a little farther down

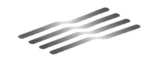

along the river, to see just a little more of that hidden gorge that reveals itself only at the occasional spot where a bridge transects it.

I grew up learning to treat rivers with respect but still to befriend them, to travel up and down them in canoes or drift down them on inner tubes or even swim across them.

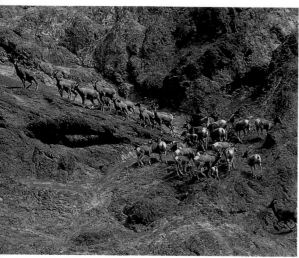

Sheep Creek earns its name from the California bighorn sheep that move through this rugged, seemingly impassable landscape. The bighorns' territory near the confluence of the Chilcotin and Fraser rivers has recently been declared a provincial park, the Junction Wildlife Management Area. In a real ecological success story, the bighorns have been brought back from dangerously low populations to the extent that they are now moved to points all over North America to be used as seed stock.

To the ranchers of the Chilcotin in the first years of the twentieth century, the Fraser was more of a nuisance. Everything coming into the country or going out of it had to be taken across the river. Once I saw the remains of an old steam tractor on a ranch in this area, and I heard the story of how it had come across Canada by train, then been driven up the Hanceville Express road and ferried across the river before being driven to its new home out on the plateau. Even after two generations, the focus of the story was the terror of rafting that irreplaceable piece of progress across unknowable river currents.

Downriver from the Sheep Creek Bridge, the view is blocked by a massive rock outcrop that towers above the water, at once calling the rafter to climb up and explore its caves, and mocking such ambition. We slipped on past, riding our comfortable raft as we entered the Junction Wildlife Management Area, designated a provincial park in 1995. A noisy trickle of gravel down the cliffs alerted our rafting group to the primary reason for establishing the park. A mother California bighorn sheep looked down at us, waiting while her new spring lamb climbed the loose gravel of the scree slope to the security of her lofty perch. As we rafted through the afternoon we saw many more bighorns among the infinitely varied browns and greens of the steep cliffs.

Most of the river along here is fast but gentle, or so it seems from the safety of a modern raft. One of our group was reading excerpts from Simon Fraser's journal as we travelled, and asked Darwin where the big rapid was, the one that gave Fraser so much trouble. Darwin, who has studied the journal closely, thought it might be Iron Canyon, just above the mouth of the Chilcotin River. Forty-five minutes later we got to the point where the river valley's gravel- and sediment-banked walls were blocked by a dramatic expanse of solid black rock rising narrow and sheer on either side. Fraser's journal is clear on this spot, and he wasn't taking any chances with it. "Here we unloaded on the left side of a strong Rapid," he wrote, "and carried all the baggage & canoes over a point which has very steep and high banks of about 1200 yards long, and incredible it is to relate the trouble and misery the people had in performing that office. On debarkation we found the horns of that animal the Tahawteens call the Sassian, and the Mayatué of the Crees, or Rocky Mountain ram . . . The course of water in this Portage is about S 5 E 1/2 [mile], and the rocks contract themselves to within 30 yards of one another, and at [the] lower end is a rocky Island on the left shore. It is terrible to behold the rapidity and turbulency of the immense body of water that passes in this narrow gut, and no less do the numerous Gulphs and whirlpools it forms constantly striking from one rock to another. The rocks are particularly high and craggy, particularly on the right side, and the water in a manner seems to have forced a passage under them and flows out here and there in numerous whirlpools and eddies that surpass any thing of the kind I ever saw before." These are strong words from a man who has crossed the continent by canoe.

On the raft we shared Fraser's trepidation, but there would be no portage. As we came into the top end of the canyon, the currents grabbed at the raft and pushed it down through the narrows toward a hard left bend, and drove us toward the west wall. Darwin revved the outboard to push us away from Fraser's "particularly high and craggy rocks." After a tense moment the prop bit into solid water and moved us to safety. Darwin grinned as the raft shot down the tongue of rapid at the bottom of the canyon, and cold white water broke over the bow to freshen the faces of the young people sitting at the front. The portage had cost Fraser four hours and a dram for all hands; the water passage had taken us only a few minutes.

As the Fraser cuts its path through the Plateau, occasional rock outcrops like this one at Iron Canyon, near the confluence with the Chilcotin, give the sunlight graphic play on their faces. But they also form a narrow passage which made this stretch of river virtually inaccessible by canoe. Simon Fraser travelled around this canyon on land; and even now, in a modern river raft with a skilled guide, Iron Canyon is an exhilarating passage indeed.

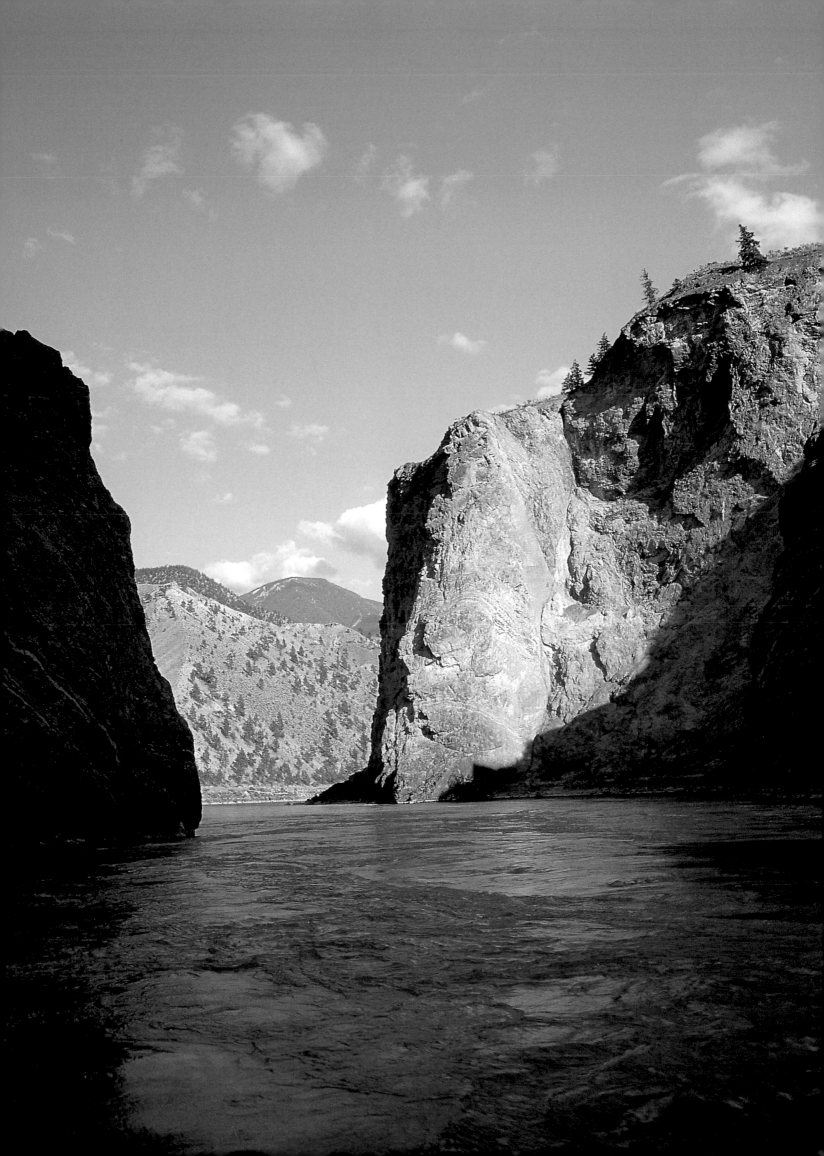

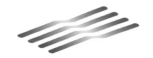

As the river spat us out the bottom end of Iron Canyon, the place Fraser named Portage de Barriel for the barrel from which those drams had come, Darwin swung the big raft into the back eddy on the east bank. He wanted to collect some driftwood for that evening's camp, and to show us some ancient petroglyphs carved into a huge rock. If Simon Fraser saw those carvings, he failed to mention them. The representations of mountain sheep would have matched his own observations, but did he see the beautiful rendition of a person on horseback, complete with a delicate trail of hoof prints? Iron Canyon was obviously an important spot long before Fraser memorialized it in his notes.

A short distance downriver, Darwin put the raft in for the night's camp, at the mouth of the Chilcotin River. The flat on the south side of the junction of the rivers is a reserve belonging to the Alkali Lake (Esk'et) band. It is here that the Secwepemc (Shuswap) people had a village before the community was devastated by the smallpox epidemic of 1863 and the influenza epidemic of 1918. In the 1970s, when I sat with my friend Amelia Dick in her kitchen, she spoke of the people who were gone from the land west of the Fraser. Now, in the 1990s, I looked at this land and thought of the continuum of history that has caused the confluence of the Chilcotin and Fraser to be the only major river junction on the Fraser system that has no town. In fact there were no people and no standing habitation here, other than our scattering of little nylon dome tents.

Some of us walked across the flat through the sage and bunchgrass along the banks of the Chilcotin. I was looking for the distinctive turquoise blue lent the river by glacial silt from Taseko Lake far to the southwest, but it was spring and that magical colour had been masked either by the silty brown of the Fraser or by slides farther up the Chilcotin. We climbed a steep slope past the white-flowered saskatoon bushes to the first gravel bench. In the open country we could see for miles, yet we observed nothing that Simon Fraser wouldn't have seen 188 years earlier, except a half dozen Hereford and Charolais bulls in a newly green pasture of the Alkali Lake ranch. Then, smelling our supper on the wind, we circled back to the camp. We came out above a low bench along the river, about 2 acres in size, marked by carefully arranged piles of rocks and boulders that looked like neat windrows in a rancher's hay field. They were probably the work of the placer miners, most of them Chinese, who reworked so much of the river in the 1880s and '90s. If the work was done by hand, it represents the labour required to build a small town. How much gold was in the field? How did they pump enough water to wash the rocks? How long did it take? Where are the descendants of the people who left this monument to their labour? Everywhere we saw any amount of flat land alongside the river, we saw more of the windrowed rocks and boulders. We could also see the remains of their tiny cabins, many dug into the hillside.

Farther downriver, we passed a massive cliff face on the east bank. We could not see the lush grass that grows on top of it, on Wycott Flat where the Alkali people have wintered horses for decades. Nor could we see, as we passed the outlet of Dog Creek, its enormous importance to the ranchers up the valley for irrigating hundreds of acres of timothy, brome and alfalfa. In the hot, arid climate of the Cariboo, ranching depends on the little gravity-fed side streams of the Fraser, because along most of this stretch the banks are too high to permit river water to be pumped up for irrigation.

The land along the west bank of the Fraser below the Chilcotin has for many years been the domain of the massive Gang Ranch. From an airplane the huge hay fields, irrigated from Gaspard Creek, shine amber against the brown hills, but from the river we could see only the brown hills. A bridge built here in 1912, of the same design as the original Sheep Creek Bridge and the bridge at Lillooet, is still in use. In the days before the Pacific Great Eastern Railway reached Williams Lake from the Lower Mainland, the Gang Ranch suspension bridge served the Hanceville Express road between Chilcotin and Ashcroft.

To Know the Chilcotin

For me the Chilcotin River, like the land and people of its name, was reserved and difficult to know, but once known it was lodged forever in my mind and my heart. I first saw the Chilcotin when I was fifteen. It was that time in the 1950s when Kodachrome bestowed a picture-postcard blue on all bodies of water. But here was a whole big river whose colour was more vibrantly turquoise than any chemistry-enhanced image. A decade later I came to live near this beautiful river with the cold opaque gemstone waters, at the Tsilhqot'in community of Stoney on a bench high above those waters. I walked the river's banks and I rode my saddle horse along the river, but I didn't swim or canoe the rapids. It would have been too intimidating on a river that I couldn't see into. Once my father came to visit, and we spent a wonderful day fishing a stretch—not fishing so much as learning a feel of the water.

But it was only when I went to the Chilcotin River with the local First Nations people that I gained some insights into the river. The Tsilhqot'in are named for the river. The *qo* in their name means river as in Chilko, Nechako, Atnarko, and the *t'in* means people. In Canada, the Tsilhqot'in are the southernmost of the Athapaskans. Named for a river, they are people of the meadows and mountains and they treat water with cautious respect. In fact, I think they are most comfortable with the river in its headwaters. In the years I lived in the rolling hill country of the Chilcotin plateau, I often heard people speak with a kind of reverence about "going to the snow mountains," a place of good hunting and powerful memories.

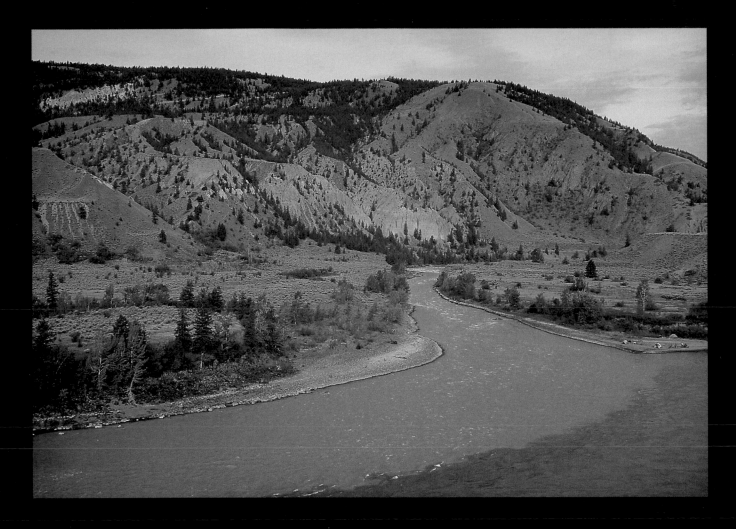

Tseman

The confluence of the Chilcotin and Fraser rivers is the only major junction on the Fraser that no longer has a town, but it has not always been so quiet. It was here that Simon Fraser met a Tsilhqot'in on a horse; a large Secwepemc village once stood here, and later a settlement of Chinese placer miners. Now it is well cared-for camping spot for rafters, who find it a wonderful place from which to marvel at the rich turquoise of the Chilcotin waters.

To follow the Chilcotin River back through its many miles, to the 55-mile long (88-km) Chilko Lake, is to follow the linking of many lifetimes. In the autumn of 1993, my daughter Helen and I made that trip. We went to Henry's Crossing, just a few miles down the Chilcotin River from the outlet of Chilko Lake, to visit Helen's cousin Dinah Lulua. She was camped by the river with her husband James and James's grandmother Emily Ekks. Each of the fishing camps I have visited along the Fraser and other watersheds is unique, but they all have

something in common—an air of transient pleasure and serious purpose. James and Dinah's camp, set in the shelter of aspen trees just on the verge of turning to fall colours, was comfortable and welcoming. The intense red leaves of drying sockeye hanging from the rack built into the green and yellow aspens attested to good fishing by the men and careful cutting by the women. There was harmony in the rhythms of the camp, in the talk over coffee around the morning fire.

James and I walked down to the river to see how his son Jeremy was making out in his first fishing. From the single-lane wooden bridge that gives Henry's Crossing its name, we watched as Jeremy stood rock-steady on a patch of grass beside the swift-flowing river. The water is clear here, as the lower river has not yet picked up its turquoise colour from the glacial silt-laden waters of the Taseko. Through a yard or two of fast-moving water we could see the dark shapes of sockeye darting up over the jade green river bed. Jeremy held his long pole with its harpoon-style gaff

hook suspended just above the surface. From time to time he lowered it quickly into the water at the same time as he pushed it outward at one of the darting fish. After several tries, he impaled a salmon. The hook slipped from the rubber lashing and swung at the end of a bit of twine as Jeremy lifted the fish and swung it to the grassy bank. He looked up at his father on the bridge, and smiles of pride mirrored each other on the faces of father and son. It was Jeremy's first sockeye.

James told me how he had caught his own first sockeye at the same spot, and I realized I was in the presence of more than the ritual of passing a skill from father to son. This was the linking of a hundred generations that have fished the sockeye at this spot in this river. It was the linking of the Tsilhqot'in people with the tseman, the sockeye that have shared their lives on the river since the people and the animals found harmony, since the first days of the first ancient stories.

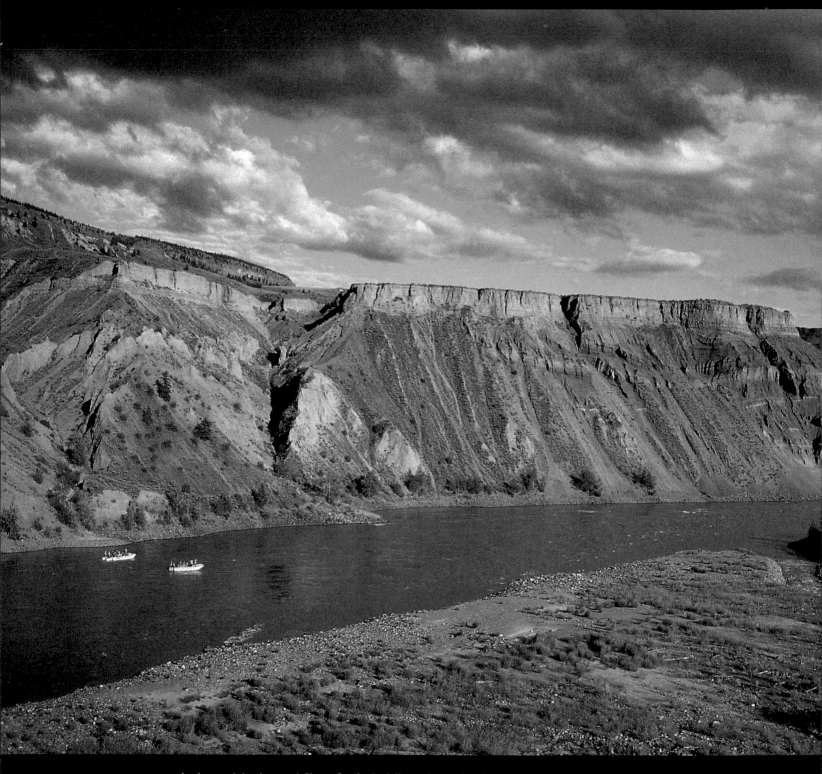

In the ranch land around Churn Creek, the hills on the shores of the river continuously add silt to the distinctively coloured waters, which then carry the sediments hundreds of miles downriver and deposit them on the growing deltas of the estuary.

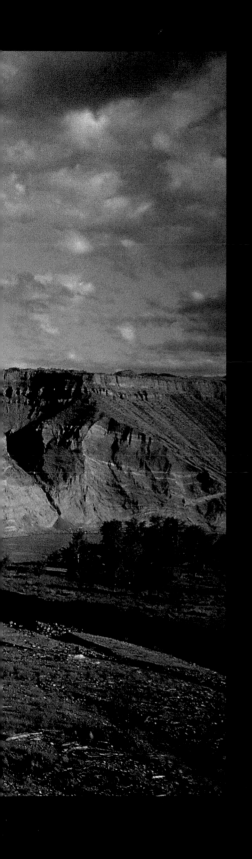

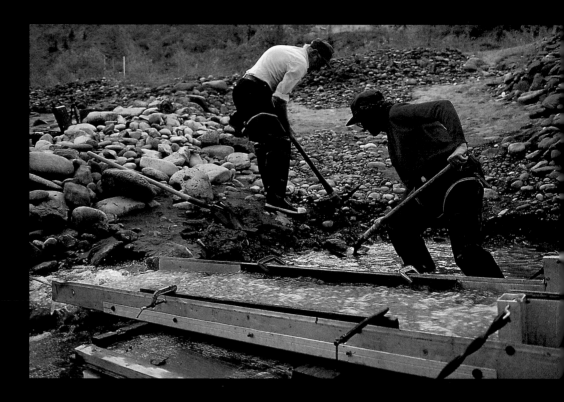

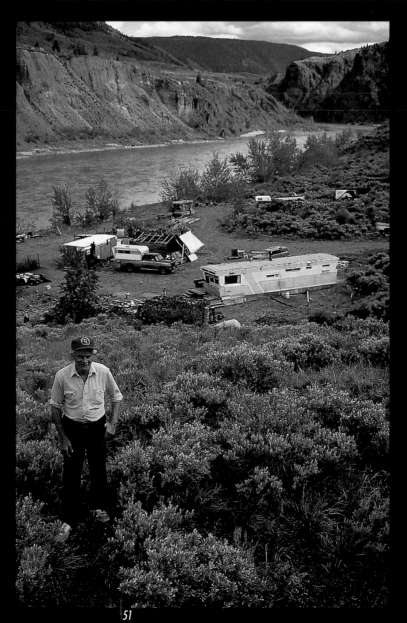

Near Churn Creek, above a stretch of fine sand beach, is Wal-Pat Mining, a placer operation run by Walter and Pat Haenschke. They love their life on this part of the river, where they work hard to recover fine grains of gold with specially designed sluice boxes. Their riverbank is a much-worked one—an ancient hydraulic mining monitor, neat rows of washed rock, a winch and a rusty old drag-line bucket bear witness to a century's worth of gold-hunters in this area.

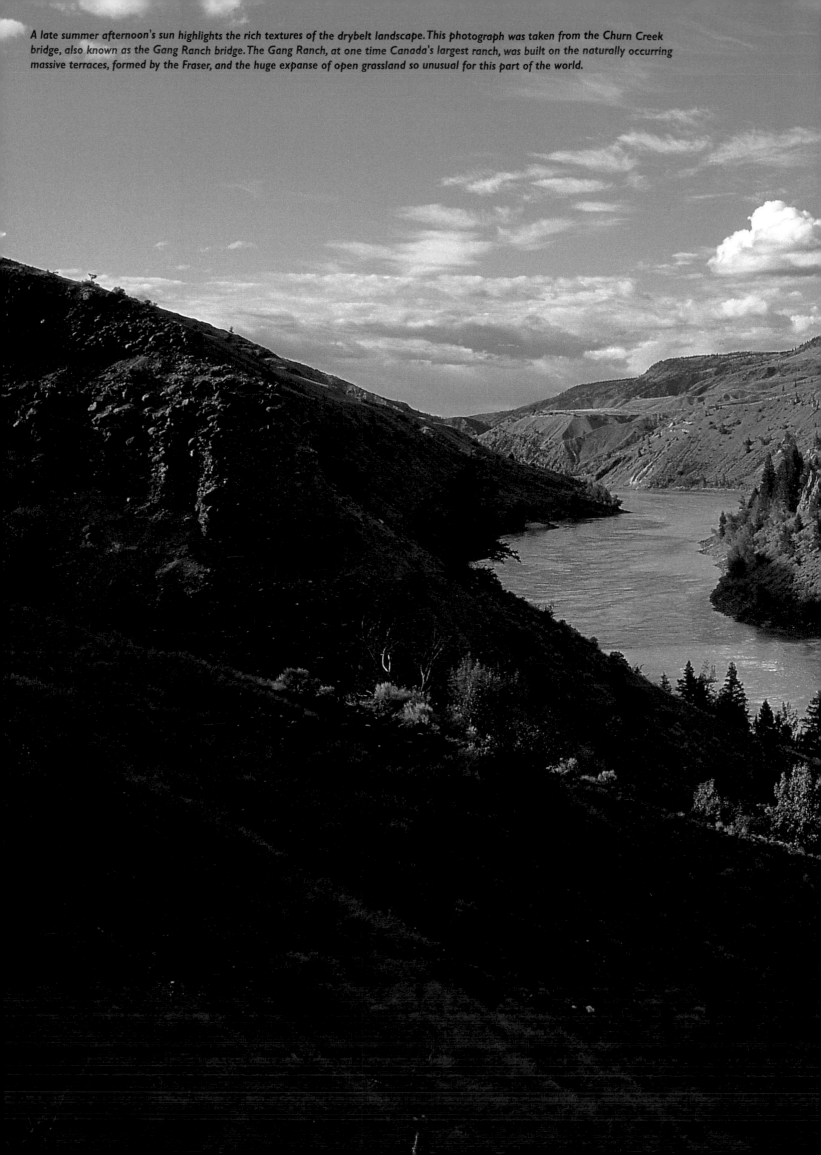

A late summer afternoon's sun highlights the rich textures of the drybelt landscape. This photograph was taken from the Churn Creek bridge, also known as the Gang Ranch bridge. The Gang Ranch, at one time Canada's largest ranch, was built on the naturally occurring massive terraces, formed by the Fraser, and the huge expanse of open grassland so unusual for this part of the world.

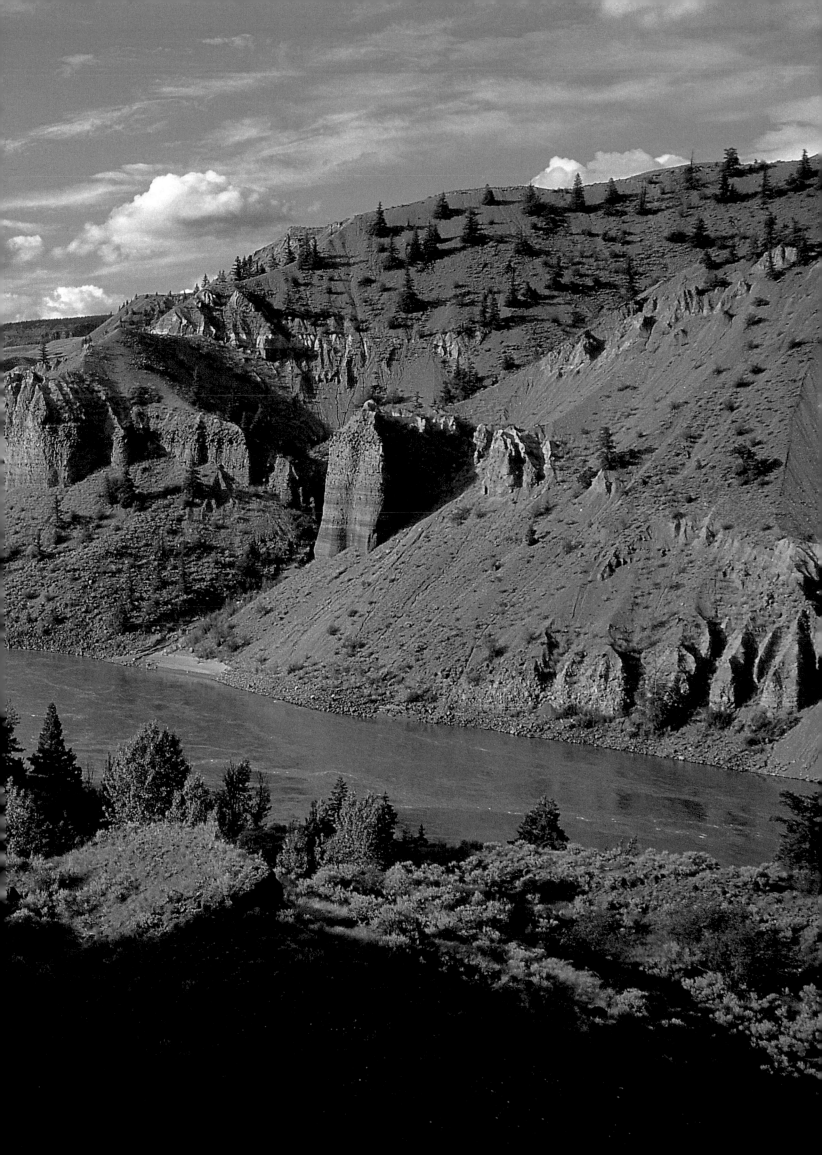

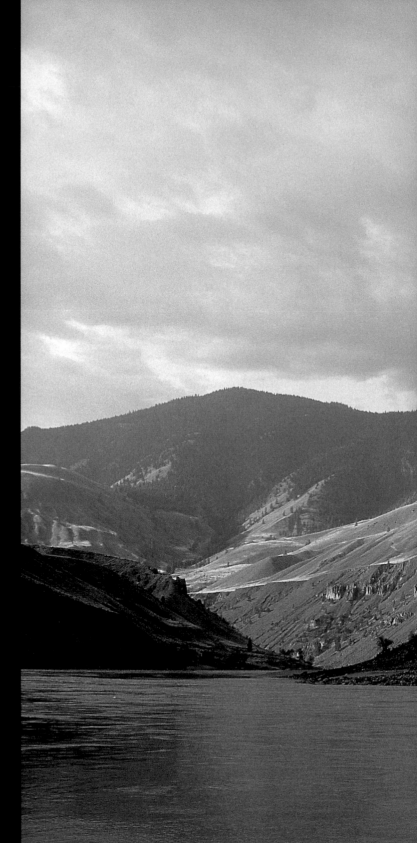

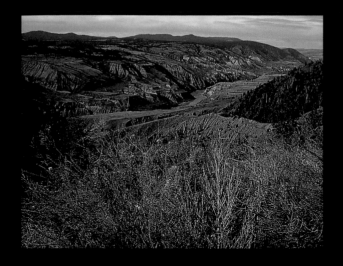

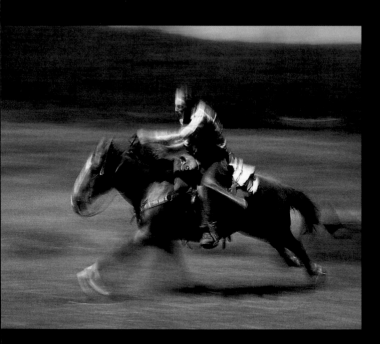

Top: Looking west across the Fraser from Canoe Creek Road near Alkali Lake, one gets a great view of the forests, rolling hills and mixed grassland of the Chilcotin plateau.

Bottom: The Chilcotin is a big land that has attracted people who love open space.

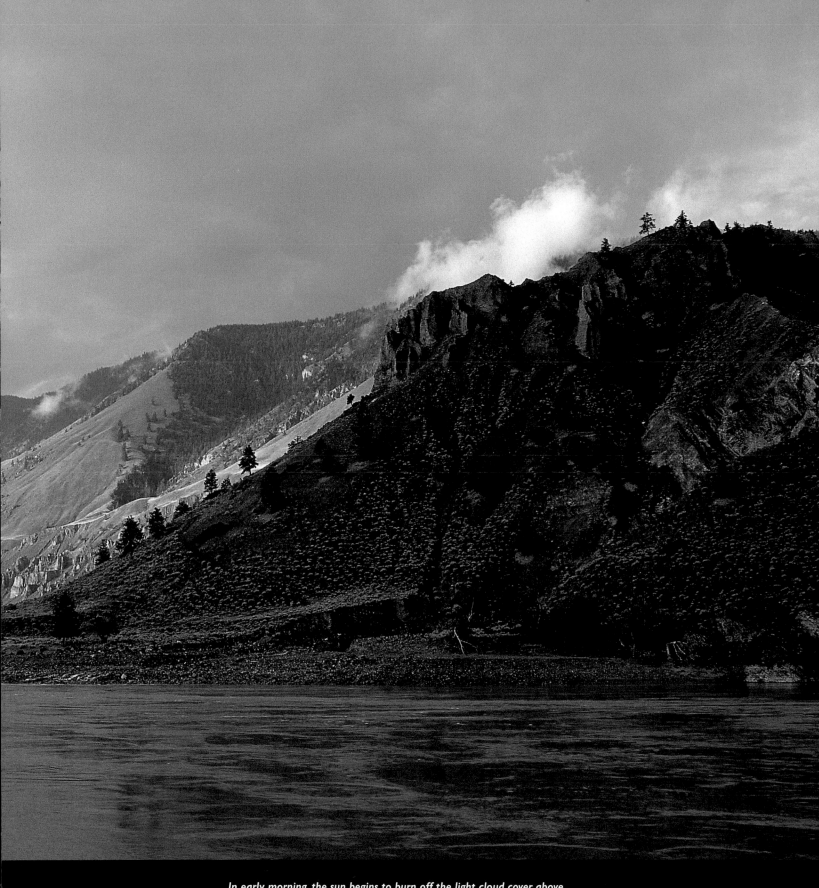

*In early morning, the sun begins to burn off the light cloud cover above
the deep valley of the Fraser at the Cathedrals.*

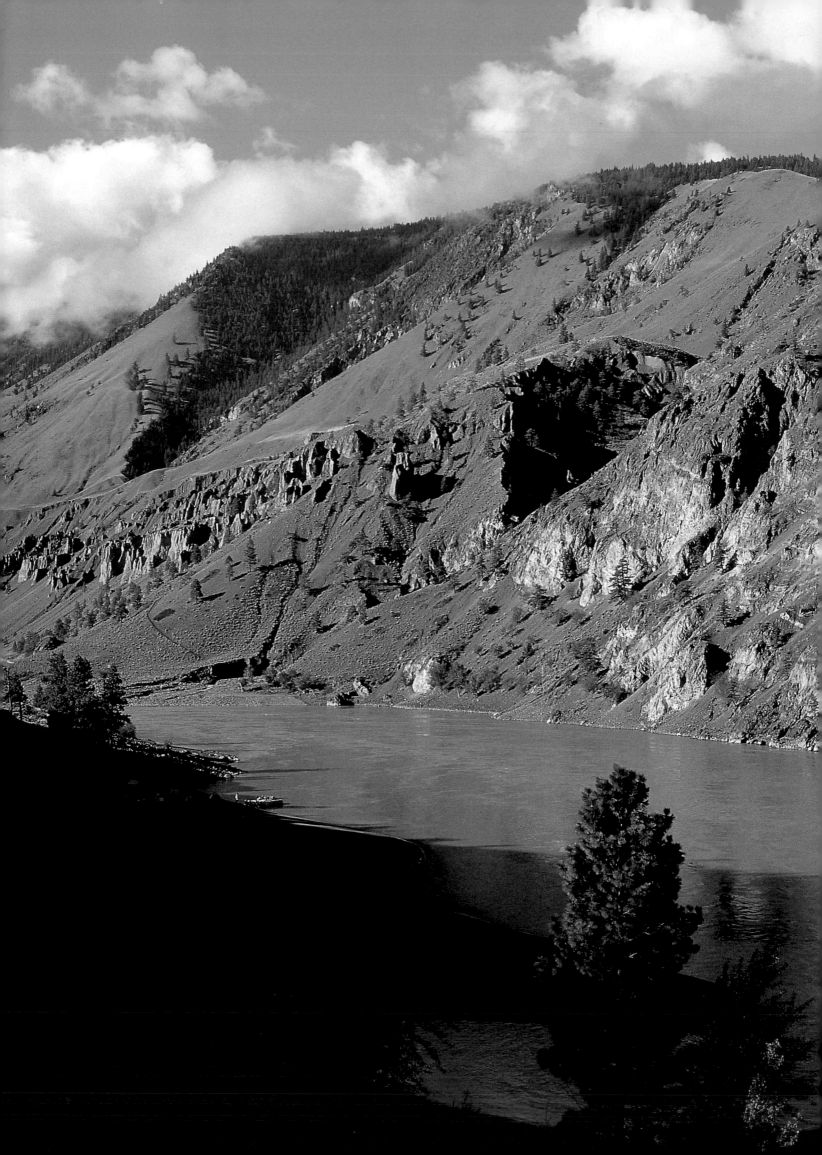

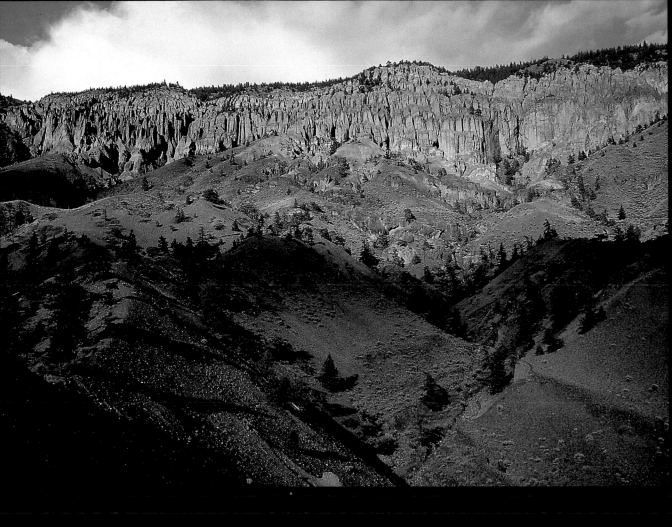

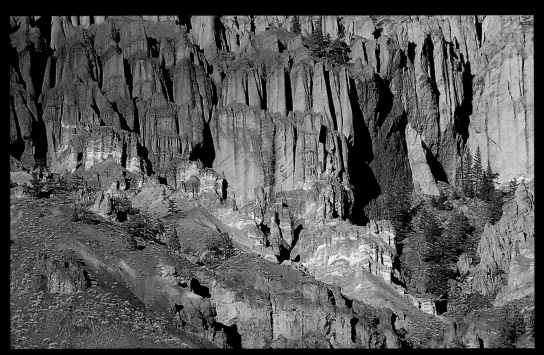

The Cathedrals, rock formations carved into the steep riverbanks by natural forces, are among the most breathtaking sights on the Fraser River. The rock here is a limestone–sandstone mix, soft enough to be carved by wind, rain and sand, but resilient enough that these elemental sculptures hold their shape over a long period. Like most sights on the river and its banks along this stretch of the Fraser, the dramatic, complex Cathedrals are best seen from a river raft. The river has carved its path so deep into the Plateau that it can hardly be seen from the edges of the land.

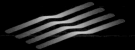

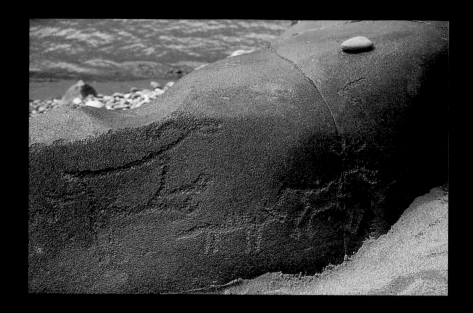

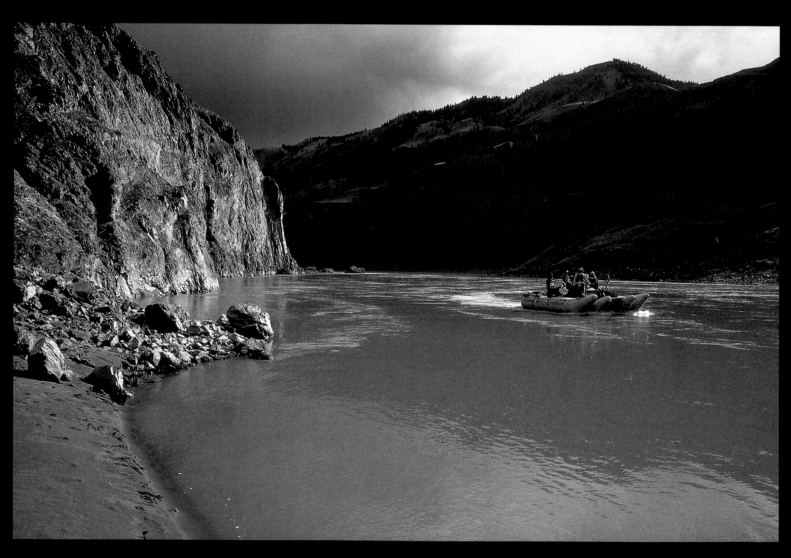

Above French Bar Canyon, early people have honoured the bighorn sheep and a wolf in petroglyphs (top).
In this stretch the river begins to gain speed as the sides crowd it into a narrower course.

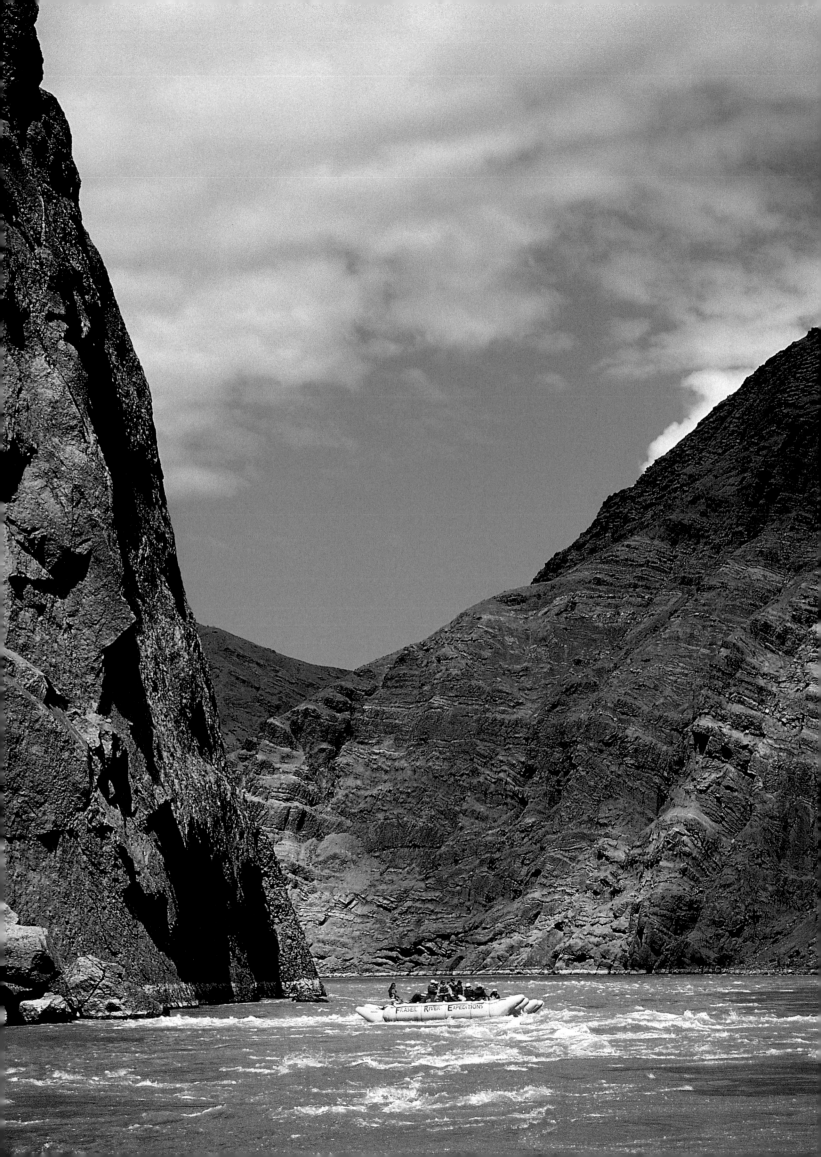

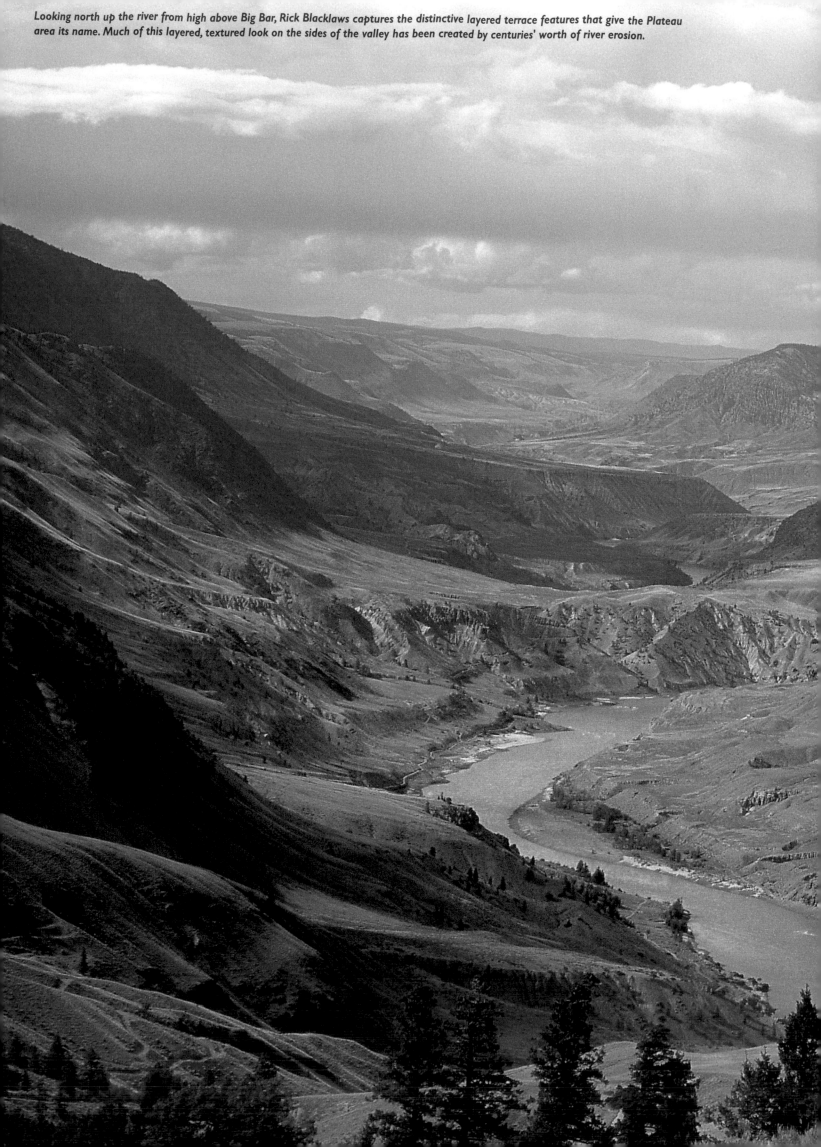

Looking north up the river from high above Big Bar, Rick Blacklaws captures the distinctive layered terrace features that give the Plateau area its name. Much of this layered, textured look on the sides of the valley has been created by centuries' worth of river erosion.

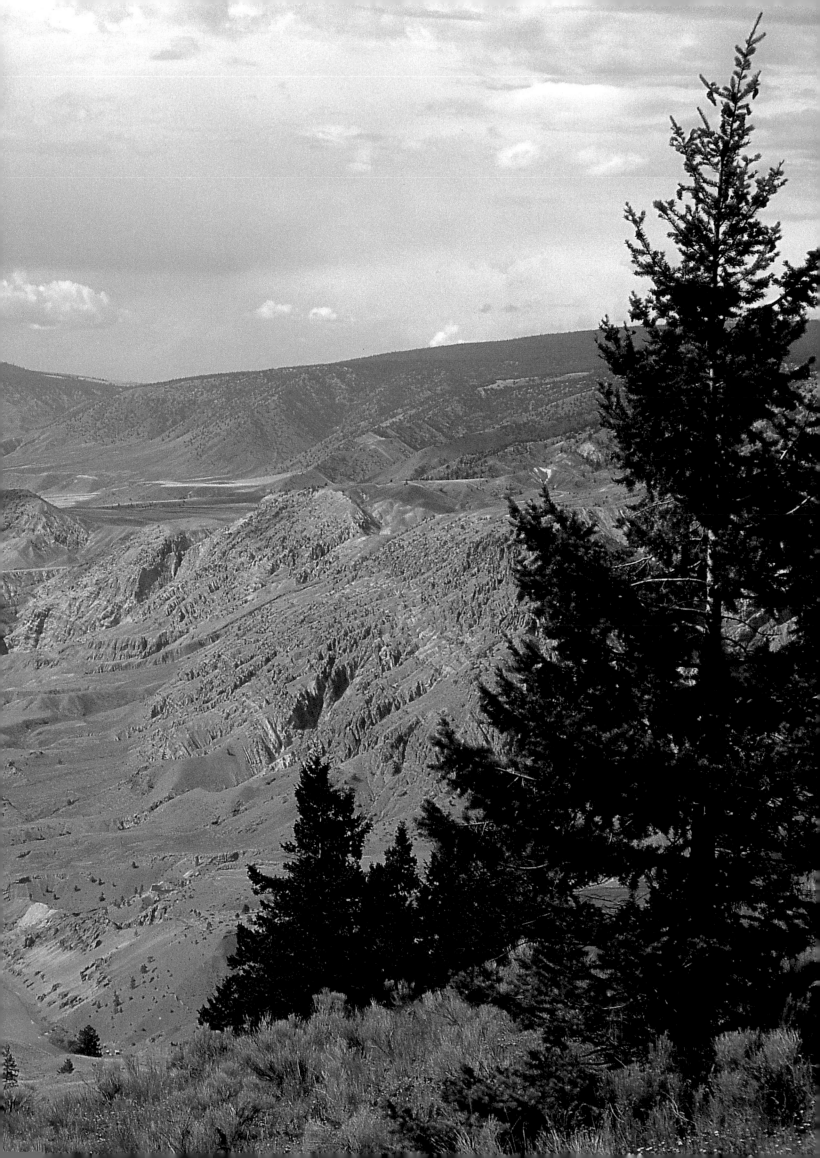

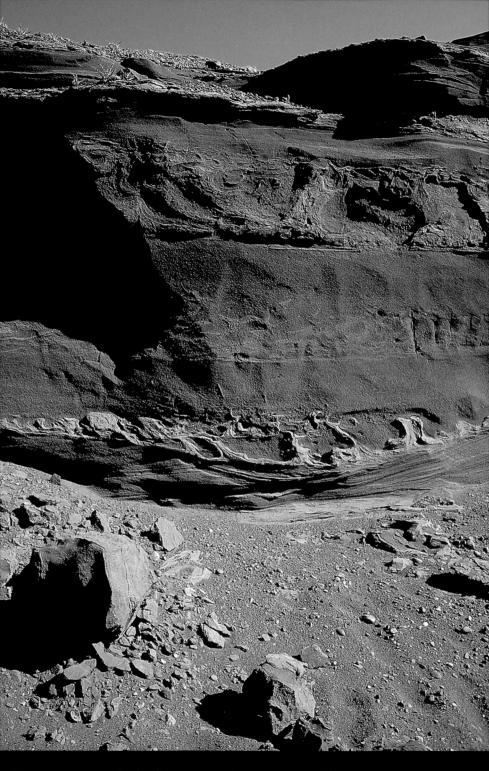

The textures in this cutbank, telling a history of streams, lakes and floods over long periods of time, are gradually being erased by the river to be reshaped in a new story somewhere downriver. At French Bar Canyon (right), the river rafts come to feel quite tiny in the landscape, as the hills begin to crowd the river.

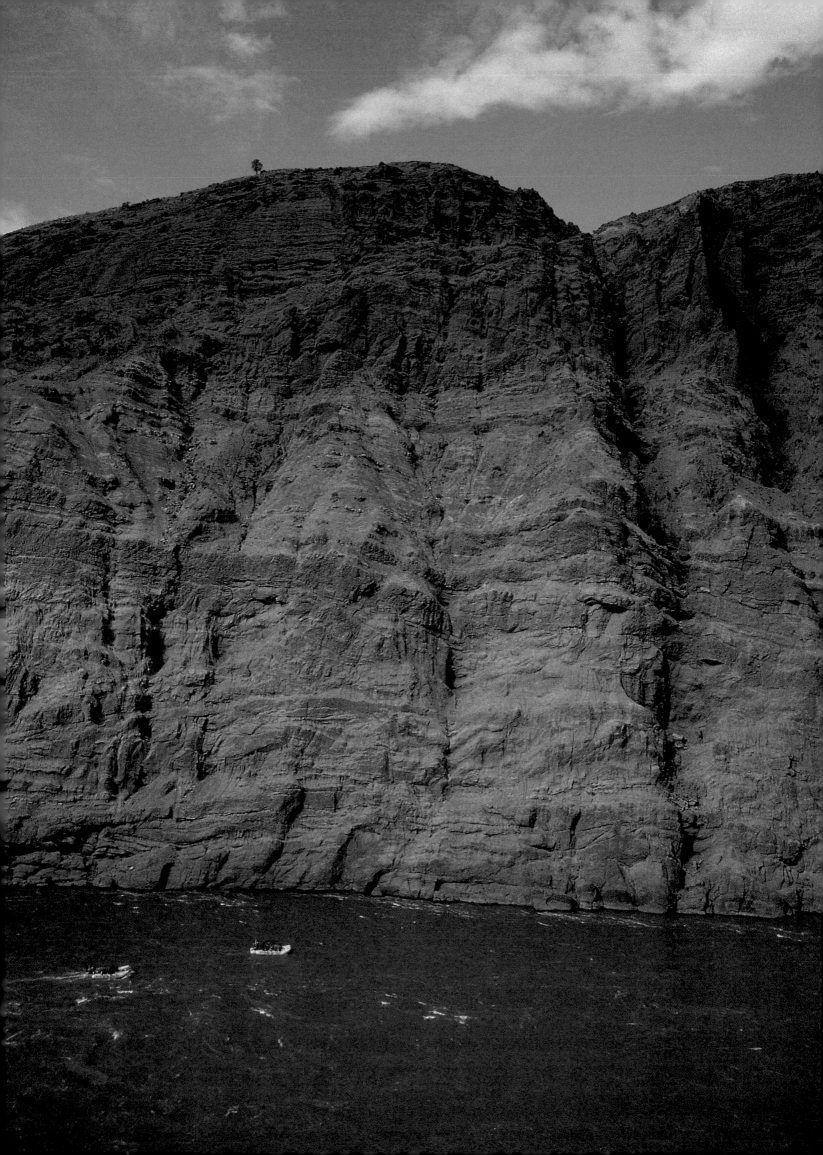

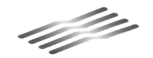

From Churn Creek, the Fraser carried us down past Canoe Creek, whose waters serve the historic BC Cattle Company Ranch, and on to China Gulch and Grinder Creek, named for a ranching family famous for their rodeo performances. At Lone Cabin Creek, and some distance back from the river, rise the Cathedrals. In a river of superlatives, these monumental columns give the impression of some fanciful secret storehouse for all the world's Ionic and Corinthian columns. Our group could only raft past the Cathedrals in awed silence.

Just downriver, little French Bar Creek tumbled in from a broad flat on the west bank. Darwin told us that French Bar Frank worked the gold bars along here until his recent death, and is said to have lived in a utopian little world farther up the creek.

Some 20 or 25 miles (35–40 km) downriver from Churn Creek, we passed under the cables of the Big Bar reaction ferry. The operator waved at us from his office on the shore, in our second contact with humans since leaving Soda Creek. Some of the low river benches along here have encouraged settlement over the years, possibly the millennia. Rick Blacklaws, who has worked with First Nations people in excavating an ancient fish camp on the west bank, estimates that occupation of this site extends back at least to the time of Christ and quite probably to three or four thousand years ago. Interestingly he found two "subsurface horizons," layers of soil indicating human habitation, separated by 8 or 10" (20–30 cm) of sand. Downriver is evidence of a huge slide that would have been a major blockage until the river managed to cut back through. Could the sand separating the two subsurface horizons be sediment from a lake that built up behind the slide blockage?

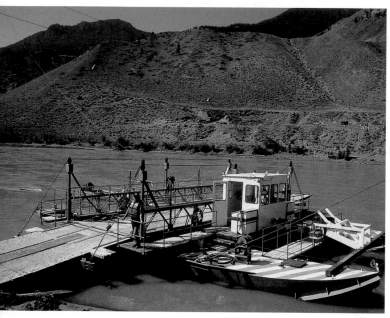

The Big Bar reaction ferry, which runs on cables and "reacts" to the Fraser's currents, serves a huge area of ranch land on the west bank of the river. The ferries and bridges of the Plateau and Cariboo are so important to human life along the river that they have shaped local history and culture as much as they have been shaped by it.

When we saw signs of human life near Watson Bar, we stopped for a visit at Chris and Rita Albeitz's ranch—the only human presence on this section of the Fraser for miles in any direction. To add to the Albeitzes' isolation, their century-old home is on the wrong side of the river. Everything they do involves getting across that ever-changing obstacle. To get to school, their sons Jim and Danny must be ferried to the other side in the outboard speedboat, then driven 7 miles (12 km) to catch a bus that takes them another 7 miles to the one-room Big Bar School. Their fourteen-year-old brother Ben is boarding in Lillooet for grade nine. In winter, several yards of ice can build out from the shore, and this is dangerous ice—the edge can be thin with the river current tumbling under it. Rita handles it by setting the bow of her boat on the ice, then gunning the engine and letting the force carry the boat up and across it. This would involve lifting the motor at the same time, but as she describes the technique it seems no big thing. "When the ice is in," she explains, "you just swoosh the boat up onto it." By January the ice buildup makes the crossing too dangerous, so they do home schooling with the kids until the thaw comes in February.

The daily adventure of crossing the river fills the Albeitzes' conversation. Hunters and hikers pester them continually for lifts to one side or the other, and more than once Chris has had to swim across the churning waters to fetch the family boat after someone "borrowed" it and left it on the wrong side. Once the electric lights went out when Chris was late coming back from town, and Rita rushed to light a signal fire for him about fifty yards up the bank so he would know where to aim the boat. "Then I heard him coming across the river and not slowing down. He hit the beach going full speed and flew out of the boat. He came up spitting sand. He saw the fire all right, but he thought I had lit it on the *edge* of the river."

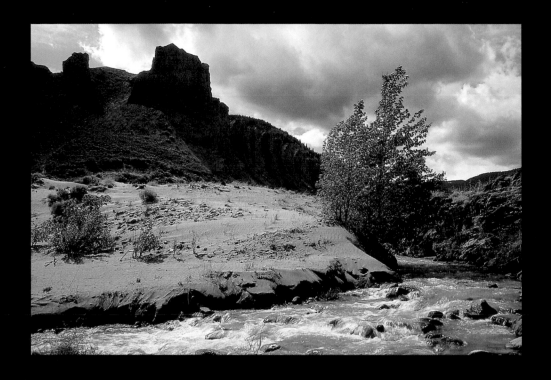

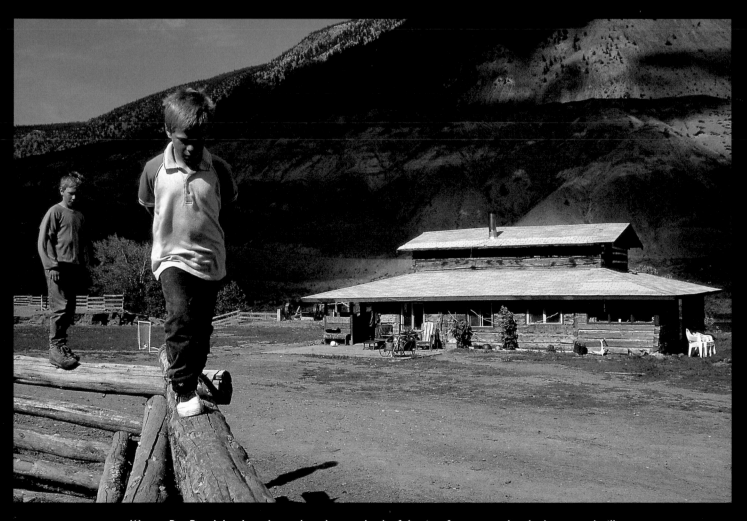

Watson Bar Ranch has been located on the west bank of the river for over one hundred years and will continue to provide families with a living—and, more important, a way of life—for many decades to come. In this generation, the ranch is the home of the Albeitz family. Creeks such as Watson Bar Creek (top) offer the only reliable source of water in this rain-starved place. Jim and Danny Albeitz (above) take great pride in their special place in the landscape. For them, living with the river and crossing it are daily adventures.

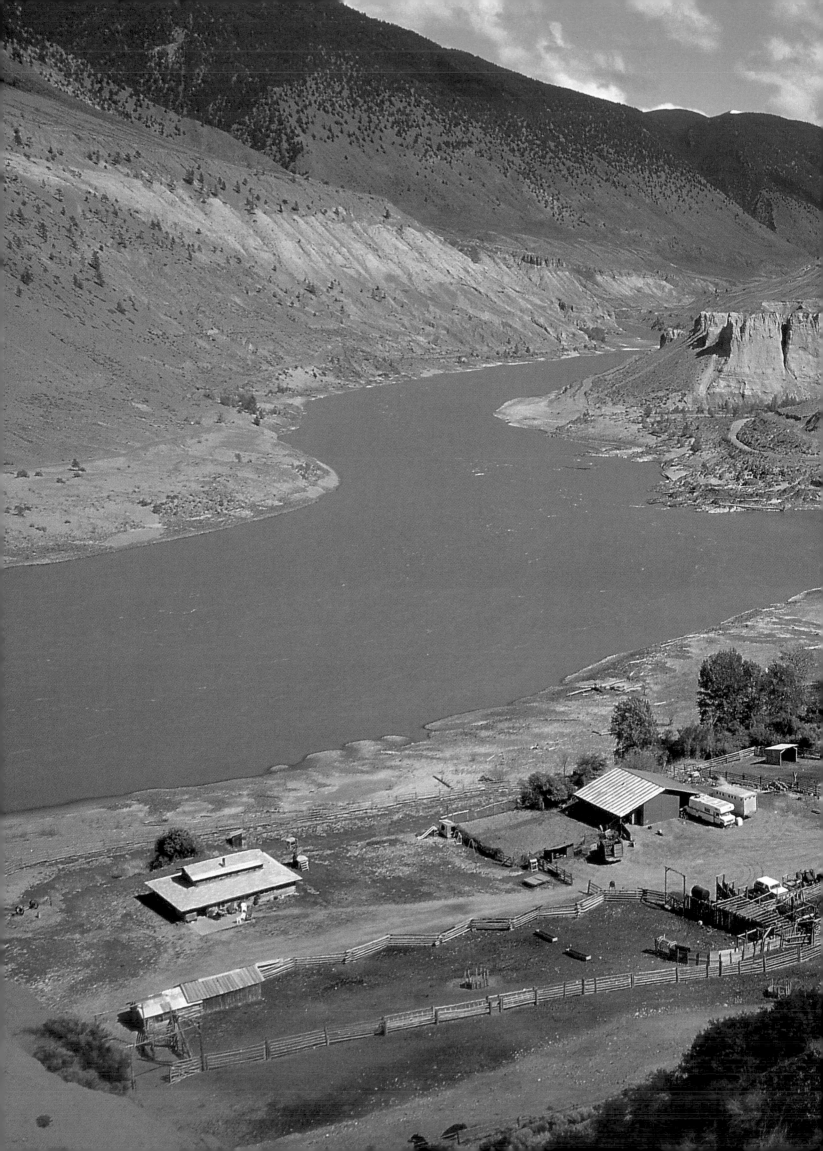

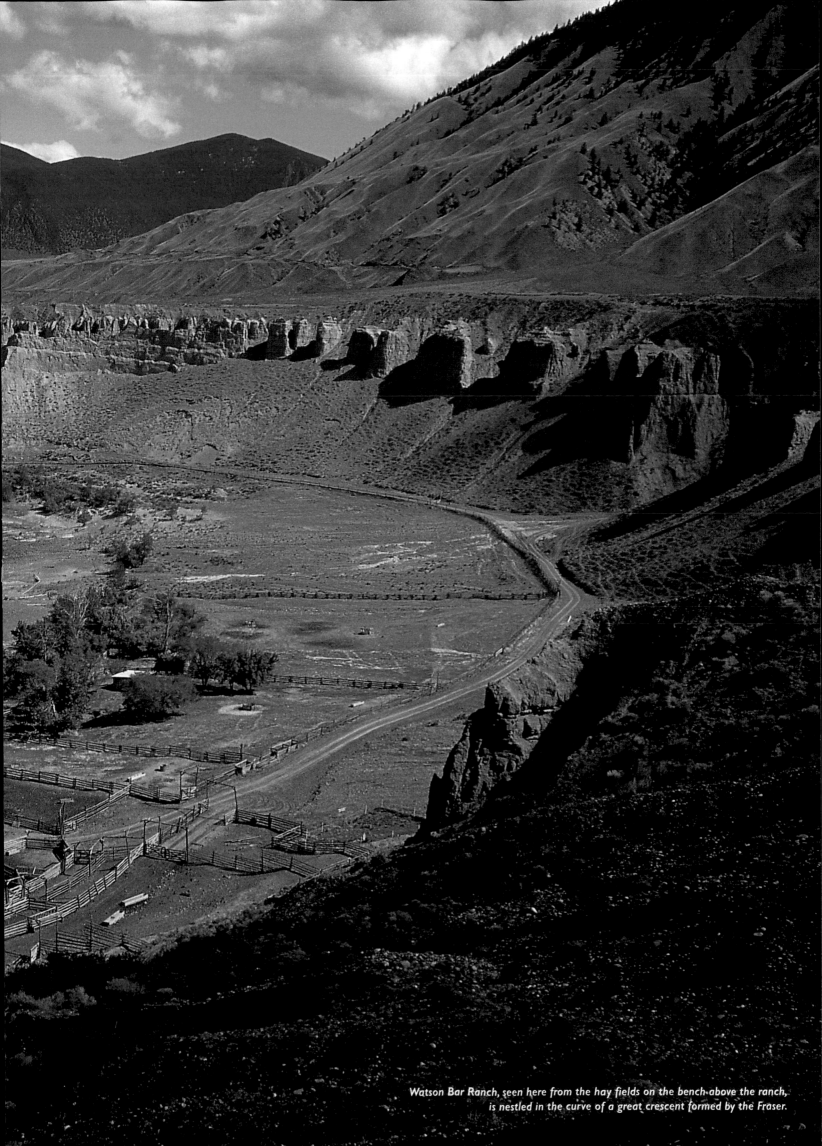

Watson Bar Ranch, seen here from the hay fields on the bench above the ranch, is nestled in the curve of a great crescent formed by the Fraser.

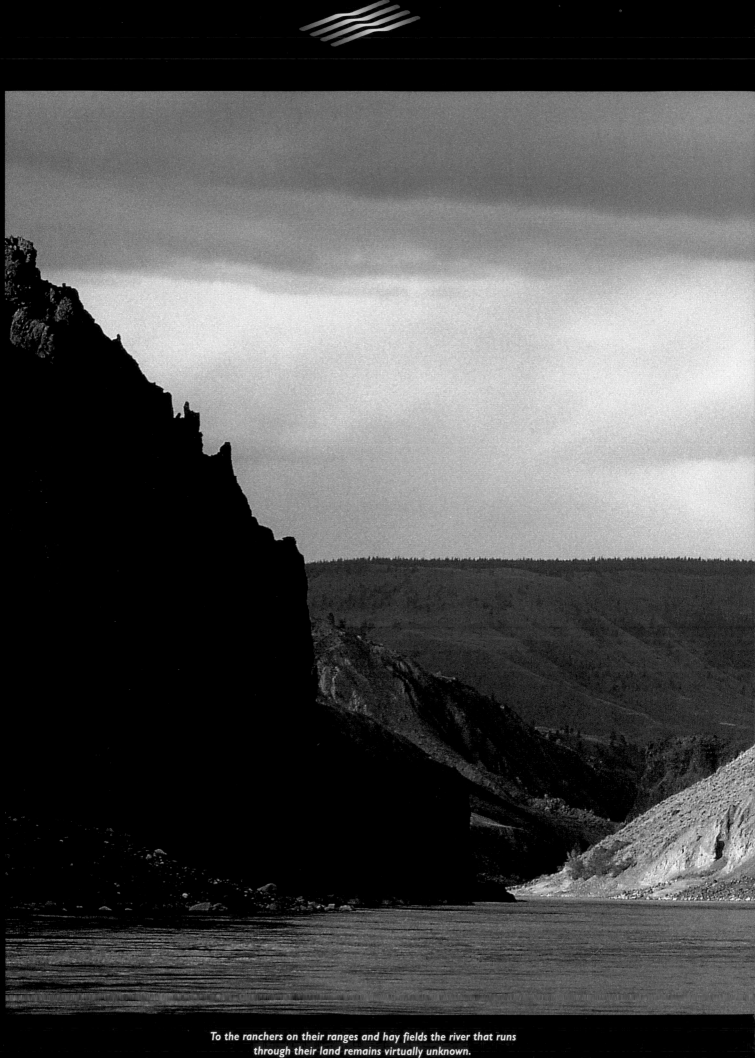

To the ranchers on their ranges and hay fields the river that runs through their land remains virtually unknown.

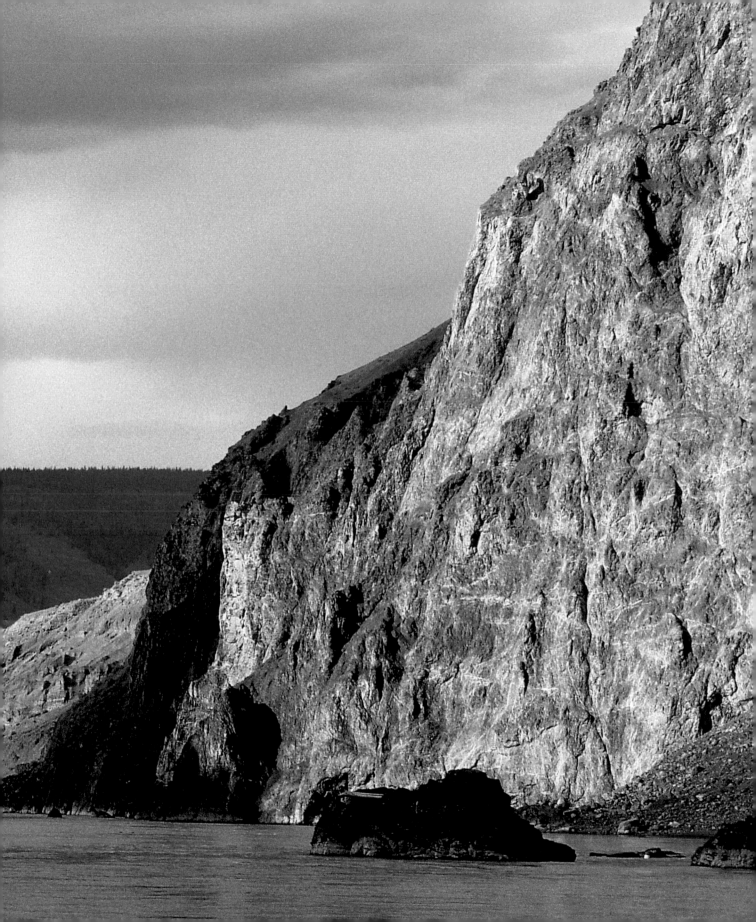

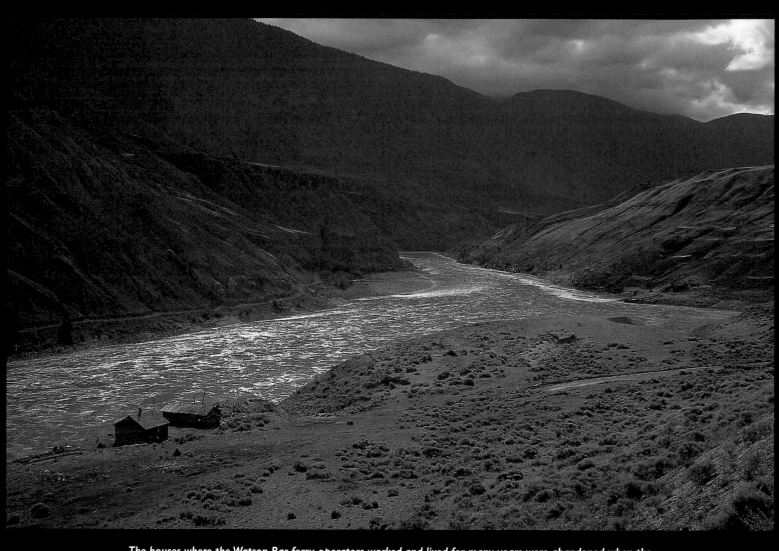

The houses where the Watson Bar ferry operators worked and lived for many years were abandoned when the
ferry was moved upriver to Big Bar. The location of ferries on the Fraser has generated much
political controversy over the years.

As south Cariboo ranches go, the Albeitzes' is unique for having its headquarters down by the river, but even here the hay fields are on benches up above the ranch buildings. Every day through the summer growing season the family goes up on the fields to move three hundred sprinklers by hand. But life is still easier than it must have been for the McDonald family, who built the place over a century ago to winter teams that worked the Cariboo Road. The house and the barn are constructed of hand-hewn timbers, and McDonald and his Native wife raised twelve children here.

After our visit at Watson Bar, the raft took us around another corner in the river to a not-so-subtle variation on the theme of cliff and colour. Except for several short canyons where the river has cut through some rock outcropping, the riverbanks through this part of Cariboo are a series of cliffs, in various combinations of fine silt sediment, layered river gravel, boulders and stone-capped hoodoos. This land is a geological and geographical treasure house of plateaus, ridges, gullies, hanging valleys, erratics, sedimentation, water and wind erosion, volcanic and glacial landscapes, and shiny black rock glazed by volcanic heat and cooled by glacial waters. It is a land all but untouched by human hand, but showing the spectacular hand of nature around every river bend. As Simon Fraser wrote, "There are so many variety along this River, that however willing I might be I am not possessed of sufficient abilities to describe it."

Not much later, our raft took us deeper into the mountains that had begun to crowd the Fraser on both sides. Here the river narrows slightly and seems to run faster, more urgently on its journey. Still we felt quite safe in our well-designed raft, with our knowledgeable guide. How must it have been for Simon Fraser in his much-patched and far less stable canoes? "The mountains are close [to] the River and steep, with no interval of even ground to the top," he wrote on June 9, 1808. "In this last Rapid much water was taken, the Canoes often wheeled about, and what rendered our situation more dangerous was not to be able to stop or find a place to put ashore on account of rocks."

Rafting over the Fraser's "big water" is great fun—exciting, but safe.

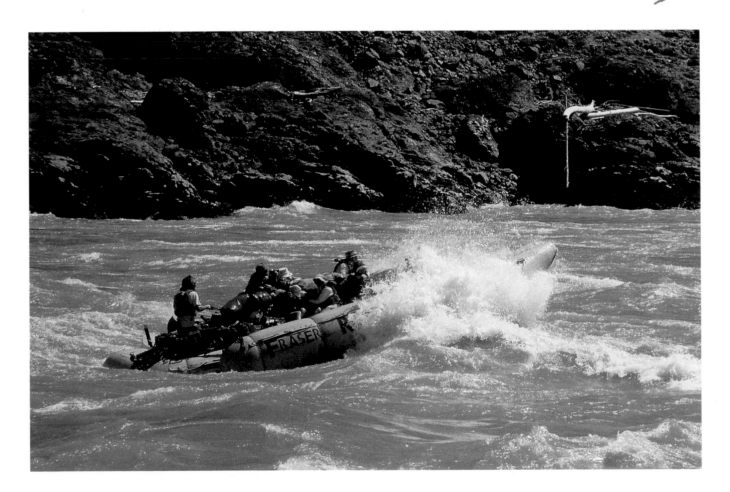

*Because the river runs from north to south between Prince George and Hope,
by late afternoon each day much of it is in shadow.*

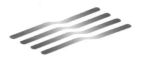

For us, in our modern craft, the turbulent waters were more exciting than frightening. Rapids occurred more frequently now, and from time to time dumped buckets of ice-cold river water over us. Our faces were always wet with the spray. Here, in a place where no person appeared to live, where great long stretches of canyon around us had never been touched by human beings, where the only forces to be seen were the timeless ones of rock and wind and water, it was easy to imagine ourselves in a pristine wilderness. Still, I could never quite forget that to swallow any of this water would be akin to swallowing water in an urban swimming pool. Before the river splashed our faces here among the mountains, it had removed the sewage and industrial effluent from all the towns upriver from us. Concerned people in Prince George, Quesnel, Williams Lake and dozens of smaller communities are struggling to clean up the waterways; regional districts such as 100 Mile House, Quesnel, Interlakes, Wells and 150 Mile House are preparing Official Community Plans for growth management; people living in the Plateau area have cut their landfill waste by half and their per capita water consumption by 13 percent. Even so, it will take decades for all the damage to the Fraser to be repaired. I envy Simon Fraser's men being able to scoop up a cup of the river's silty clean waters whenever they grew thirsty.

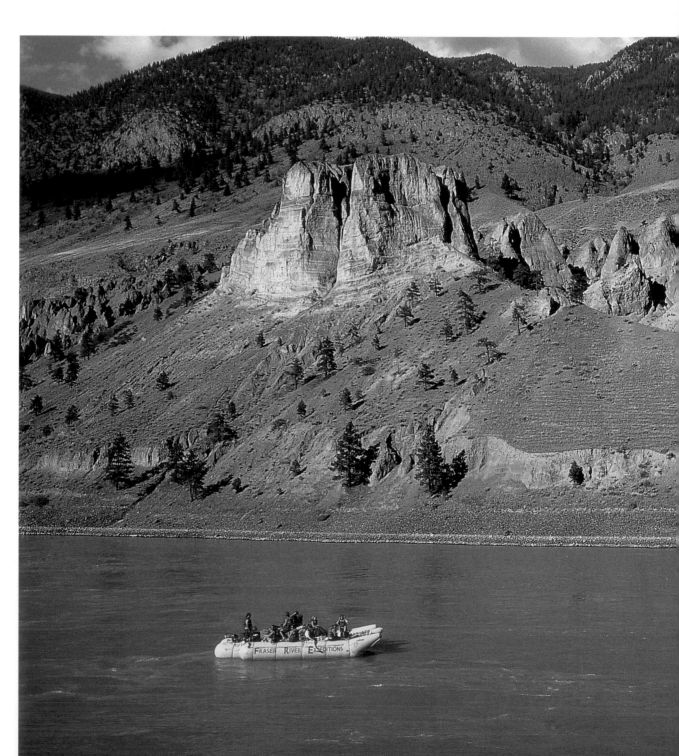

A few miles later, we arrived at the point where Fraser finally abandoned the river to trek over land. Darwin put the raft in at Leon Creek, and we made camp near where Fraser had done likewise 188 years earlier. Where his fragile canoes—particularly the one named *Perseverance*—were in bad repair and in constant need of pitch patches, Darwin's raft had been unscathed by the passage.

In the morning we started down the river into the steepening canyon country. A short distance along we stopped at the Big Slide Mine (also called Grange Mine) that was built into the edge of the greatest red scree slope imaginable. We climbed up to look at the wreckage of the mill, and the younger people did a little scree sliding—a combination of leaping down a sand hill and skiing down a snow hill along the angle of repose of the great slide. The mine had not been worked for many years, but we could see the vein that the shaft had followed into the mountainside, and a rugged road snaking down the mountain on the opposite bank.

We went on downriver, and before long we were rafting around a rock wall that rose straight out of the water, twice as high as any we had seen on the trip. We took wild guesses at its height—five hundred feet? A thousand? More? Clearly we had left the plateau country. We were in the middle of a mountain surrounded by mountains.

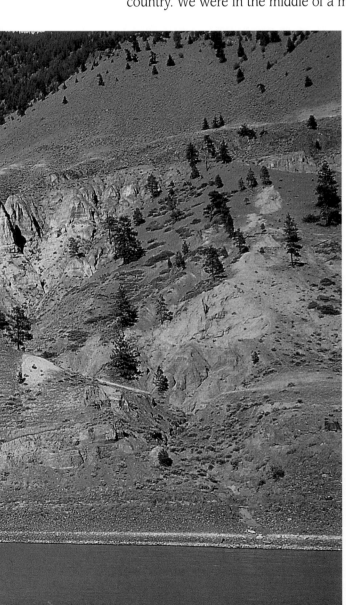

I gazed up at the dizzying heights and realized I had arrived at one of those places which even the most extravagant artist could not exaggerate. We really are like tiny mites travelling in to the deepest interior of a huge land. It was an indescribable privilege to be here. I wished everyone on earth could experience the beauty and awesome magnitude of this land and the rugged, majestic river that flows through it. Should we require every young person in BC to make this trip before we let them vote in a provincial election? Surely then there would be no hesitation in spending tax dollars to control pollution in our interior communities. Surely then we would not have to debate our collective responsibility to the fish, the bighorn sheep, the human beings and all the other species that depend on the Fraser River for their survival.

A raft approaches Leon Creek, moving past the southernmost Cathedral-type landforms on the Fraser. Many of the formations on this bank are true "hoodoos"—columns of rock eroded at the base so that they resemble pillars holding up larger rocks. It was at Leon Creek that Simon Fraser realized the character of the river was about to change; so he abandoned the water, stored his supplies and trekked overland to the site of present-day Lillooet.

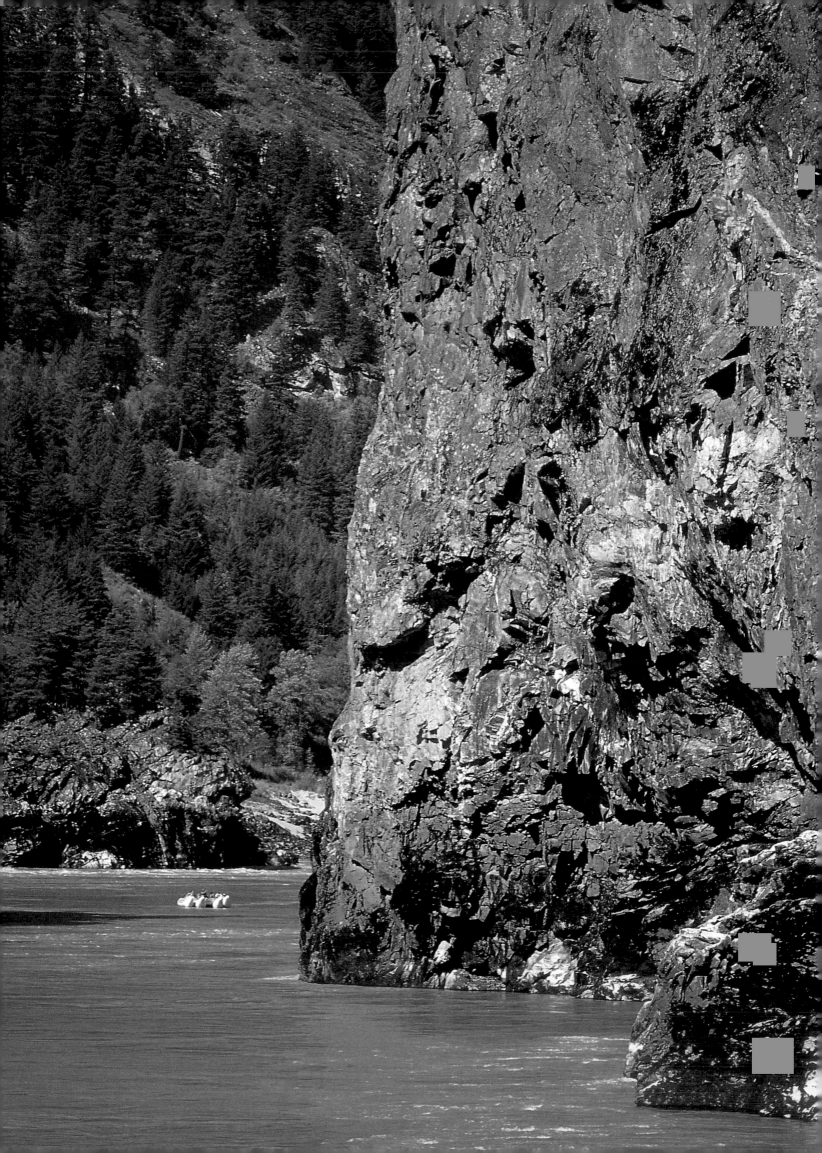

5

CANYON

The canyon, that magnificent stretch of the Fraser between Lillooet and Hope, is the best-known part of the river, probably because it is the most dramatic. Near Lillooet the mountains begin to tower over either side of the water, and the river narrows and begins to fight its constraints. The water's impatient work shows in rock walls that seem to have been cut by a giant saw, and matching veins of coloured rock prove that the two banks were once connected.

As you travel downriver, the rock canyon is interspersed with layers of glacial lake sediments, outwash sediments and glacial till, which is actually the ice deposits. The Fraser River fault line runs along the river from around Hope, but then leaves the Fraser to run along the Bridge River, up the Yalakom River and along the base of the Coast Mountains through the Chilcotin country. This fault line creates a valleylike place more easily eroded by the Fraser than a mountain canyon. Before the last ice age, there was another river working at eroding that valley; then, as the ice receded, the valley was largely filled with glacial moraine. Since then, the Fraser has eroded most of that material and is cutting into the rock once again.

The Moran Canyon, about 18 miles (30 km) above Lillooet, is the first of a series of canyons along the way to Lytton, where the Thompson River adds its green waters to the Fraser's muddy torrent. Between Lytton and Yale the Fraser Canyon continues in a jumble of sheer rock walls, broken only by the occasional crevasse to bring in a creek or river bench. From an airplane it is almost impossible to see the water. Unless the plane is directly over the canyon, the path of the river looks like just another defile among the ranks of mountain peaks.

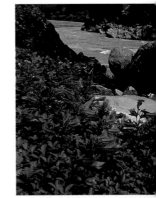

Through the lower slopes of the Coast Mountains, the Camelsfoot Range between the river and the coast range, Mount Bowman and the hills and small mountains behind Big Bar, the river continues steadily southward. The ancient fault line has carried the Fraser in a nearly straight course all the way from Prince George but here, for the first time in hundreds of miles, the Fraser fault line meets solid steep rock. It is this topographical shaping that has made the Fraser River attractive to hydroelectric engineers for many decades.

In places in the Fraser Canyon, the sheer rock walls rise in perfect verticals from the water's surface.

Various dam sites have been proposed over the years, but the most favoured was the Moran canyon. I remember a day in the 1950s when I stopped on the road above Lillooet with my father, and he pointed up the river and spoke ominously of this threat to the river.

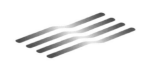

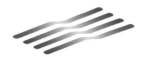

Later he wrote, in *The Living Land*: "The Fraser watershed is by far the largest salmon producer in the province; it is also, potentially, one of the largest power producers. Realizing its full power potential would entail construction of a large number of main-stream dams, which would completely change the character of the watershed and wipe out every important salmon run. But the construction of even one of the projected main-stream dams, the seven-hundred-foot dam proposed for the Moran Canyon site, 23 miles above Lillooet, would destroy every major sockeye run on the watershed except possibly the Adams run."

He went on to describe in horror some of the probable consequences of the dam and the 150-mile (250-km) lake it would create, including dramatic temperature changes, the problem of getting adult salmon up over the dam, and the virtual impossibility of getting the fry back down.

About 6 miles (10 km) below Moran Canyon, the Bridge River joins the Fraser in a dramatic rush of white water. The Bridge River rapids are set in a spectacular landscape— a sweep of river flowing through deep-cut hills covered with sage. The rapids are formed by great ridges of bedrock jutting up from the river bottom, slowing the upstream migration of salmon and making this one of the great fishing sites on the river. Sockeye heading upstream to the Nechako, Quesnel and Chilcotin rivers all pass through these rapids. Local people have names for at least two spring salmon runs and four sockeye runs.

Arthur and Marilyn Adolph fish here every year, at a place called Sxetl' on the east side of the Fraser six miles above Lillooet. Art, from the Fountain Band of the upper St'at'imc people, was born in 1955 and raised by elders Sam and Susan Mitchell. He can't recall when he first went fishing down at the river. "I was probably carried down there in a sling on my mommy's back," he says. Marilyn, from the Bridge River Band above Lillooet on the west bank, was raised by her parents Gordon and Dorothy James. She doesn't remember her first trip down to the river either, but at five years of age she was sent away to the residential school at Kamloops, where like many other First Nations children she spent ten months a year being forced to give up her language and culture.

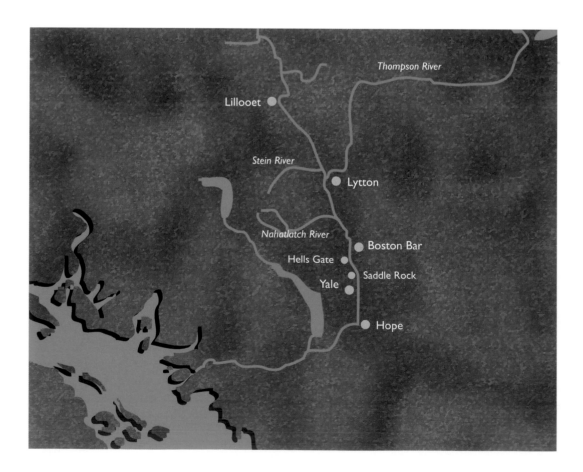

Through all of that time, elders like the Mitchells were confounding the experts by teaching their age-old laws and practices to young people like Art Adolph. And Marilyn, like other St'at'imc people, is reestablishing the traditions she learned in early childhood, with the aid of those who stayed home to learn from the elders.

Depending on the height of the river, there are about ten good fishing rocks at this spot. People share the rocks and the nets. Fishing permits are issued by the band, but everyone who has a right to fish at this spot is known by the others who fish there. If someone from outside wants to fish with a friend or relative at a Fountain fishing station, that person must get permission at the band's spring fishing meeting. Because it is a one-mile hike down to the fishing spot—which feels a lot longer going back up with a load of fish—not many people drop in uninvited.

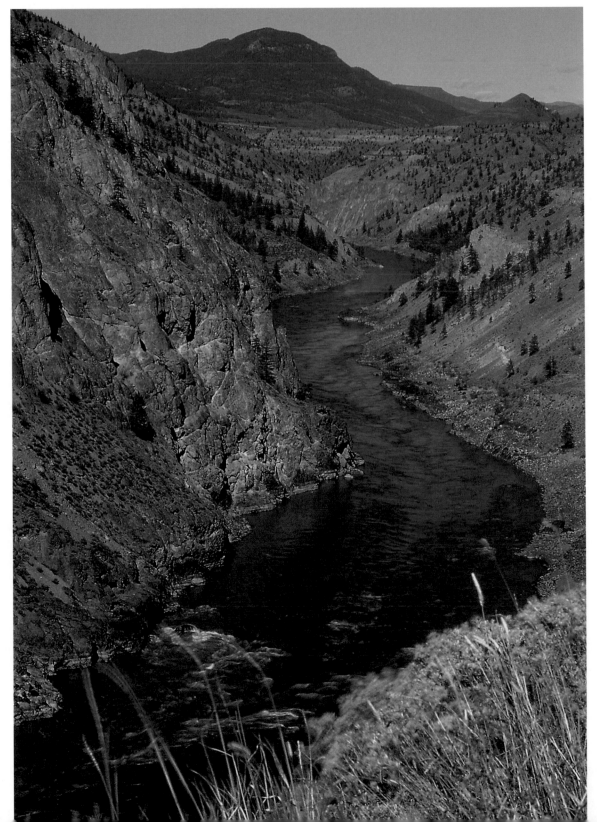

Distances on the old Cariboo Wagon Road, built in the 1860s, were measured north from Lillooet, where the road began. At Mile 12 on the east bank, the road begins to turn away from the river to avoid impassable mountains.

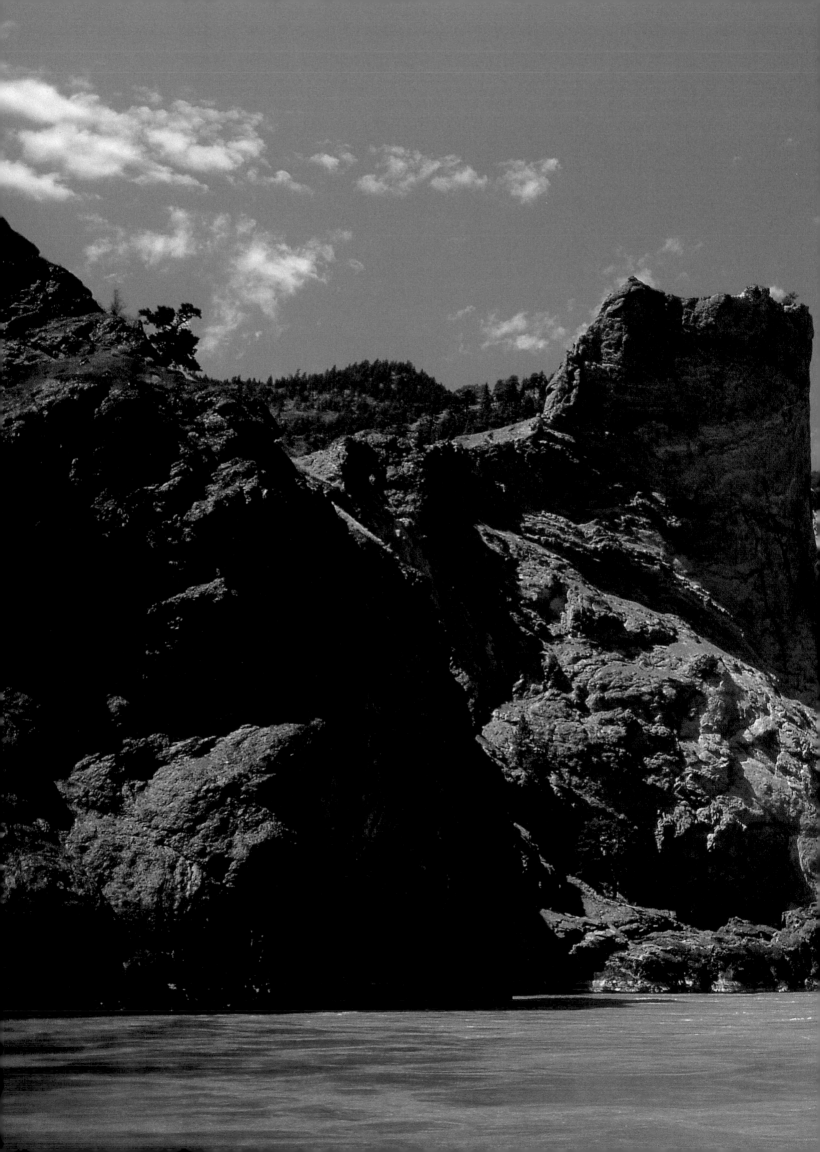

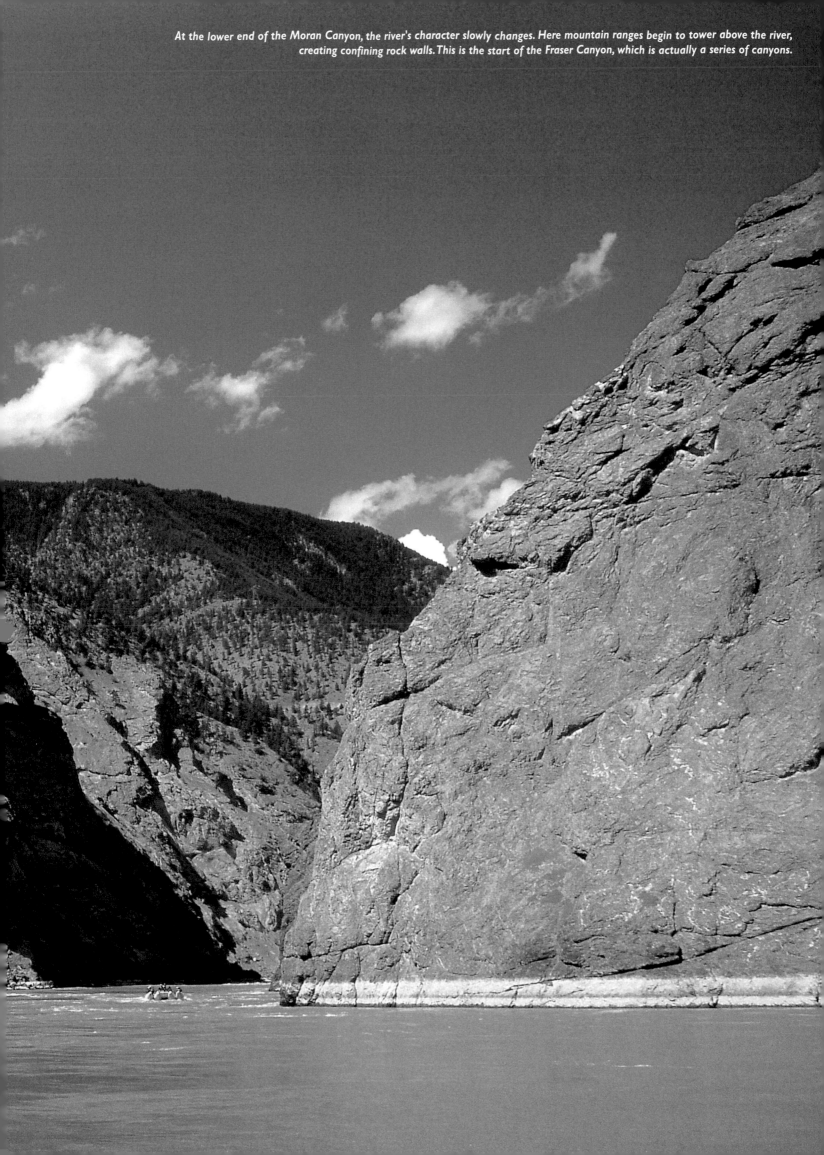

At the lower end of the Moran Canyon, the river's character slowly changes. Here mountain ranges begin to tower above the river, creating confining rock walls. This is the start of the Fraser Canyon, which is actually a series of canyons.

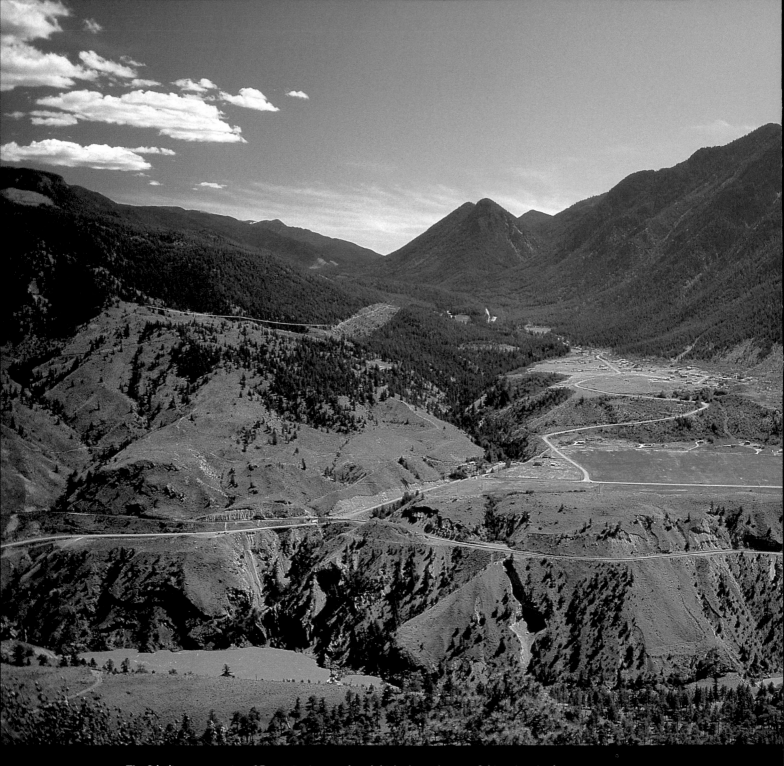

The St'at'imc community of Fountain sits on a bench high above the river fishing sites, in the same manner as the nearby precolonial village of Keatley Creek. Archaeological work is currently taking place at Keatley Creek, one of five sites of ancient villages in this area. These communities, developed on the bounty of Fraser River salmon, were rich, populous and sophisticated.

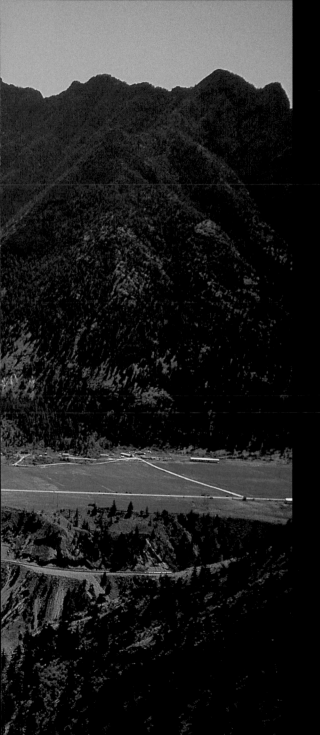

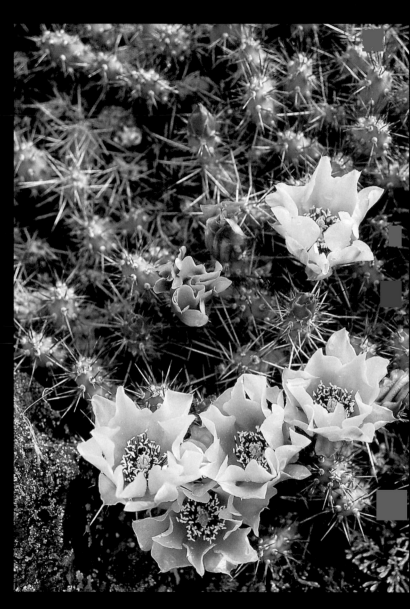

In the dry land around the Bridge River area of the Fraser Canyon, the prickly pear cactus flowers for about a week in early summer. Rick Blacklaws knows the river and its banks so well, he arranged to travel to Bridge River during the one week in June when he knew he would find this exquisite bloom.

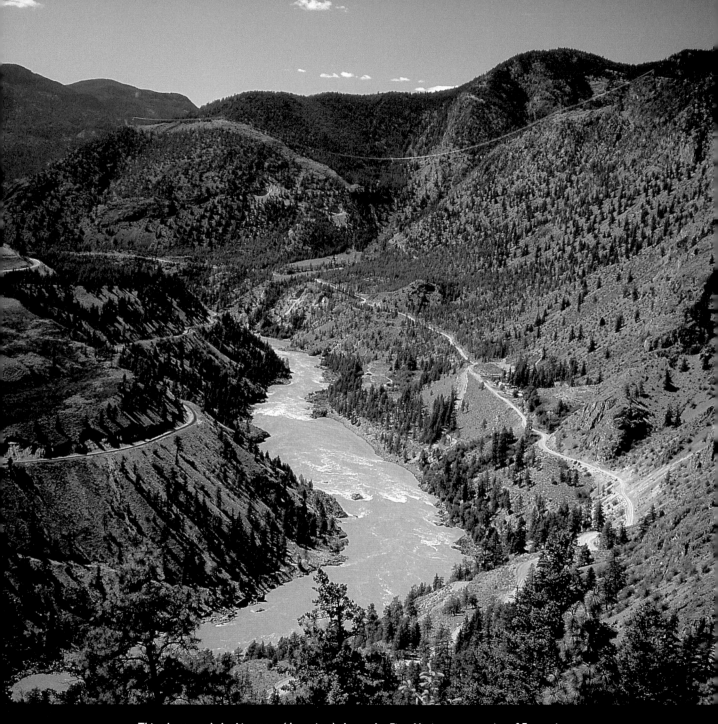

This photograph, looking west (downriver) shows the First Nations community of Fountain on the south bank (at left). This area is home to several excellent fishing spots.

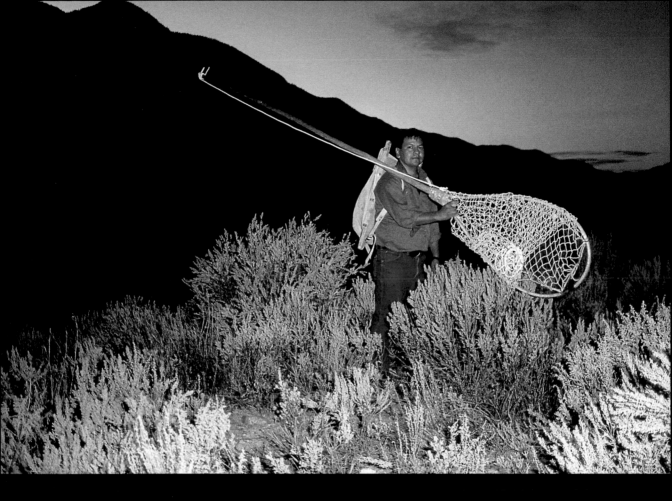

Dip Nets and Cowboy Chaps

For Art and Marilyn Adolph, who fish at Sxetl', near Lillooet, the Fraser River is a vital element in their culture. "Traditionally our people caught and dried large numbers of salmon," Art says, "and a lot of this was traded to the east. My dad, Sam Mitchell, told me it was this trade that brought the first horses to our people."

Three types of fishing gear are used in this part of the Fraser. Gillnets are set out with pulleys on the end of poles guyed out from the beach or, in some cases, across the mouth of a small bay. A smaller dip net on a pole is used in places like the Bridge River rapids, where fish make their way up through fast currents but close to the fishing rocks. The third method employs a set net, larger than the dip net. Each of these nets has rings around the hoop so that a line can

be dropped, closing the mouth of the net. A bridle attached to the hoop is tied to a rock so that the net can be held in a back eddy in such a way that the current holds the bag open, and fish making their way upstream through the back eddy will swim right in. Art's father told him that the second run of spring salmon, the one that comes when the wild roses are in bloom, is very fast and will turn back out of the net if the line closing the bag isn't dropped quickly. In the old days, when there were more fish, special spring salmon nets were made with larger meshes to allow the sockeye to pass through.

Art and Marilyn can or freeze the sockeye from the early Stuart run, as it is too fat to dry well, and each summer they freeze, can, dry and salt enough fish for their family of five and for elders and relatives who can't make it down to the fishing site. The salted fish are especially enjoyed by elders, who come to visit and

to recall times past when this was a more common method of preserving the fish.

Today many people dry fish by cutting a fillet from each side and hanging it over a pole, after making the cross-grain cuts in the flesh that allow the summer breezes to dry the meat. Often called "cowboy chaps" because they look like a pair of old woolly chaps hanging over a fence rail, these fillets are relatively easy to cut and dry. Art and Marilyn prefer the older method, in which the whole fish is left attached to the backbone and is held open with sticks. The extra oily belly meat needs special care in drying so as not to go rancid, but it is an extra treat when boiled in soup on a cold winter day. Another treat Art was told about as a boy is made by boiling fish heads, then mixing the oil with saskatoon berries and salmon flesh that has been roasted, dried and pounded.

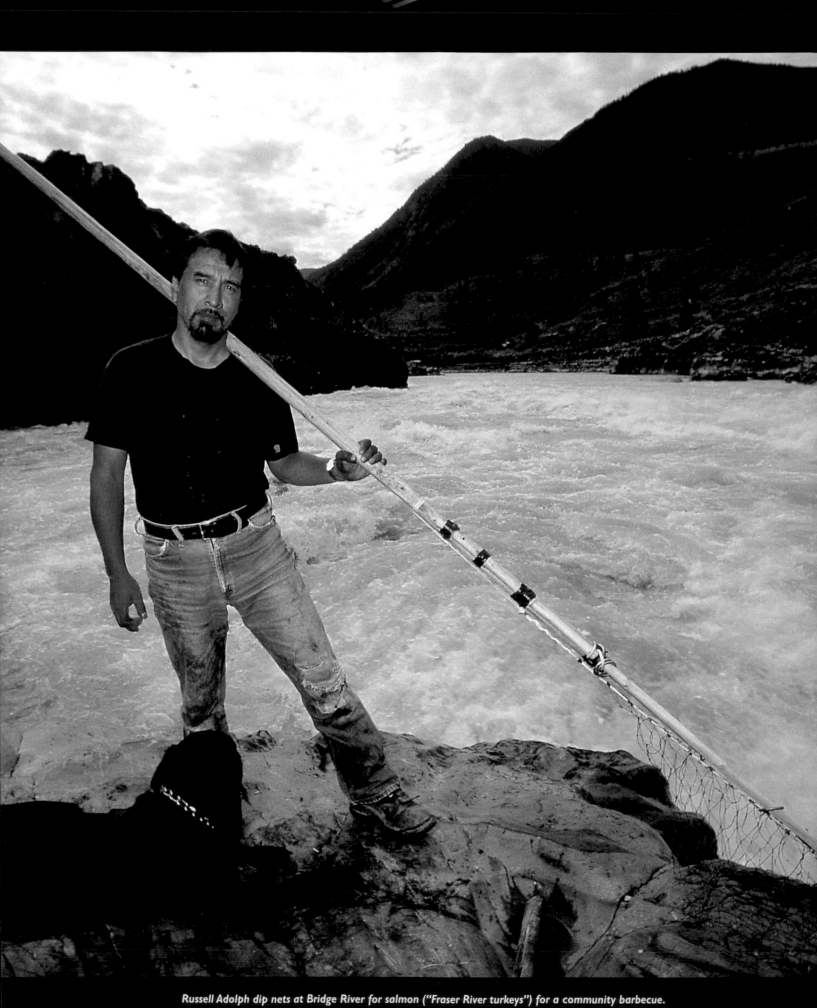

Russell Adolph dip nets at Bridge River for salmon ("Fraser River turkeys") for a community barbecue.

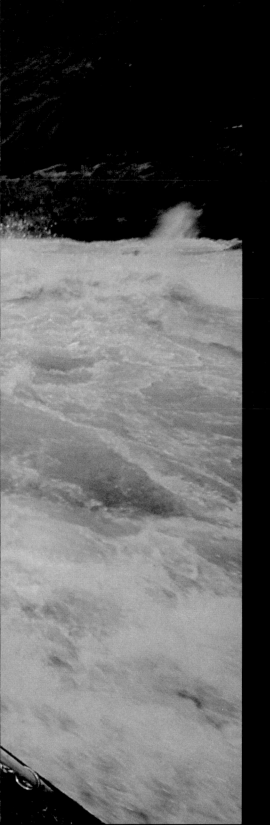
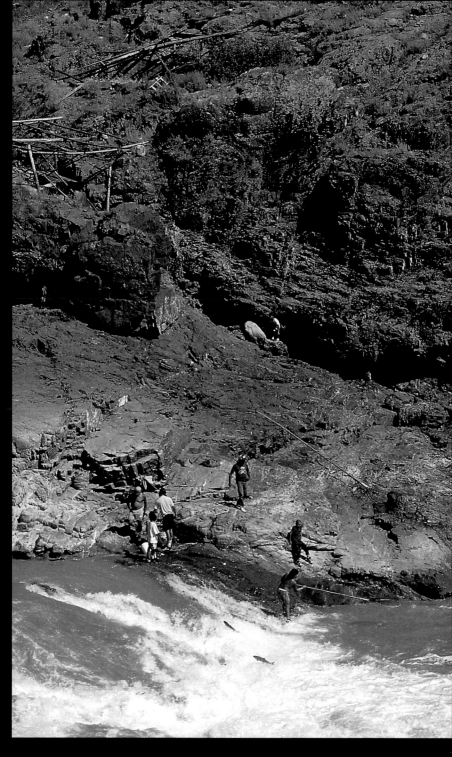

Bridge River is one of the most productive First Nations fishing spots on the Fraser.
It has supported an entire community for millennia.

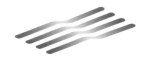

The Bridge River rapids present as difficult a passage for river rafts as they do for the salmon bound upriver. Darwin Baerg, the rafting guide who first took me along this stretch of the Fraser in 1996, says that these rapids are the most treacherous on the lower river, "the only ones that the Registrar of Commercial River Rafting won't allow us to take passengers through." Darwin supports the registrar's safety regulations, established in 1988 after some rafting accidents on other BC rivers, so his rafting guests walk around the Bridge River rapids just as Simon Fraser did. But unlike Fraser's guides, Darwin and his guides take the rafts through the rapids while the guests walk the shore rocks. "The characteristics of any set of rapids depend on the water levels," Darwin explains. "The Bridge River rapids are safe at the high water levels in early spring, but at that level Hells Gate is not safe, and we aren't allowed to run Hells Gate at more than 6,000 cubic metres per second of water flow." Our rafting party has not yet reached Hells Gate, the narrowest passage in the Fraser Canyon and famous for its fiercely turbulent waters.

In late April, when I rafted the Fraser with Darwin, the river was nearing the safe level. He had two rafts to take through the rapids, one 26 feet (8 m) long with extra tubes lashed on the outside, the other 23 feet (7 m) with no extra tubes. We raft passengers walked along the ridge above the rapids with Trevor, a guide Darwin was training for the coming season. Trevor would take the larger raft, as its extra tubes gave it greater stability. Darwin, who had never gone through in a single 23-foot (7-m) raft before, admitted to a few butterflies as he and Trevor scouted the rapids from the bluff trail.

The Bridge River rapids occur in two sections. In the first, the water breaks hard, but evenly, over a rock ledge. The second is more complex. "You come down just to the right of that eddy line on the far side," Darwin explained to Trevor, "but don't get sucked into the eddy or it will turn you broadside to the rapid below. As you come down the eddy line, try to time it so that you come down the left side of the *V* on the big rapid tongue when it is smoothed out. That curl is well over twenty-five feet high, and if it is breaking back it can turn the raft and roll it over. The river surges so the volume of water isn't always the same. You don't have much control once you are committed, but by slowing or speeding the motor you can vary your time down the tongue by a few seconds. I'm going to try to sneak the 23-foot (7-m) raft down on this side because it doesn't have the stability to handle that big curl."

The huge Bridge River rapids, just above the Fraser's confluence with Bridge River, are formed by a ledge jutting nearly to the river's surface. This ledge creates a white-water passage difficult even for a sophisticated modern river raft. But it also slows the progress of salmon swimming upstream, making them more easy to catch with dip nets.

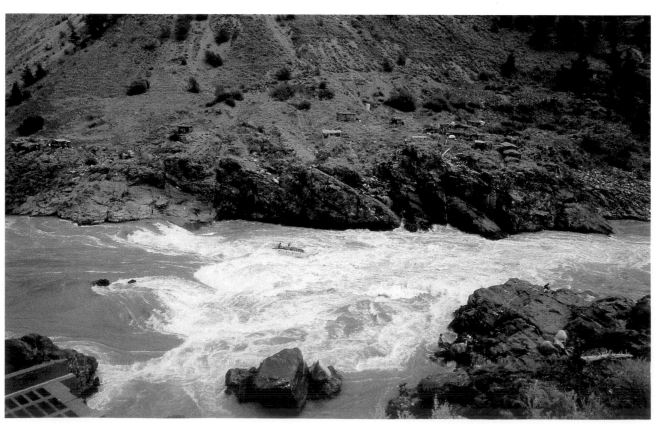

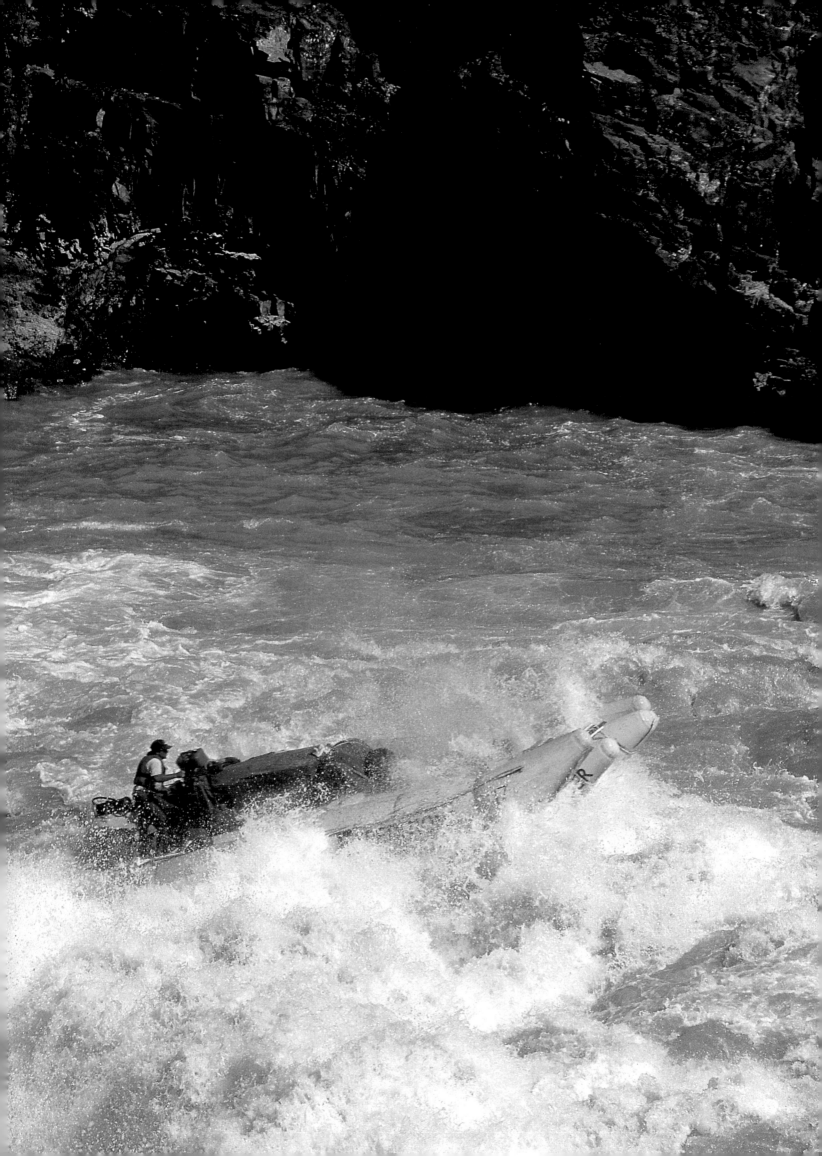

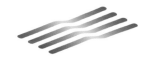

On the near side, the river rounds a barely submerged rock, which Darwin would have to slip past into the turbulence below. Then, trusting his propeller would find a purchase in that churning water, he would have to drive the boat back midstream to avoid being dashed onto the wall of black rock that juts out into the river just below the rapids.

Darwin and Trevor stood at the side of the river for a while, pointing to the water, conferring, discussing contingency plans. Coming back up the trail, they told us, "Our job is to make it look easy."

We watched from the trail as first the larger raft shot through with perfect timing, then the smaller one flew down through the right side. Just as they had planned, they made it look easy.

Lillooet, located at the confluence of the Bridge, Cayoosh and Fraser rivers, was once an important First Nations village, gathering place and burial ground. But in 1858 the old Douglas Trail was built so that prospectors could reach the Fraser gold fields without having to go through the canyon, and the trail reached the Fraser River at this point, having started at the head of Harrison Lake and run along what are now the Lillooet River and the Anderson and Seton lakes. By 1863, some 15,000 gold-seekers had flooded into what was now a town.

Lillooet was also the site of the short-lived Hudson's Bay Company Fort Berens, and in 1862 it became Mile Zero of the Cariboo Wagon Road. Today it is the headquarters for the Lillooet Tribal Council and local band offices.

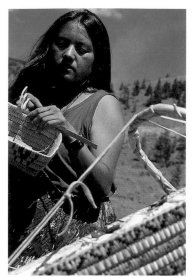

Ida Ley is a traditional basket maker and fisher who lives at Shalalth on Seton Lake, but has a fishing site on the Fraser at Bridge River.

Modern-day Lillooet is a junction town, one of those places where rivers, valleys, trails, highways and railroads bring people together before they go off to some other place. Historically it was also a great gathering place and fishing site, home to one of the largest First Nations settlements on the river. A few thousand years ago, fishing and trading supported a huge population here. The climate was ideal for drying fish, and Lillooet was the hub of a wheel of trading routes that ran in several directions.

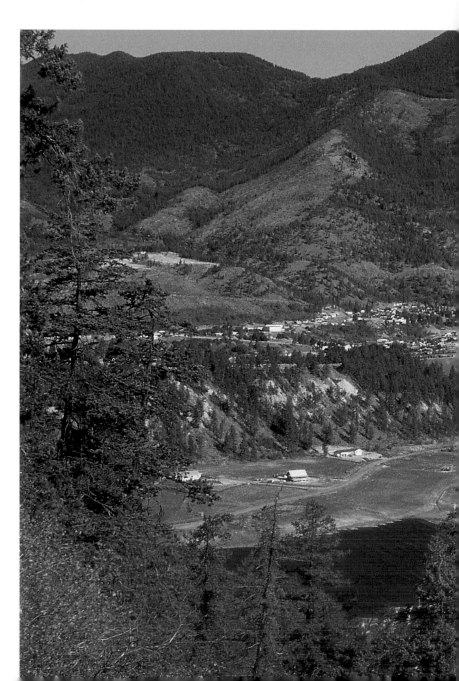

About 9 miles (15 km) downriver from Lillooet, Texas Creek flows into the Fraser. Here June Ryder is working to understand the dynamics of a catastrophic landslide that occurred around 900 AD. Thousands of tons of debris, including huge rock fragments, would have crashed down the eastern side of the river, leaving a pile of stone and rubble on the river bottom about 1,100 yards (1 km) long and 165 feet (50 m) deep. The slide would have created a lake extending 18 miles (30 km) along the river.

Meanwhile, Brian Hayden, a Simon Fraser University archaeologist, has been working at Keatley Creek, 10 or 12 miles (15–20 km) upriver from the slide site. He has been excavating among the remains of more than 120 semi-subterranean winter dwellings, in an ancient village site on a bench high above the river. One of five similar sites in the area, this one appears to have been a healthy, well-developed community, yet around the same time as the Texas Creek slide, it was suddenly deserted. The people seem to have moved away, taking all but broken possessions and leaving their many food caches empty. There is no sign of warfare or epidemic.

Hayden's archaeological evidence indicates that the Bridge River rapids area was home to a complex and thriving society based on the harvest of salmon runs at the lower end of Moran Canyon. He estimates that after the Texas Creek slide, the Fraser took several years to cut through the debris—long enough to damage local salmon runs severely and to provide "the most compelling explanation for the abrupt and simultaneous abandonment of the very large, rich, populous and socially sophisticated villages in the Lillooet region." Human populations here may never have been restored to their former levels, although "the

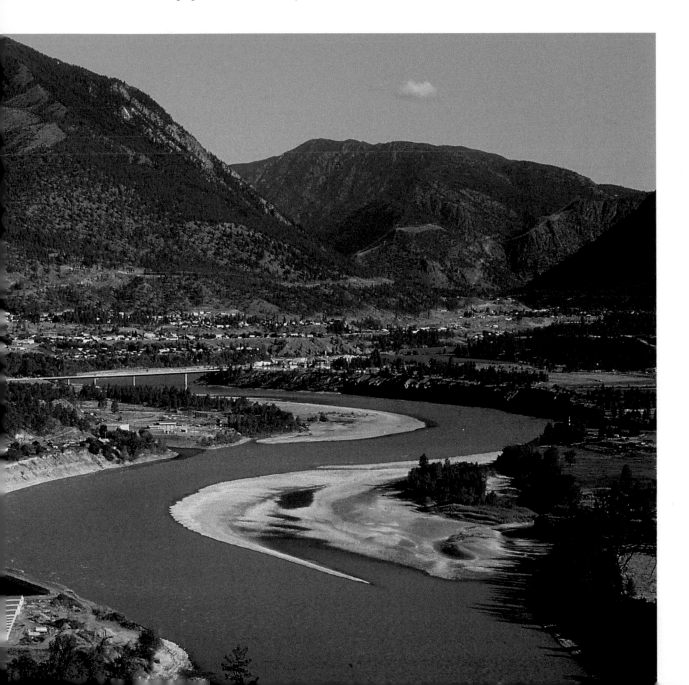

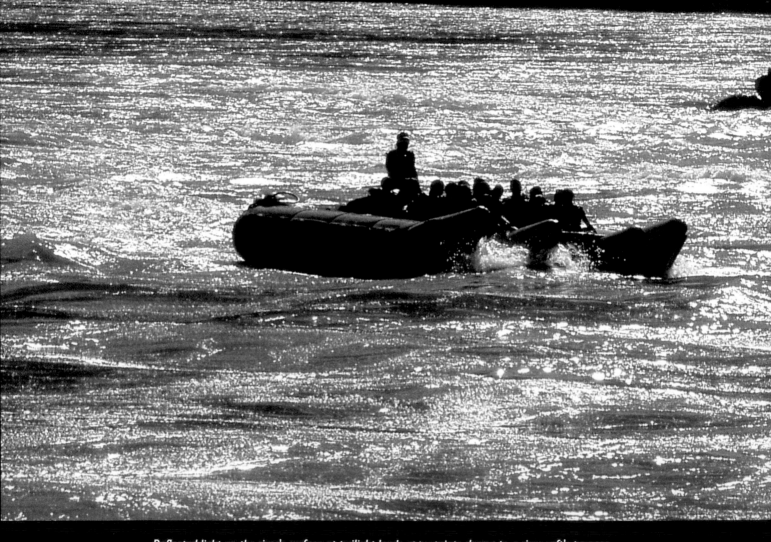

Reflected light on the river's surface at twilight lends appropriate drama to a river raft's passage.

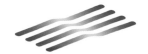

historic Lillooet bands were well on their way to reestablishing the kind of cultural complexity, trade, and social structure" that their ancestors had enjoyed."

For 15 or 20 miles (25–30 km) from Bridge River on down past Lillooet to Lytton, the river has created its own canyon, or series of canyons. But it is at Lytton, where the Thompson River joins the Fraser and the Cascade Mountains begin their long march to California, that the Fraser Canyon begins. Here, with the added volume of water from the Thompson and a river channel that is becoming increasingly narrow, the Fraser takes on a palpable urgency, and its roiling surface hides unplumbed depths. Ironically, Lytton, at the junction of these two deep, cool rivers, is regularly the hottest spot in British Columbia in summer. This results from its location tight under the shadow of the Coast Mountains that have just wrung the moisture from the air passing over them.

Like any settlement at the confluence of two major rivers, Lytton has been a strategic spot for millennia. In prehistoric times, this area was home to dense populations. In the 1850s the Nlaka'pamux (Thompson) people struggled to protect their lands from the thousands of gold-seekers who poured into the canyon, and it was at Lytton that Chief Cixpe'ntlam declared the sovereignty of his people.

After the influx of European immigrants, Lytton became another kind of cross-roads as well. Major highways converge here, and the two transcontinental rail lines join the river at this point. Just below the confluence, one of the lines crosses the river, then a few miles farther down, the two railways trade sides with the help of a pair of bridges. This strange and costly situation developed when the Canadian Pacific Railway, built in the 1880s, crossed the river to gain more favourable ground, and the Canadian Northern (later the Canadian National), built thirty years later, was forced to take the only canyon side available. Through this part of the canyon the railways are a constant presence, with trains squealing their way along one track or the other much of the time. Occasionally the rusted remains of railcars mark the spot where a whole train has toppled into the river, perhaps taking its engineer with it. These deaths only add to the fatalities amassed during construction of the railways. The toll was especially high among the nine thousand Chinese workers, who among the thirteen thousand employed in the project were treated as the more expendable.

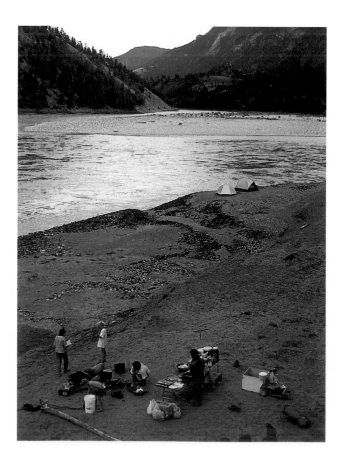

For rafters, a riverside camp like this one at Riley Creek is the perfect ending to a well-spent day.

Lytton marks a dramatic confluence. Here the green waters of the Thompson River, which has passed through lakes and slowed down long enough to drop its sediment, meets the silt-laden golden brown of the Fraser. The Thompson is known as one of the finest steelhead rivers in North America, but its runs are now threatened by pollution. Mill effluents, urban runoff, recreation developments and population growth on the river, especially in the Kamloops area, are caus-ing serious concern along the Thompson Basin.

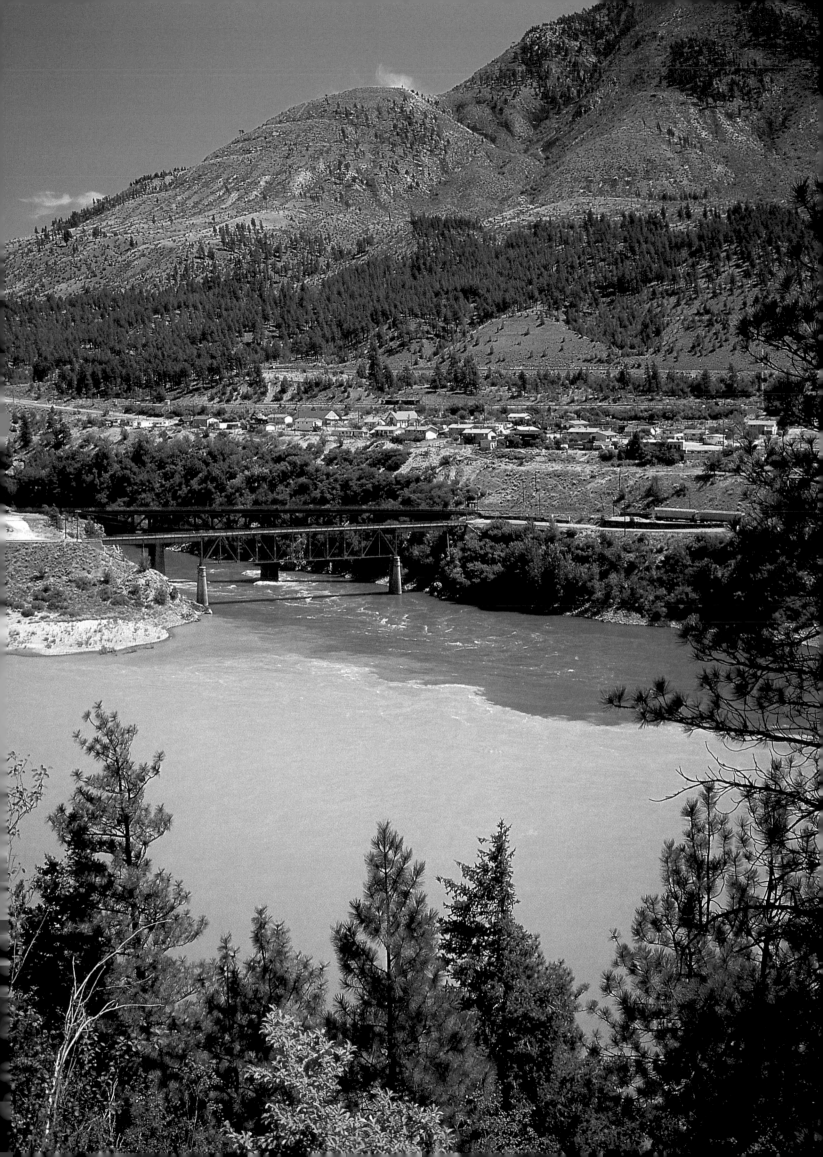

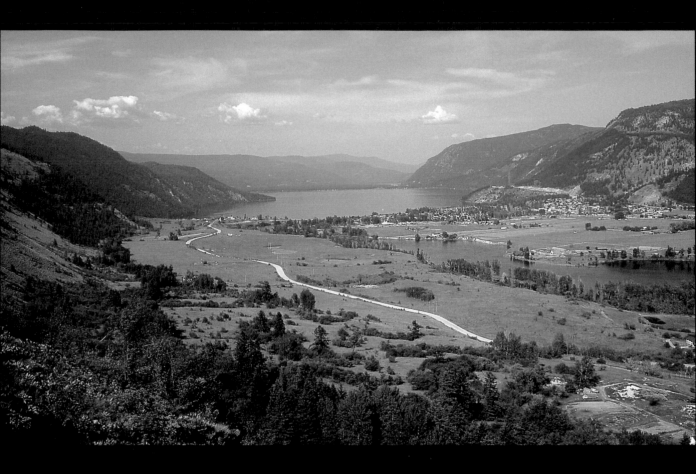

Minor Stocks, Major Concern

The Thompson River is the largest tributary to the Fraser and drains a large basin of its own. The system flows from the huge area of central British Columbia north of the Okanagan Valley and south of the Rocky Mountain trench, and the North and South Thompson rivers flow roughly south and west to join at Kamloops. Unlike the main stem of the Fraser, these waters flow green and clear. The Thompson system has several large lakes, from the Shuswap down to Kamloops Lake, and muddy sediments settle out in the lakes' calm waters. Another 70 miles (110 km) south-west, when the Thompson joins the Fraser at Lytton, it surrenders its green waters to the opaque browns of the Fraser.

Near the confluence, the Thompson passes through land that geographers classify as desert. Huge cottonwoods line its banks, providing refuge and nesting sites for birds. In early summer the female river-born merganser can be seen shepherding her brood up through the rapids in the shade of the cottonwoods,

then later in the year the whole family flies down the river in a flight pattern that follows precisely the contours of the water's surface inches beneath their wingtips. Once I stopped near the North Thompson with one of my children to watch a dipper scoot from rock to rock along the bottom of a little brook tumbling down the hill to Little Fort. In much of this part of the Thompson watershed, timber stands along the river and stream banks. In the meadows where the water lies still, there are willows to carry the moose through the winter, and in spring and summer there is rich green wild mint to crush between your fingers, just for the scent.

Besides running through some of the prettiest country in Canada, the Thompson River system is home to many salmon stocks. The confluence of the Thompson and Deadman rivers is the spot where the Secwepemc (Shuswap) people have taught their children to fish salmon for centuries. Despite its English name, which it acquired in 1817 after a man was killed here in a fight, the Deadman is a beautiful little stream which once supported healthy runs of salmon, including important stocks of

steelhead, chinook and coho. Now the smaller stocks have dwindled in numbers, and Chief Ron Ignace and the Skeetchestn Band are working to save them. They have improved the stream habitat where possible, and they are also working on an insurance policy: they are collecting sperm from migrating salmon and freezing it, so that if the stock ever faces extinction, successive generations of females can be fertilized, thus restoring the fish whose genetic history determines that they will enter the Fraser River, turn right into the Thompson and turn left into the Deadman.

Just up from the Deadman River, the Thompson widens into the expanse of Kamloops Lake, then moves on to its confluence with the North Thompson, where the city of Kamloops is located. About 60 miles (100 km) upriver, the Thompson is joined by the Adams River, a tributary whose gravel bars are called the richest few acres in BC. Millions of valuable sockeye are hatched there, later to be harvested by commercial fishermen on the coast.

But among the mass of Adams sockeye that return along the coast and

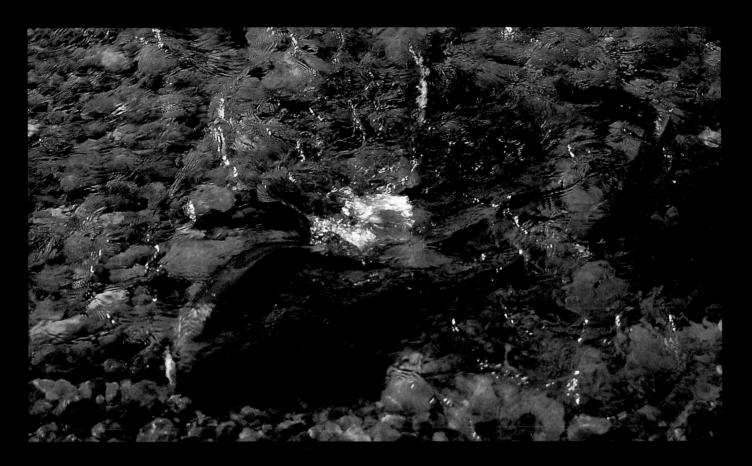

up the rivers, there are also many minor stocks of salmon from small streams. These small stocks are increasingly at risk in an industry whose management policy targets the big runs. A minor stock may number several thousand or just a few dozen, but each one has developed in the same painfully slow manner of survival and loss as the larger, more lucrative runs.

The Shuswap Nation Fisheries Commission, just across the bridge from Kamloops, is working with the federal Department of Fisheries and Oceans on stream enhancement and other ways of saving the smaller stocks. "The main problem is managing our weak stocks in the mixed stock fisheries," says Pat Matthew of the Commission. "The present agreements on the Fraser River system are not meeting our needs in this area." For example, Pat is concerned about the future of the Barrière River, which flows into the North Thompson about 100 miles (60 km) above Kamloops near his home community of Chu Chua. The river, named by Europeans for the "barrière" (fish weir) they saw here, has a run of sockeye that regularly returns between 8,000 and 40,000 fish. It also

has much smaller runs of chinook and coho, which spawn in the Barrière and some smaller tributaries of the North Thompson, including Lemieux and Dunn creeks. The Chu Chua community, Pat says, "is at the end of the line in that fish spawn and rear in our area. We don't have well-defined escapement targets for chinook and coho in our streams, which makes it hard for us to develop harvest targets. The Department of Fisheries manages to aggregate numbers for the whole North Thompson system, but our Band is interested in the well-being of each little creek."

Coho are considered the most opportunistic of salmon species. Over the centuries they have found their way into the smallest of streams along the coast and into the headwaters of major rivers like the Fraser. A 1967 study estimated that coho spawned in 970 of the 1,500 known salmon-bearing streams in BC. In some years, in some of the smallest streams, only a few dozen fish may return.

"We have separated rights issues from management issues," says Nathan Matthew, chief of the Chu Chua band. "The Department of Fisheries manage for

the big sockeye runs like the Chilko, Adams and Quesnel. We are interested in the biodiversity of each stream."

One late March day, I accompanied the band's fisheries manager to an interior coho creek. The snow under the birches and cottonwoods had been reduced to patches where the spring sun hadn't reached through the winter drifts. We followed the North Thompson to Lemieux Creek, and the creek to a side channel that flows through a rancher's field. Fed by a groundwater spring that keeps it relatively warm in winter and cool in summer, the channel widens from a point where you can jump across it, and becomes a deeper weed-filled pool. This tiny waterway, which feeds a creek that feeds a small river that feeds a tributary to the Fraser, is located some 360 miles (500 km) from the sea. This is how rivers and coho are born.

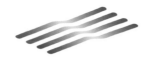

The years of railway construction through the canyon saw another noteworthy event in BC history—the only time a steamboat ever made passage upriver through the Fraser Canyon. Built to order for Andrew Onderdonk, the CPR contractor, at Spuzzum in the lower canyon, the *Skuzzy* was intended to be used in construction, to haul freight between Lytton and Boston Bar. But first she had to be taken to Lytton. It took several tries and three different captains to get her up through Hells Gate, and then only with the assistance of the steam winch on her bow, pulling cables affixed to ringbolts set in the rock walls, and 125 Chinese labourers who helped pull her through on yet another line. In the race to take steamboats through waters nobody else had dared, the *Skuzzy* set a high-water mark that was never equalled.

In 1882 when the *Skuzzy* made her passage, Hells Gate was a very dangerous piece of water, but not as dangerous as it became in 1913, when construction of the Canadian Northern Railway dumped tons of rock into the river along the east bank. The slide was observed to be slowing and even blocking passage of the sockeye along that run, which had been producing record catches—up to 32,000,000 fish in one year. The crisis was compounded in February 1914, when a slide caused by railway work dumped 100,000 cubic yards (76,000 m³) of massive granite chunks into the eddy just above Hells Gate. The channel was narrowed from 110 feet (33 m) to only 80 feet (25 m), and the river was partially dammed so that it dropped 16 feet (5 m) in a stretch of only 80 feet (25 m). Within a month, attempts were being made to remove the slide—with some success. Workers dumped smaller rocks into the river to be carried away by the current, and lifted larger boulders to the high west bank of the river. They kept working until the summer runs arrived, then tried to dip net the fish around the obstruction. A temporary fishway was built, and a small number of salmon managed to get through. The following winter, 59,000 cubic yards (45,000 m³) of rock were freed, a third of it lifted to the west bank and the rest dumped into the fast water to be carried away.

After these tiny attempts at repair, the horribly violated river and its fish were left to heal themselves. But rivers move rock slowly, and salmon runs die quickly. In 1918 the dearth of fish on the spawning ground was blamed on over-fishing, rather than the desecration at Hells Gate. It wasn't until 1941 that the decline of Fraser River stocks was officially attributed to the obstruction in the canyon, and funds were made available by the United States and Canada to plan and build fishways there. Construction of the first fishways along both banks was completed in 1946, and additions and improvements were added over the next twenty years.

Growing up on Vancouver Island, I knew little about the Fraser Canyon. In my Socials text it was an ominous barrier, the place where Simon Fraser and his men had to inch their way around a mist-shrouded rock wall, possibly about to drop into the cold fires of Hades at any moment. Then, when I was fifteen, I travelled through the canyon with my father. We walked down the trail to Hells Gate to see the fishways, and he told me with some reverence the story of the man-made fish-blocking slide of 1913 and the enormous international effort that had been necessary to help correct that human folly. It is a good story, but at the same time it is a tale of senseless vandalism that we have heard again and again in this land, in the name of progress.

Close-Up on the River

Darwin and Susan Baerg's rafting company, Fraser River Raft Expeditions, takes five hundred people down the Fraser Canyon each year and they raft a number of tributary rivers as well. About five rafting companies operate on the Fraser system, two of which, including the Baergs' company, run through Hells Gate. All of them are developing a new recreational tradition that is as much a calling as a business. "The river runs through most of the province, and yet it is taken for granted," Susan says. She knows that anyone who experiences the river close up will be committed forever to protecting it.

In 1995 the Baergs provided an escort boat for Fin Donnelly when he undertook the ultimate close-up river experience—swimming the full length of the Fraser from Tête Jaune Cache to the sea.

Near Siska, just below Lytton, twin bridges over the Fraser allow two transcontinental rail lines to trade sides. When the Canadian Pacific Railway was built in the 1880s, the first bridge was put in because the opposite bank was more favourable for railway building. Later, when the Canadian Northern (later Canadian National) Railway was built along the other bank, it was forced to change sides at this point, as there was nowhere else to build. From Lytton downriver to tidewater, rail tracks run along both sides of the river.

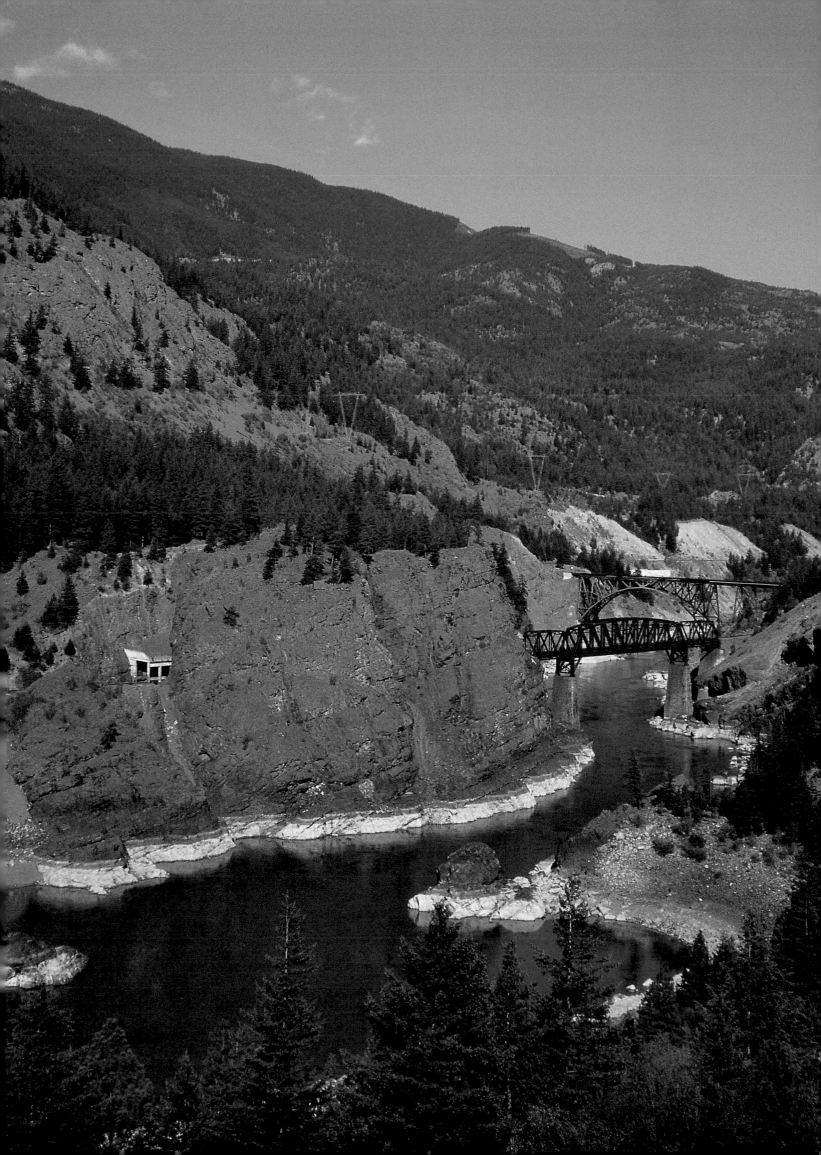

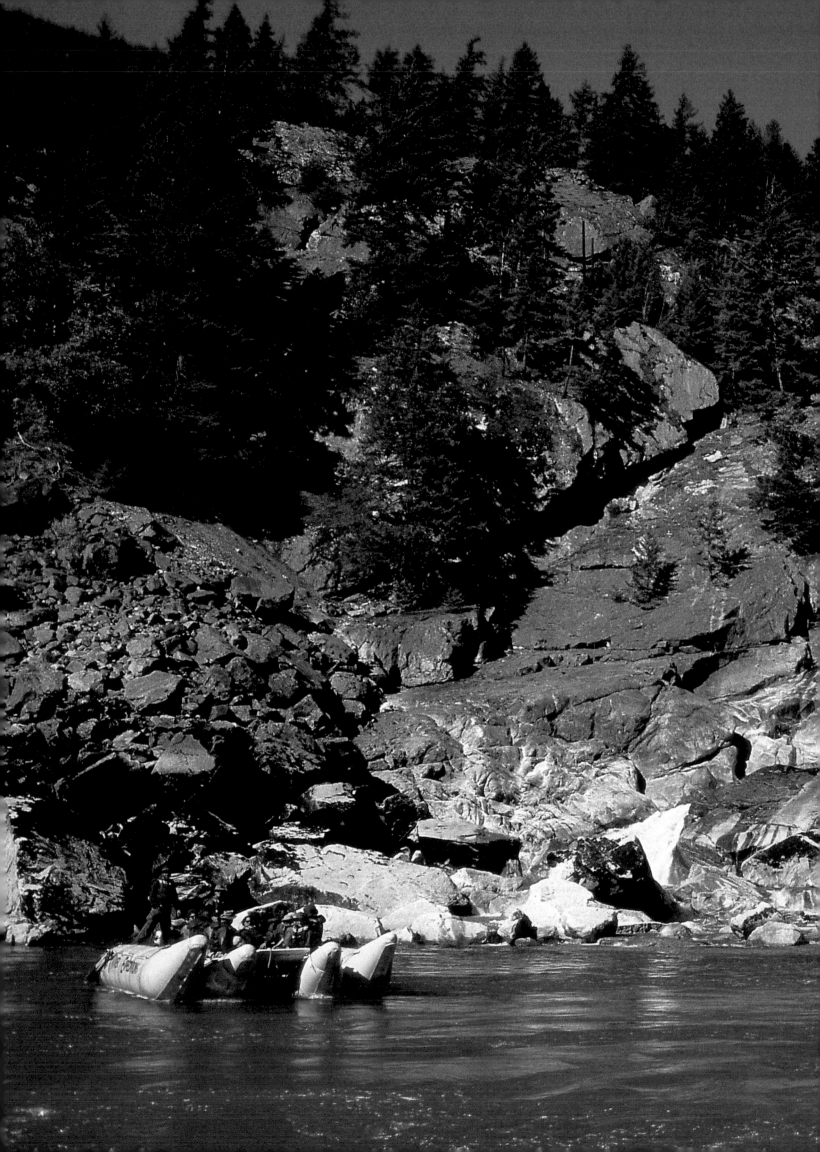

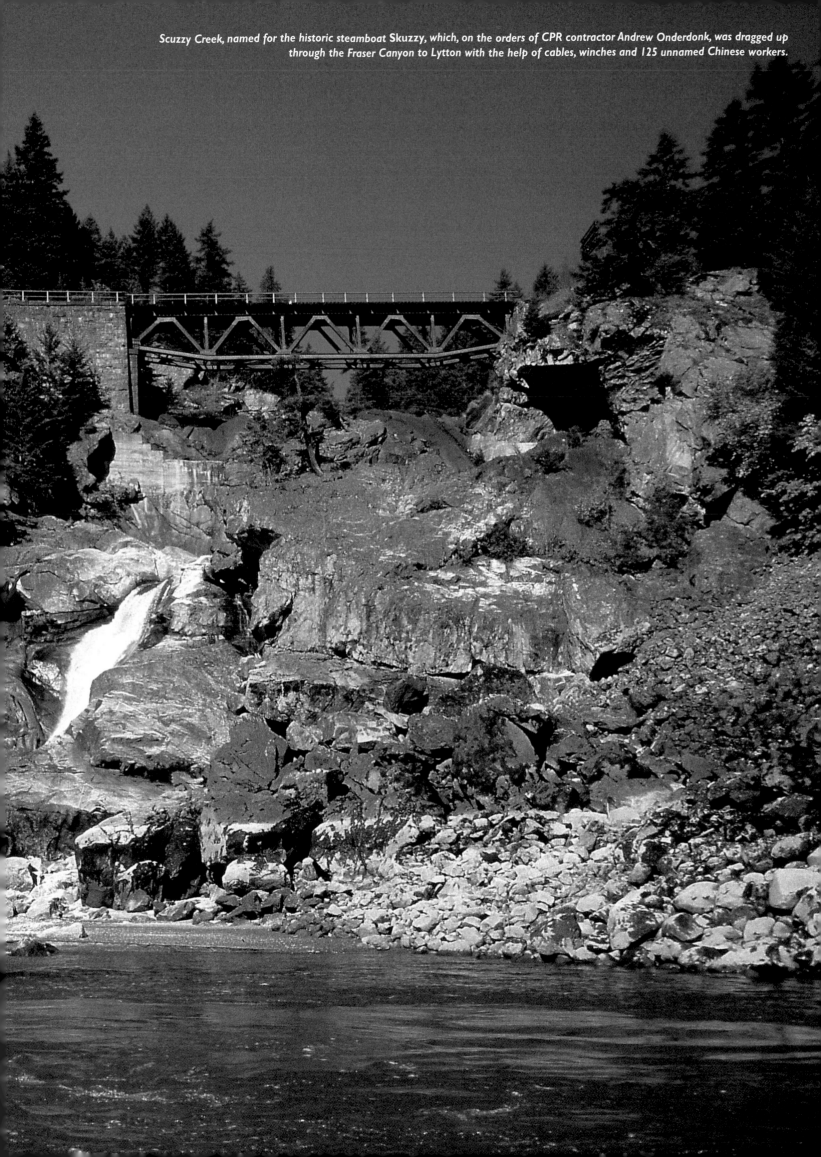

Scuzzy Creek, named for the historic steamboat Skuzzy, which, on the orders of CPR contractor Andrew Onderdonk, was dragged up through the Fraser Canyon to Lytton with the help of cables, winches and 125 unnamed Chinese workers.

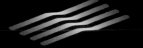

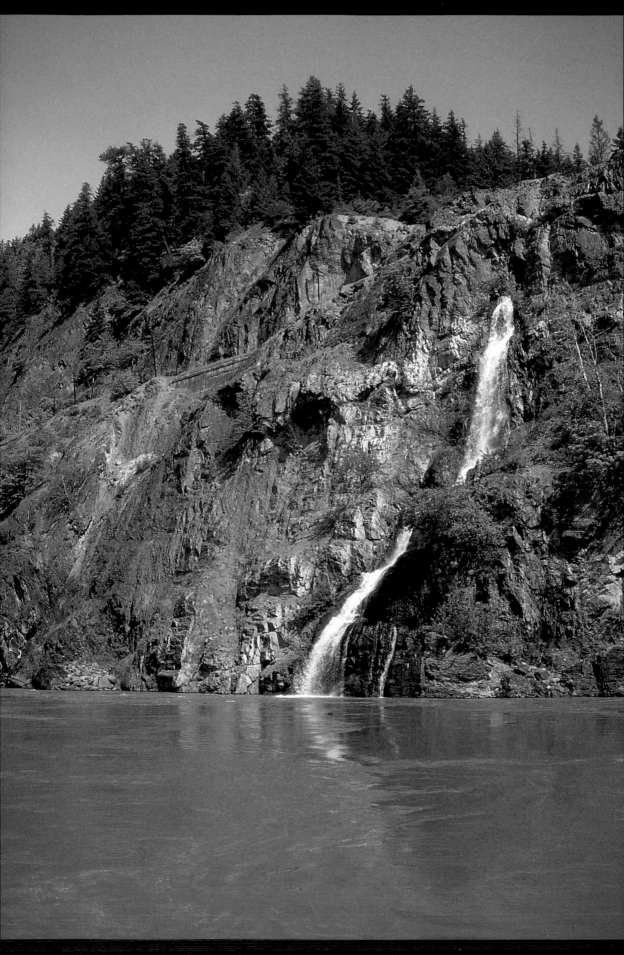

Derailment is a constant danger for trains moving along the steep sides of the Fraser Canyon. Substantial property damage is unavoidable, and people have died in derailments.

As I stood there in 1957, on the edge of Hells Gate, the thundering waters impressed on me that I was at a great fulcrum of our province. So much of BC relates directly to this spot. Fishing Fraser-bound sockeye in Johnstone Straits or listening to Tsilhqot'in legends of the boy who went down the river on a pad of ice, I have so often realized that much of what is good about this land passes through the constriction at Hells Gate.

I know the canyon best from the road and the tunnels. As my children grew, they learned to recite the tunnel names from north to south and the other way around, as we drove from our Cariboo home to the coast and later from our coast home to the Cariboo. Yale, Saddle Rock, Sailor Bar, Alexandra, Hells Gate, Ferrabee, and the longest, China Bar. And I have my favourite spots along the road for stopping and looking at the canyon, like that wonderful sandy point of land at Lytton where the green Thompson joins the muddy Fraser. But it wasn't until I rafted the canyon that I felt the river and experienced the strength with which it reshapes the landscape. From the water, I could see how the river slows momentarily to deposit its load of gravel and flakes of gold, which forms the bars that have named the highway tunnels.

Darwin Baerg is entirely comfortable but never casual about rafting the turbulent waters of the Fraser Canyon. Before each trip, he gives a full safety lecture, acting out several basic survival techniques. Before he took our rafting group through the canyon, he showed us how to sit facing downstream with our feet out in front to fend off the rocks, and how to breathe through our teeth to keep out the river water, and how to rescue someone who has gone overboard. Then he checked that everyone was properly buckled into their life jackets, and we were off. From Lytton, where we began, it was about 30 miles (50 km) to Hells Gate.

Two of North America's major mountain ranges overlap in the Fraser Canyon. The west side of the canyon from Lillooet down is formed by the Coast Mountains, which extend from Vancouver to Alaska. The east side of the canyon is formed by the Cascade range, running from Lytton to California. Darwin turned the big raft around with the outboard so that we all got to see the full panorama of canyon walls and river, a spectacle that went on for tens of miles and was breathtaking all the way. In places the rock walls rose 100 feet (30 m) or more straight up to the rail or highway ledge, and then up again in a sharp *V* to mountaintops hundreds of yards above us. From time to time we spotted a secret little beach tucked into a crevasse in the canyon wall.

As we approached Hells Gate, a mere 110 feet (33 m) wide but 200 feet (61 m) deep, with river depths that vary up to 100 feet (30 m) over the years, Darwin reminded us to sit astride the inside raft tubes with both hands on the safety lines that run along their sides. He had already warned us that the front person takes the brunt of the water, and I was sitting in front. We glided downriver in the powerful water, past the concrete fish ladders, and as the river narrowed abruptly we passed beneath the tourist structures. A gondola swings from cables high above the river, bringing people down across the water. A coffee shop and museum crowd the small bench above the west side of the canyon, and there is a foot-traffic suspension bridge. All of this focusses on the river, which is itself focussed by the narrowing rock walls.

As we slipped down the water into the great curl of rapid, I felt no fear, only an overwhelming joy at the sensation of being one with the river. A moment later we entered the curl and a lot of water—what felt like the whole river—crashed into my lap, the weight of it tugging enticingly at my arms. It was one of those moments I wished I could live in slow motion so as to experience fully the pleasure of it. But the water sloughed off and the excited, relieved laughter of the other rafters rose above the roar of the river. We were through Hells Gate. I was in awe.

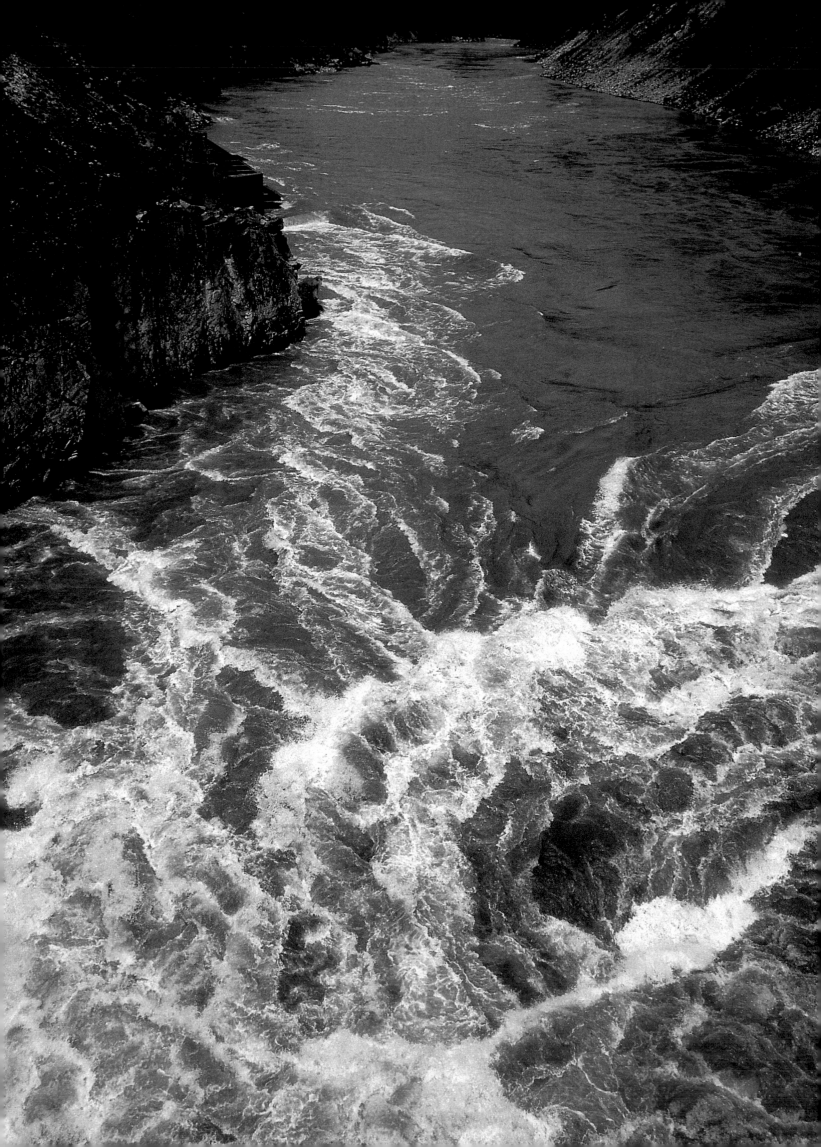

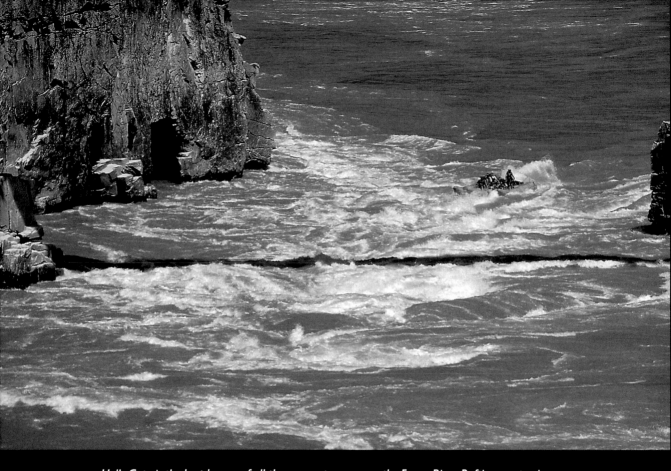

Hells Gate is the best known of all the narrow passages on the Fraser River. Rafting companies are not permitted to make the passage in water levels higher than 7,800 cubic yards (6,000 m³) per second. Some years it is mid-July before freshets have tapered off and flows have reached that level. But even at safe levels, the passage is an exhilarating experience.

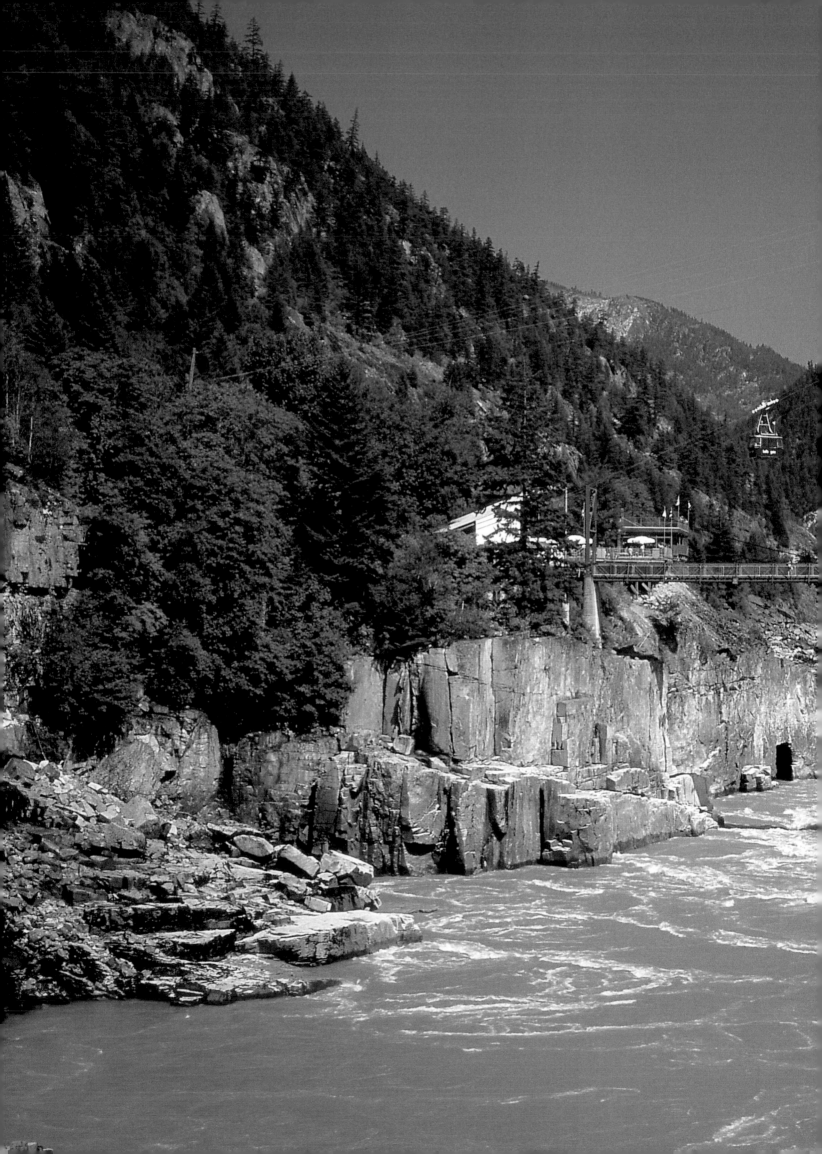

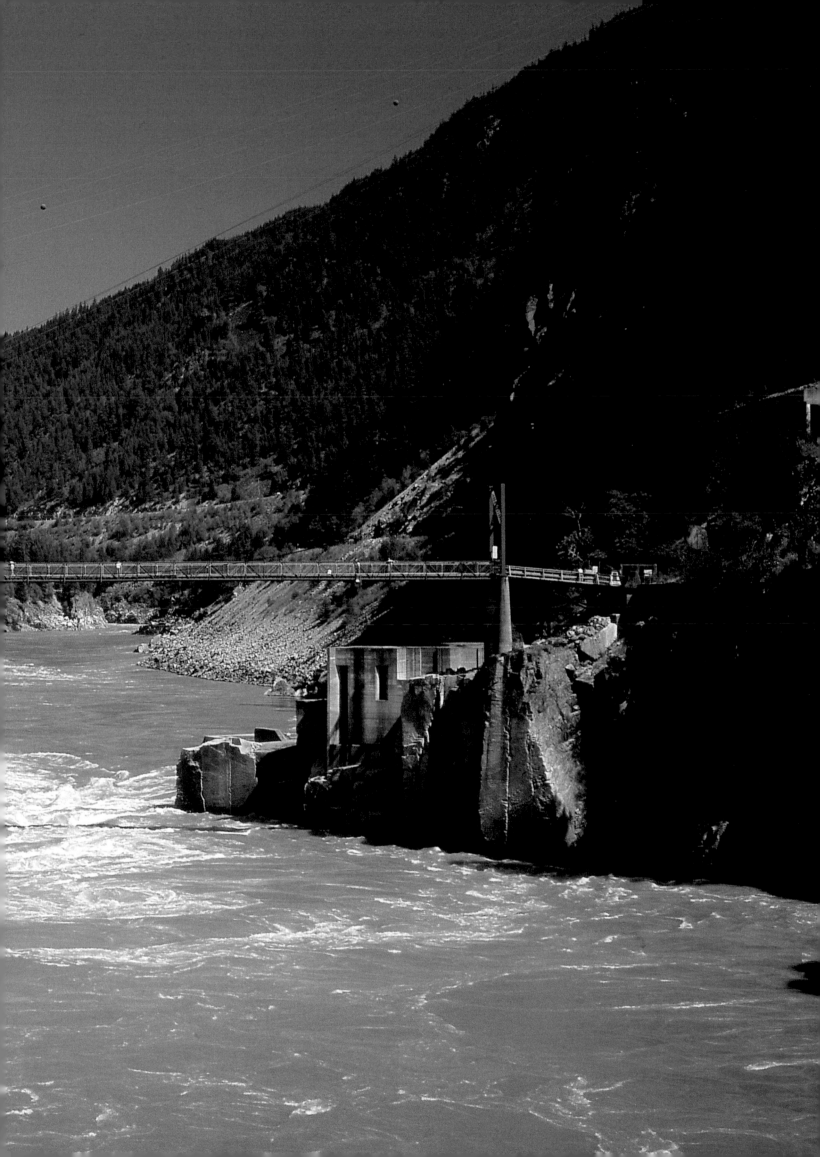

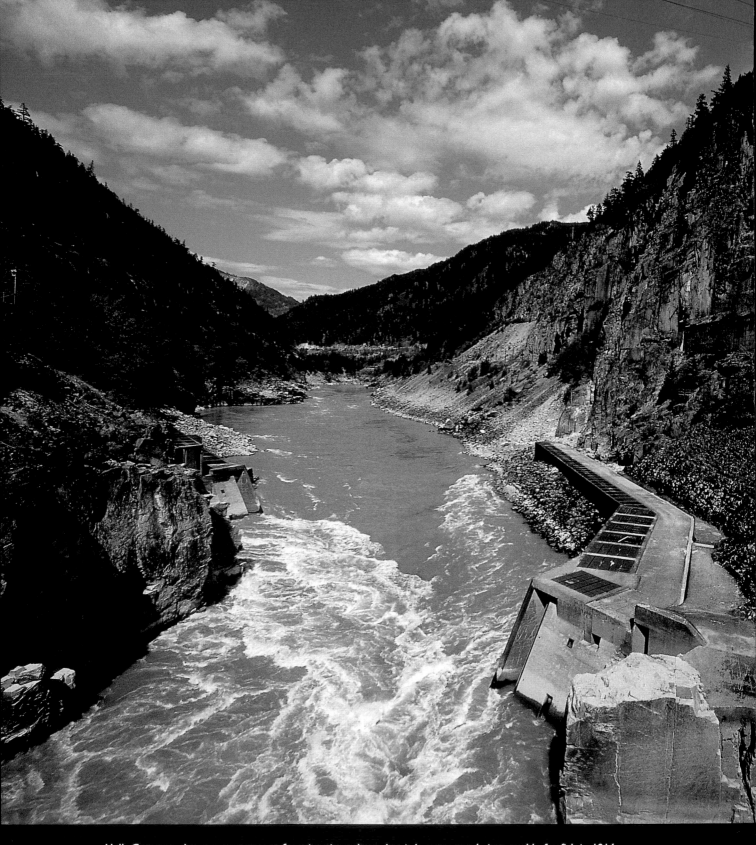

Hells Gate was always a narrow spot for migrating salmon, but it became nearly impassable for fish in 1914, when a huge slide of granite chunks was dropped into the river during railway construction. Workers began clearing the rocks immediately, but decades passed before proper fishways were installed and runs began to move upriver at pre-slide rates. Even now, the Gate can be a formidable obstacle to salmon at some water levels.

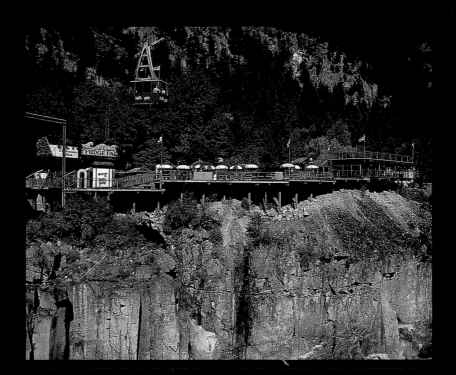

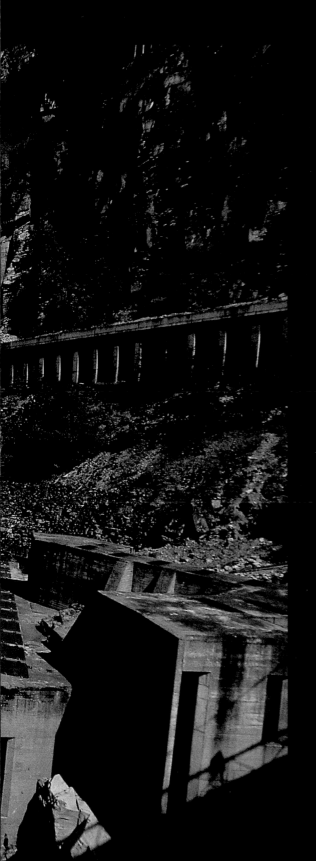

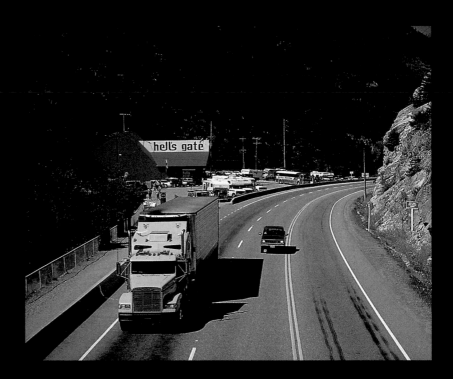

An air tram takes visitors from the high canyon walls down close to the river
to view the excitement of Hells Gate, while trucks beat their way along
the Trans-Canada Highway, far above the river's waters.

Later I asked Darwin what he had been doing while his passengers crashed through the narrows in wild exhilaration. I wasn't surprised to hear that he had been thinking and planning every second, from setting us up at a point above the rapids, to calculating how far and how fast the river would drop, to checking constantly for water that would take us through without tossing us into a whirlpool. "Sometimes not much happens," he said. "It's what I call the magic carpet ride. But you have to be cool-headed and ready for anything, because the river doesn't stop. It's not like you can hit the brakes, pull over and figure out what you're going to do next."

The waters below Hells Gate are relatively quiet, and as we drifted we gazed up the sheer walls of the inner canyon to the steep mountain slopes. On either side the train tracks snaked along their ledges, while still higher on the east bank we glimpsed the highway tunnels, so familiar from the road and so remote and distant—in every sense—from the water. We were at a timeless remove, sharing a moment in the infinite life of the river. Like the silt from the bank at Prince George and the few fine grains of white mica from under the Yellowhead Highway bridge, at this instant we lent definition to the river that carried us. We were very far away from the highway.

Downriver, at Alexandra, we came upon the old suspension bridge that reaches from a rock abutment on the east side to carry the old Cariboo Road to another rock abutment on the west side. Named for Princess Alexandra of Wales, the bridge was built in 1926 to replace the original 1863 structure. Apparently the first bridge deck was 10 feet (3 m) lower than this one and was actually awash during the great flood of 1894 that overwhelmed so much of the Fraser Valley. Now the old bridge is used only by tourists. They walk down from the little park on the highway after they cross the newer Alexandra Bridge, which soars on a great red steel arch over the river.

Suspended from a rock pillar near the bridge was a pulley supporting a yellow rope, which marks a Nlaka'pamux (Thompson) fishing spot. We had passed many such sites in the upper canyon, each rigged to take advantage of the particular rock formations and river eddies. The day we went by, fishing was closed, but when it opened, the people who have rights to that spot would come with a short piece of gillnet, attach one end of the net to the loop of yellow line, and run it out like laundry on a clothesline to hang down in the turbulent waters.

Train tracks run through the Canyon on a scree slope of apparently unstable rock.

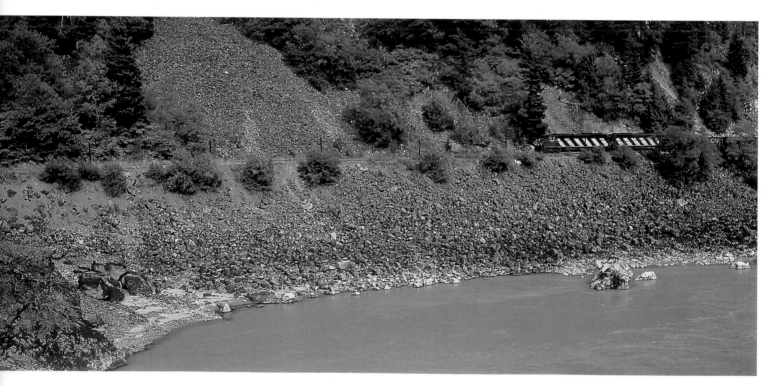

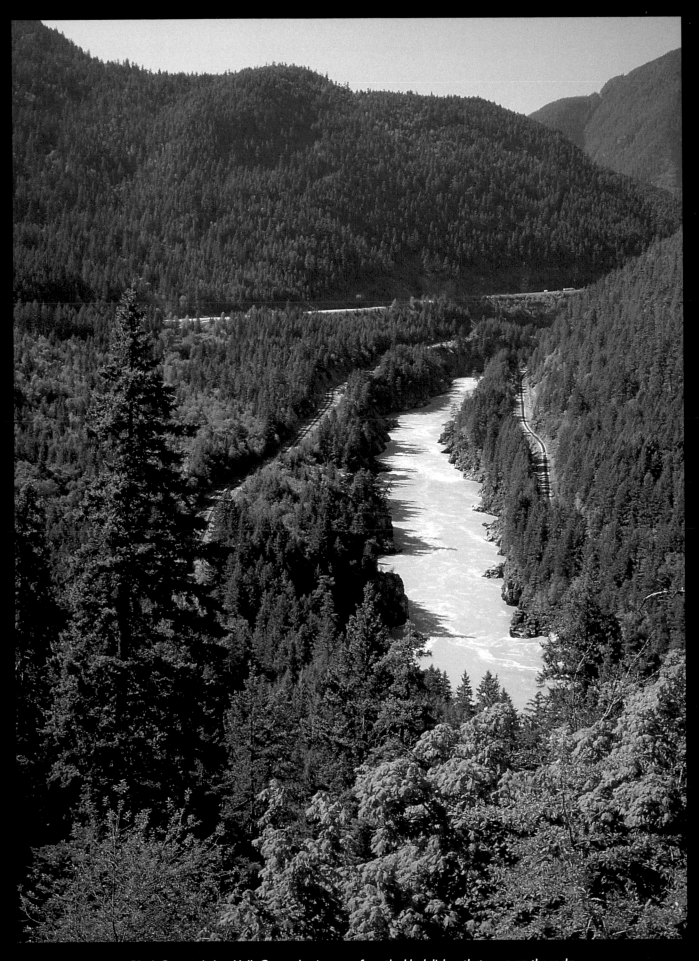

Black Canyon, below Hells Gate, takes its name from the black lichen that grows on the rocks along the edge of the river.

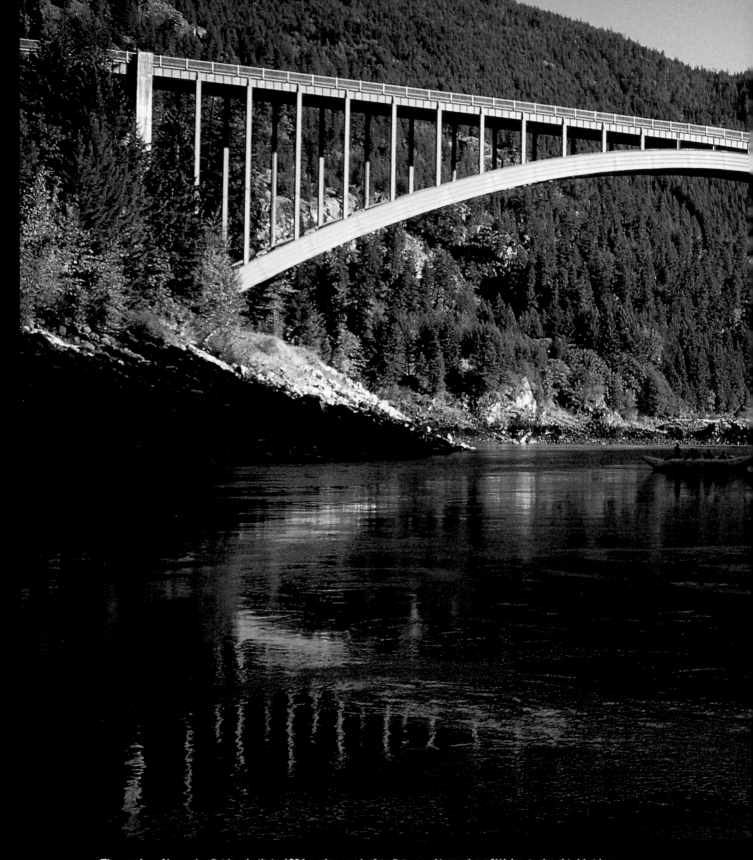

The modern Alexandra Bridge, built in 1926 and named after Princess Alexandra of Wales, is the third bridge to cross the Fraser near this point. Its dramatic sweep forms a frame into which our raft floats.

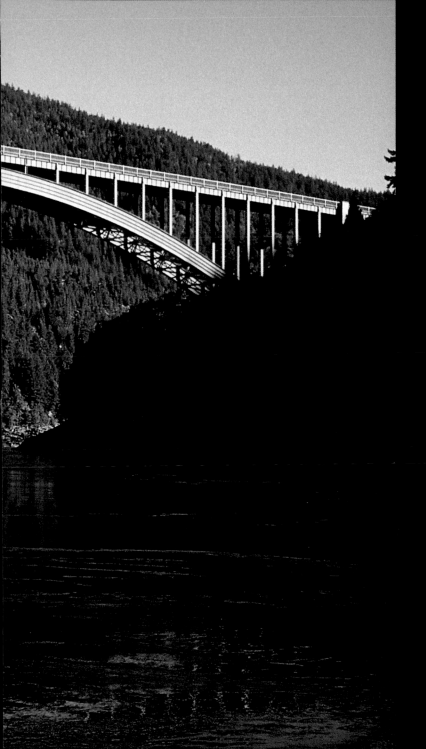

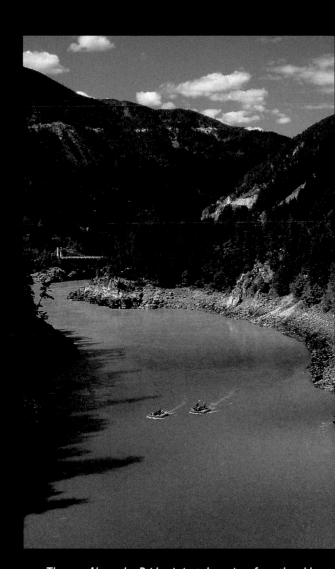

The new Alexandra Bridge is just downriver from the old
suspension bridge built in 1926 that still spans the river. An early
bridge was built at this site in 1863, some 10 feet (3m) lower than
the 1926 bridge. It is said that during the great flood of 1894, the

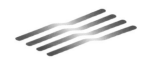

Just down from Alexandra and the little community of Spuzzum on the west bank is the boundary between the Nlaka'pamux and Sto:lo First Nations. Downriver from there, we floated by a lone rock pillar crouching dejectedly beside the river. A nearby rock ledge with a gap near one end is said to be a group of Nlaka'pamux men who came down to play the lahal stick gambling game against the Sto:lo. The gap was left by the dejected loser, still waiting upriver for his comrades. The story served to remind us, as we moved comfortably through the river in our high-tech craft, just how little we know of human history on the Fraser. It was just downriver, at an ancient midden known as the Milliken site, that Charles Borden, an archaeologist at the University of BC, excavated the charred pit of a chokecherry that some early aboriginal salmon fisher had spat into a prehistoric camp-fire, and by radiocarbon dating found it to date back nine thousand years—long before the building of the pyramids or the writing of the Dead Sea scrolls.

Some years ago, on a day in early February just as the ice was leaving the river, two of my children and I went out on this part of the Fraser with Kenny Malloway and two of his children. Kenny's winter home is down in the valley at Ch'iyaqtel (Tzeachten), near Chilliwack, but he lives for the canyon, where he has fished since he was a child. Pointing to the mountaintops above us, he said, "If you look way up, you can see a sort of finger of rock. Just beside that is a cave where the people stayed during the big flood, the one when Noah built his boat." In February the upper reaches of the Fraser watershed were still frozen, the river was low and still wearing its winter colour of rich opaque green. Kenny was scouting in anticipation of an opening for the early spring salmon. On the east bank of the river, opposite the highway, his mother camps on a particular point of land for two months every summer. "The land belongs to the Ohamil Band," Kenny told us, "and the spot was fished by a couple for many years until they drowned in the river. When my mom started fishing there, we used to come up on the train that they called the way freight. It would bring us up on Wednesday and back down to Chilliwack on Saturday. The fare was six fish." Every point, bar and rock on the river has not one but many many stories, some buried deep in the past and forgotten, others still forming in the experience of today's river people.

Much of the Fraser Canyon has been burnt at one time or another by fires that start along the railways. Fires can be ignited easily when sparks are generated by rail traffic.

Once again, as our raft approached the treacherous Sailor Bar rapid, it was time to get ready for rough water. Feeling like something of a whitewater expert after the rapids

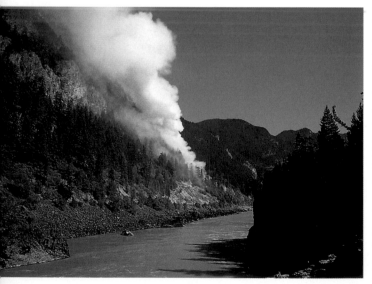

at Hells Gate, I confidently wrapped my hands around the safety lines and prepared for the ride. Darwin drove the raft into the rapid, and I only had time to see the tail that arched out of the bottom of the rapid before I was under water. The weight of it crashed down and pulled harshly at my body, and the sense of elemental oneness I had experienced at Hells Gate was replaced by a force that threatened to tear me from the raft. Maybe the river was reminding me that I had grown a bit presumptuous about my place in the scheme of things.

Darwin ran the raft up the back eddy and we repeated the passage several times. It was exhilarating to play with such large natural forces, even though it was always clear that in this game we were mortal and the river was a benevolent God. By now the sun had slipped behind the canyon's western wall and we were wet and rapidly growing cold. Like good guides the world over, Darwin knows when it is time to get his charges home to hot drinks and dry clothes. We motored downriver past Lady Franklin Rock. According to popular lore, Lady Jane Franklin led a party up the river in search of her husband, Sir John Franklin, after he disappeared exploring the Arctic in 1845. In truth the rock was named to mark a visit she made to Yale in 1861, for purely recreational reasons, her appetite for adventure travel apparently undimmed by her husband's grisly experience.

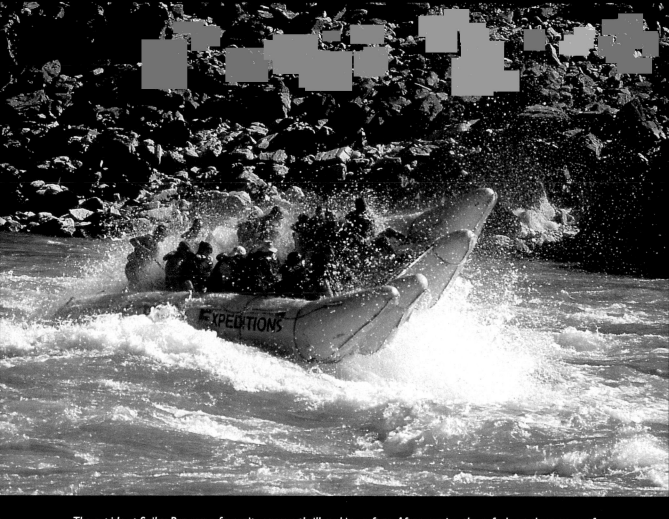

The rapids at Sailor Bar are a favourite among thrill-seeking rafters. After running the raft down the tongue of the rapid and thoroughly soaking everyone on board, the guide can take the raft up the back eddy and repeat the performance as many times as the passengers can stand.

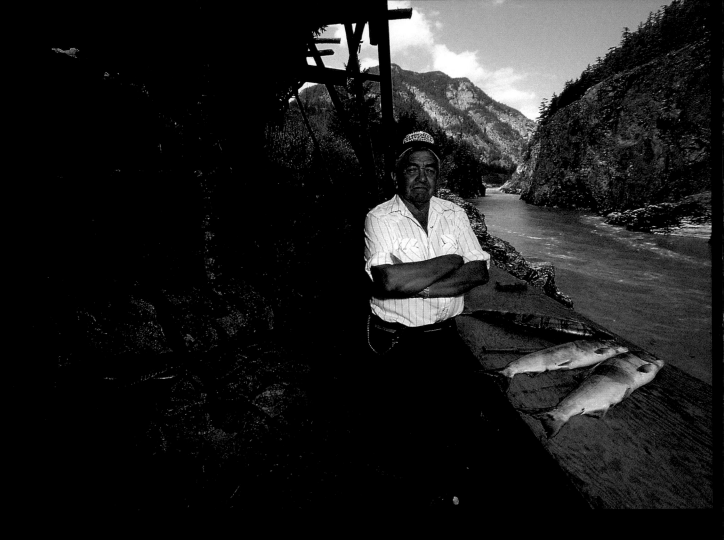

A Taste of the Stuart Run

Archie Charles is chief of the community of Seabird Island near Agassiz, but he has a fishing camp just above Saddle Bar, about 10 miles (6 km) upriver from Yale. "We use all of the fish. All we throw away is the bone," Archie says. The red flesh of his dried sockeye bears characteristic cross-grain cuts: these allow the strong, dry winds flowing down the Fraser Canyon from the interior to do their work. The winds blow best in July, and by August the wasps and flies appear, so it is important to get a good catch of the early Stuart sockeye as they pass through the canyon on their way north to their birthing gravel. This is the run that Archie's people have long depended on for the dry rack fishery. Not only has it traditionally fed the Seabird commodity. Years ago the dried fish were traded along the streams and trails that the Hope–Princeton and Coquihalla highways now follow. To this day the Seabird Island people barter with the coast people, getting seaweed, dried clams and mushrooms in exchange for the rich dried Stuart sockeye, still one of the Fraser River's finest products.

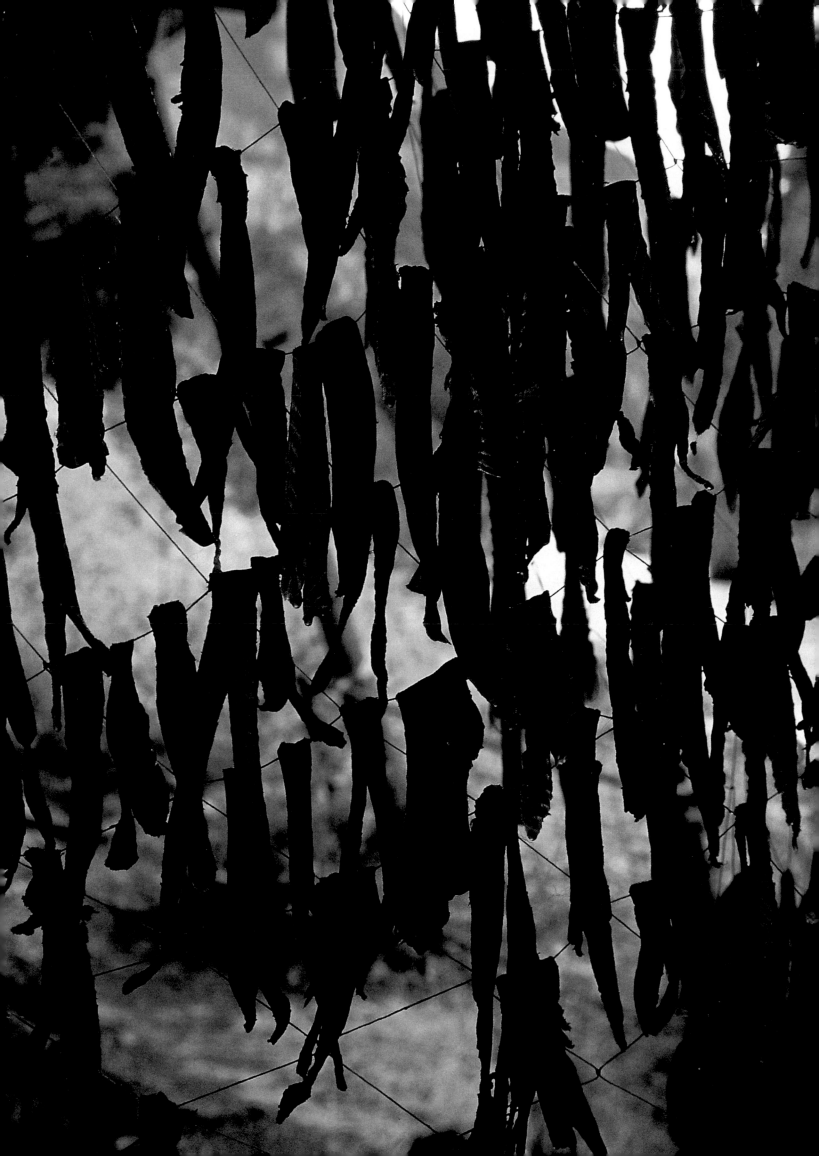

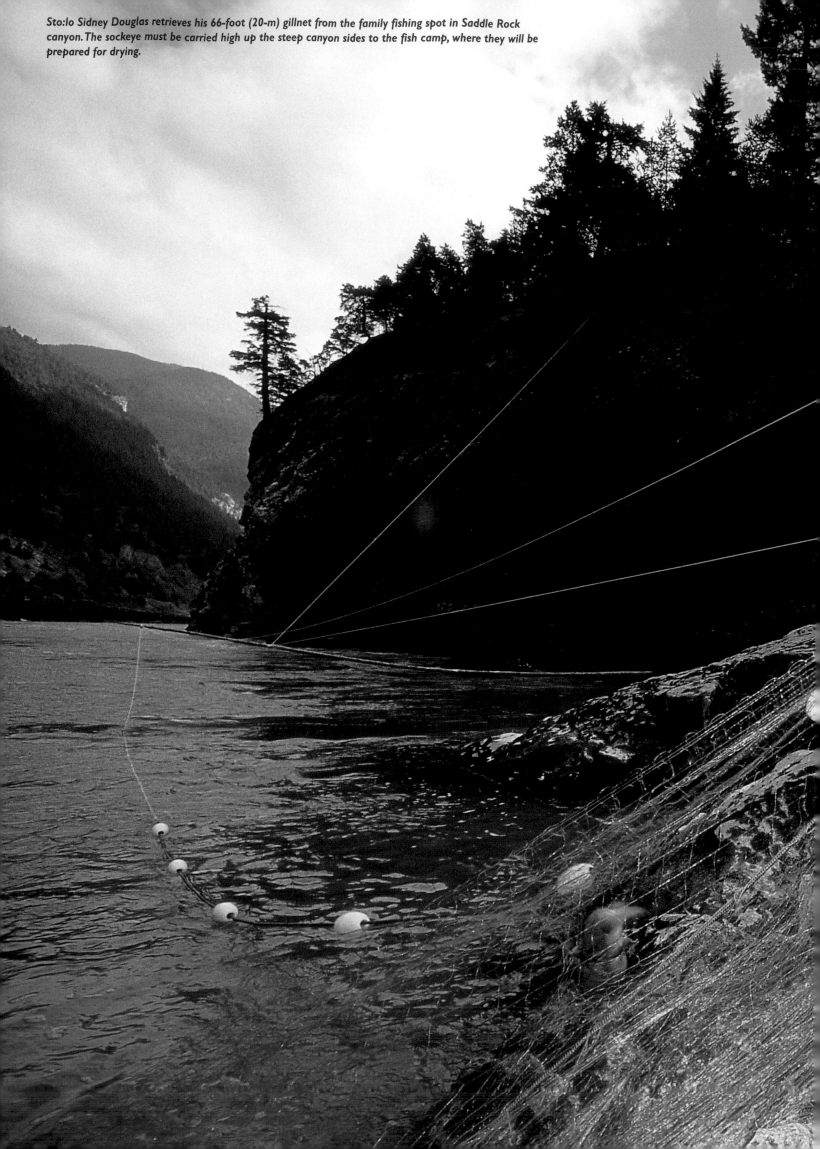

Sto:lo Sidney Douglas retrieves his 66-foot (20-m) gillnet from the family fishing spot in Saddle Rock canyon. The sockeye must be carried high up the steep canyon sides to the fish camp, where they will be prepared for drying.

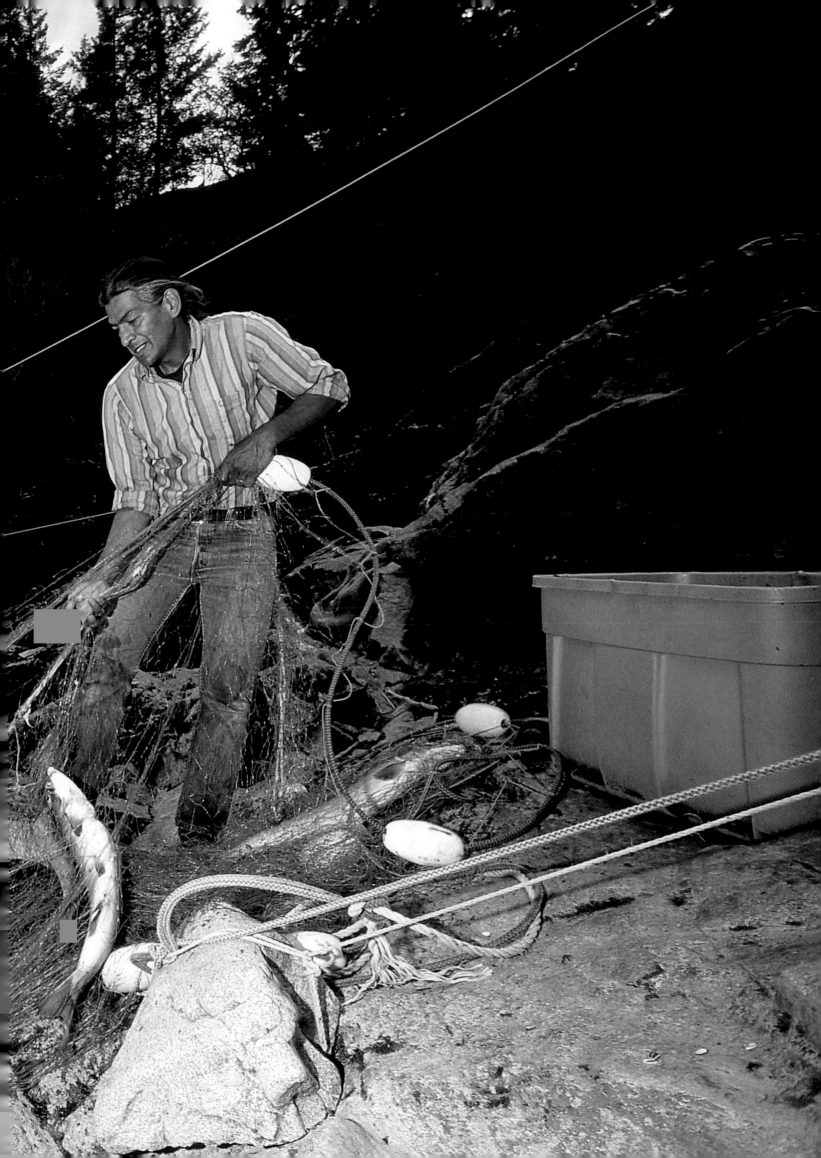

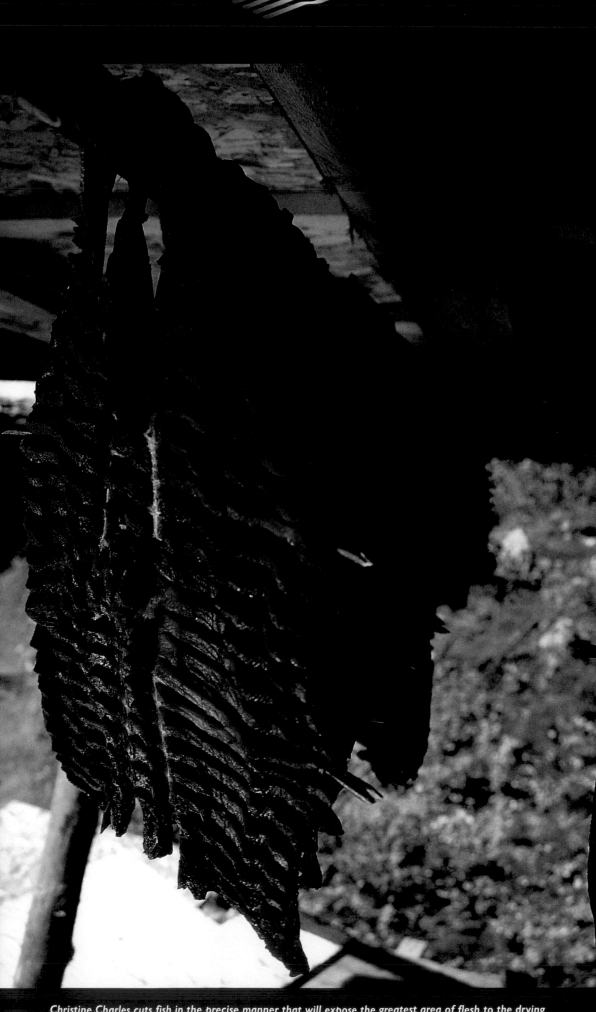

Christine Charles cuts fish in the precise manner that will expose the greatest area of flesh to the drying winds in the Canyon. The fishery here is timed extremely carefully, to take advantage of the best drying winds and to complete the work before wasp season.

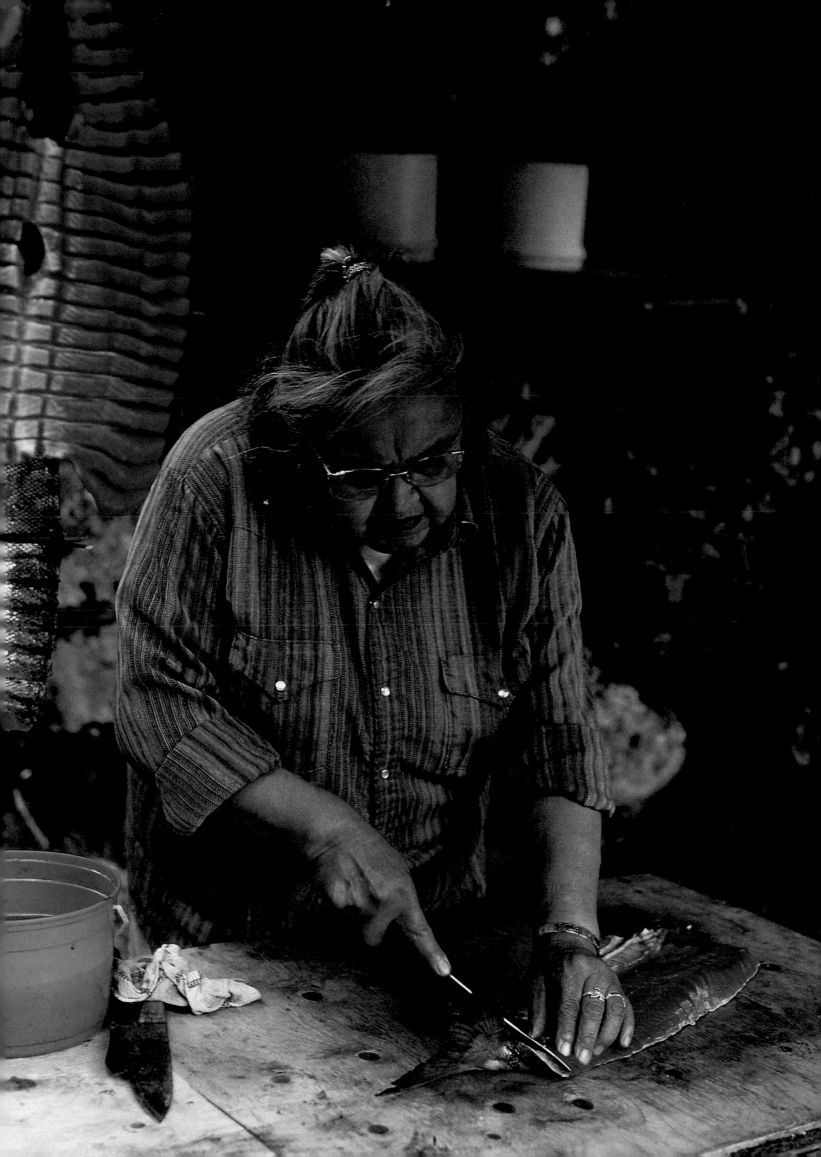

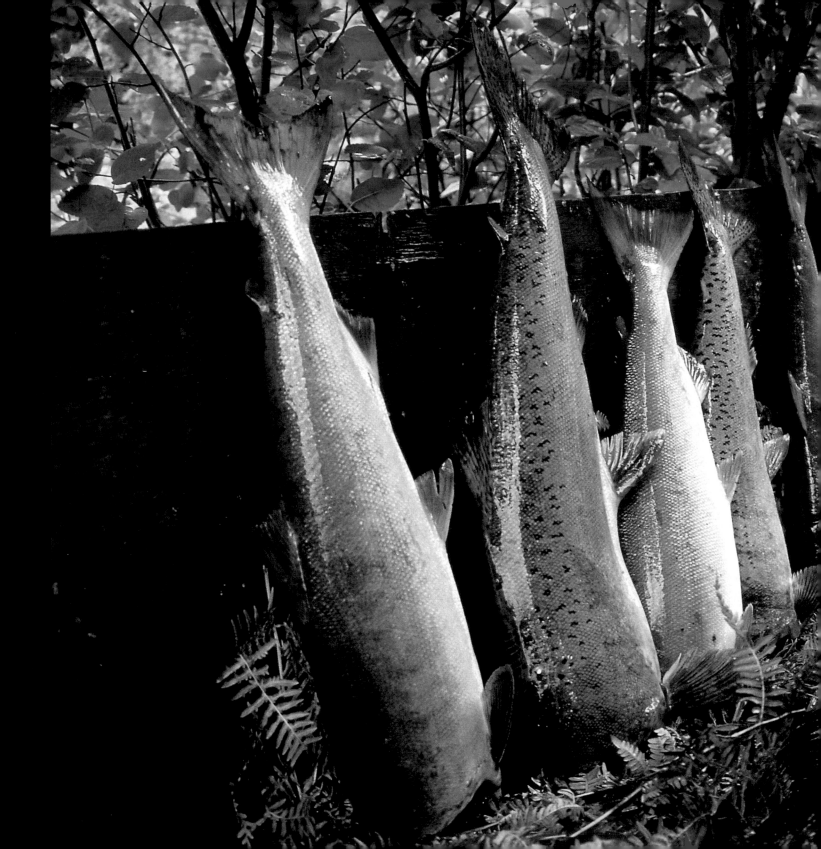

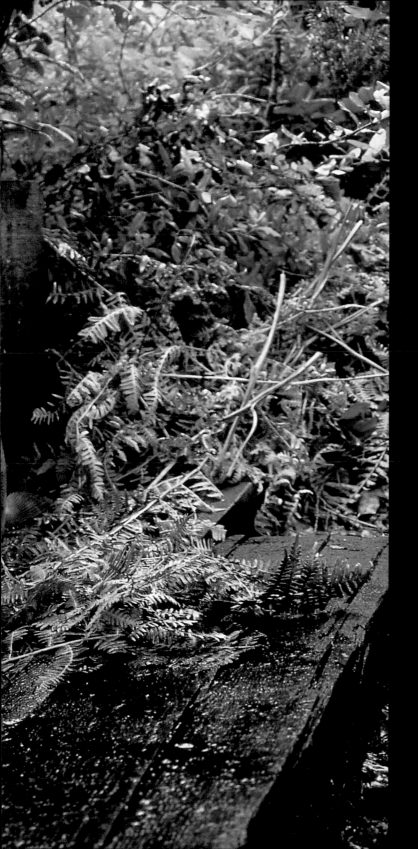

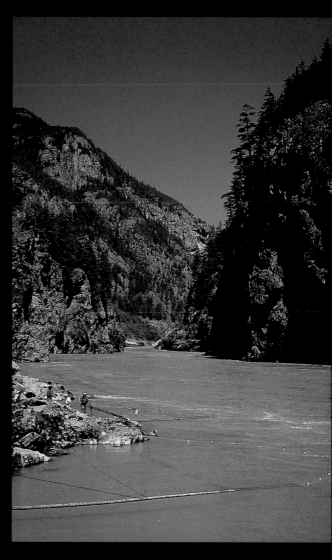

The gillnet is placed in a back eddy and suspended from a pole, which holds it straight in the current. After being taken from the net the chinook are cut and bled off (left to bleed for a time), then stripped and hung to dry.

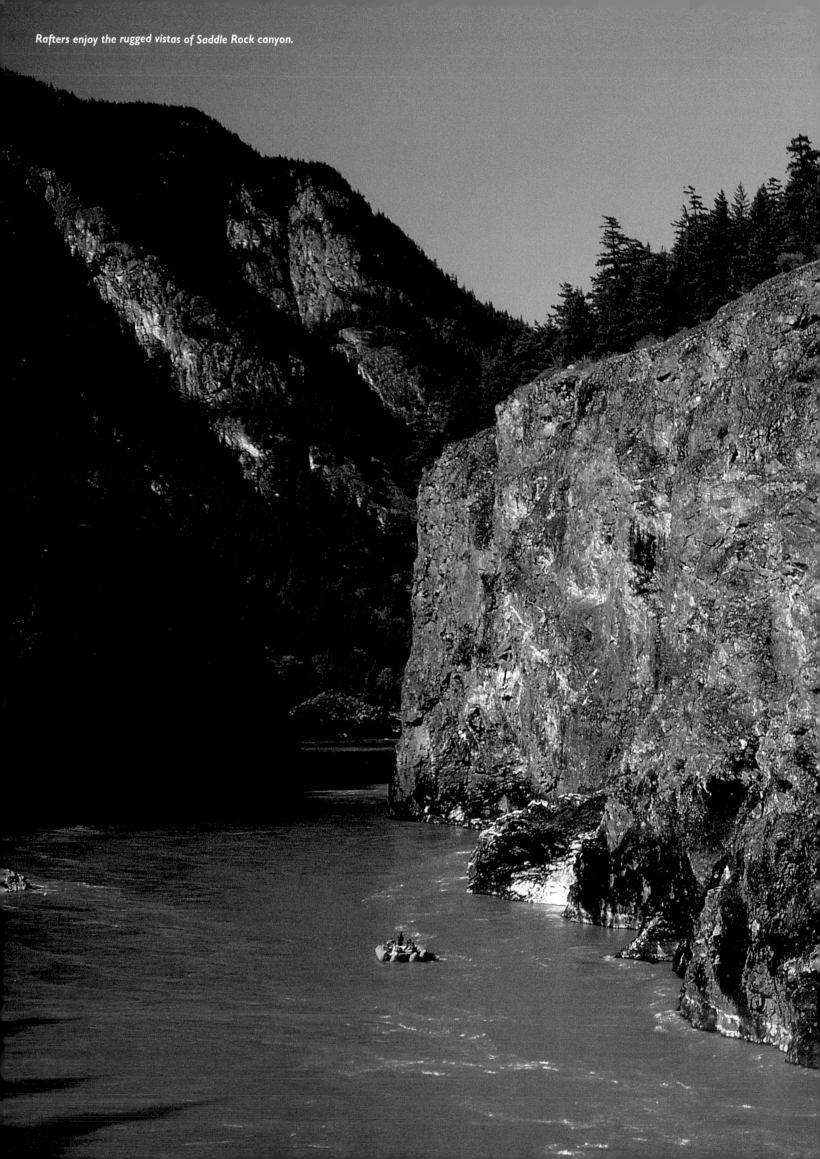
Rafters enjoy the rugged vistas of Saddle Rock canyon.

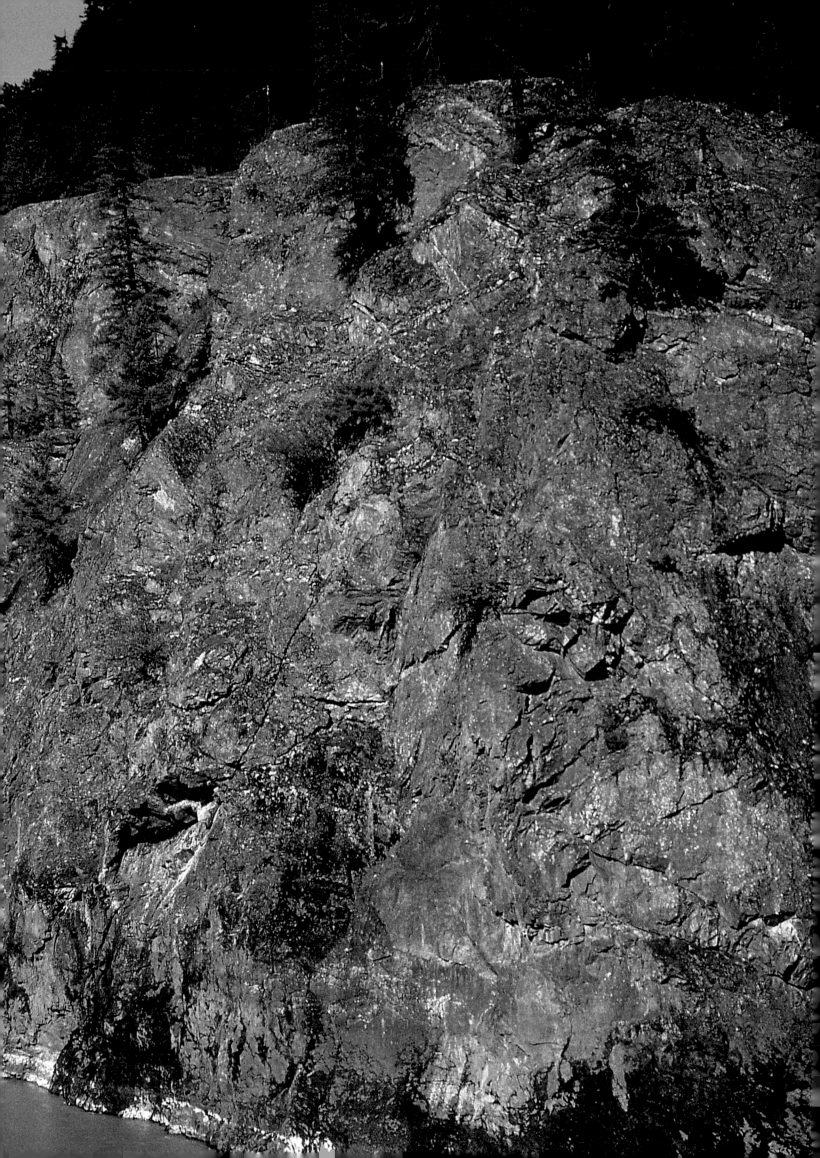

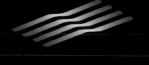

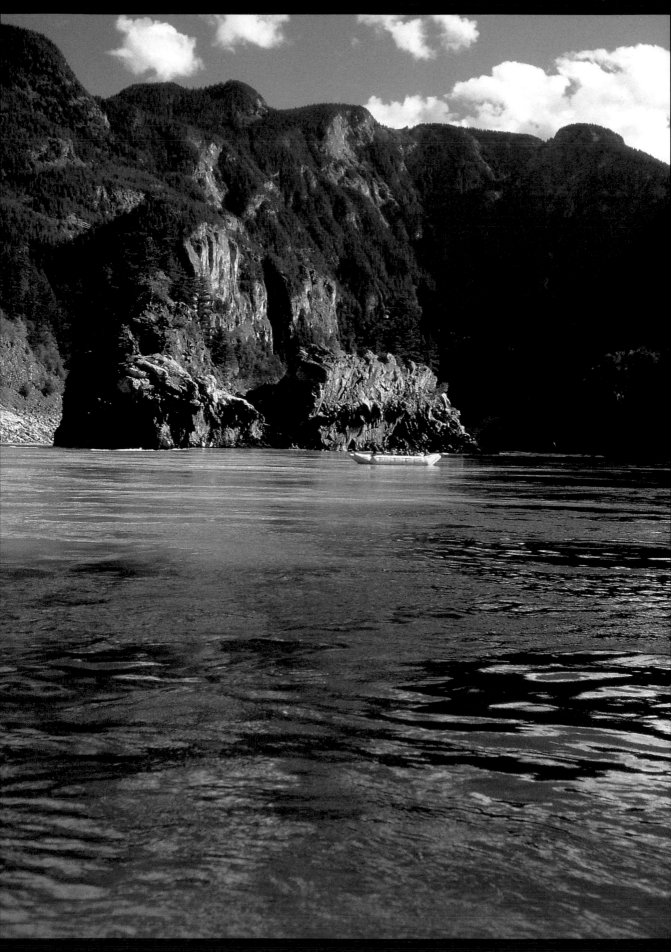

Saddle Rock is an island in the middle of the canyon, a few miles above the point where the river begins to open to the valley.

As the top end of the Fraser Canyon funnels the waters into a narrow channel, so the bottom end funnels the returning salmon upriver. Rock ridges jutting out from the canyon walls create back eddies in which the salmon rest before surging up the next stretch of water. This is the home of the Sto:lo fishing sites, where the short gillnets are set. Like other aboriginal fishing rights, these are based not on race but on inherited title—owned by families and passed down through the generations just the way property moves along under British common law. In this place, the moss grows thick and soft up under the trees. On summer nights the fishers can sleep on the riverbank's big boulders, still warm from the day's sun. The visitor is tempted to relax for a few hours and feel the years roll back a decade, or a century or a millennium. The activity below has changed very little over time, and the Sto:lo civilization, with roots deep in the wind and water and rock of the Fraser Canyon, continues to go about its business.

My father warned me forty years ago that a dam in the Moran Canyon would devastate the salmon runs, and today I tell my children that they will have to remain vigilant even after I am gone. Fortunately they will not be alone, and the travesty of destroying in one fell swoop a mighty living river and its fish seems less likely in this era of greater environmental awareness.

But there are other dangers, less dramatic but even more harmful over time, such as smaller dams on tributaries like the Nechako and Bridge rivers, proposals to divert the North Thompson into the Columbia for water exports to California, and the pollution caused by population growth. We know now that it is possible to live comfortably without fouling our own nest—that, for example, we can manufacture products in less toxic ways, and that we can produce hydroelectricity, a relatively clean and cheap source of power, in small-scale projects that do not defeat the ecosystems of our rivers. We have the knowledge to protect the river from the temptations of short-term gain. All we need to add is the commitment.

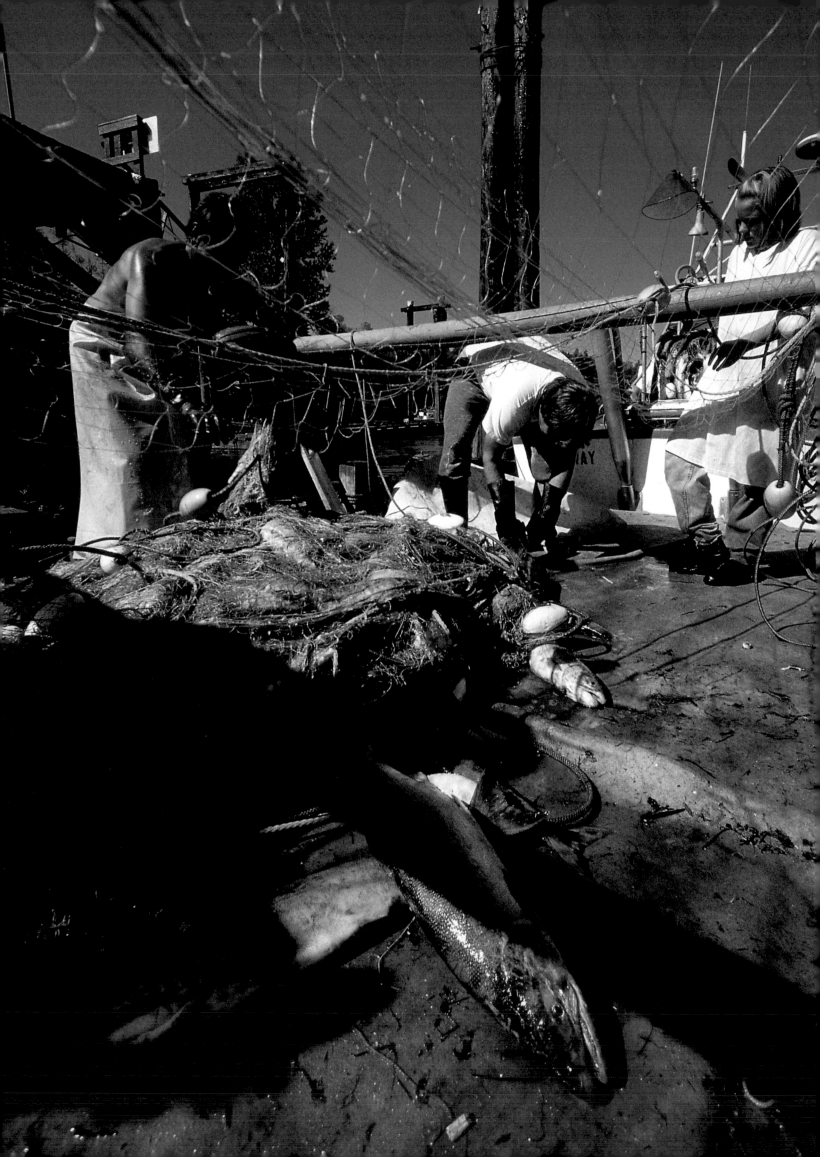

6

VALLEY & ESTUARY

*T*he best vista of the Fraser Valley and the estuary is the bird's eye view, available to anyone who flies into Vancouver International Airport from the east. Freed from the confining walls of the Fraser Canyon, the river emerges from the last cut in the mountains near Hope, spreads out along luxurious flatlands and makes its majestic way to the Gulf of Georgia. The waters seem quiet in these last 115 miles (185 km) to the river mouth. Heavy with silt, the river flows languidly through sedimented lands of its own creation.

This part of the Fraser, from Hope to the sea, has undergone dramatic changes since the last ice age. For thousands of years the upper river has been cutting into the glacial sediments, then carrying them to the lower river and depositing them. The river slows in the widening valley below Hope, so that rocks and gravel that are tumbled along the bottom in freshets, now settle out quickly. In the area around Chilliwack and at the mouth of the Harrison, the river is characterized by slowly growing gravel bars and islands. Below Sumas Mountain, the river slows even more and the coarser sands settle. Then, above Barnston Island, the river meets the tidal waters of the Pacific, which slows it to the point that still finer silt settles out.

About 13,000 years ago, when the glaciers were at their largest, great chunks of stationary ice still sat in some areas of the Fraser Valley. By 10,000 years ago, the Fraser, born from glacial meltwater, was beginning to build deltas just below New Westminster—which at that time was the edge of the sea. By 5,000 years ago, these sedimented deltas had spread west and south, almost as far as an island which is today joined to the mainland and known to us as Point Roberts. In south Vancouver, in a little park tucked away within sight of the Fraser's north arm and within hearing of the Vancouver International Airport, a small cairn commemorates the Marpole archaeological site. Sites like this one, a few miles from the Musqueam reserve, have helped British Columbians understand that the history of the Fraser and its people reaches back centuries before the European "discovery" of the river. When the Marpole site was occupied, 400 BC to 500 AD on the Christian calendar, the sea still lapped at the shores of the village, and the land on which the Vancouver International Airport would be built was still part of a river bank 240 miles (400 km) north, in BC's Cariboo country.

That is how fast the river changes the coastline, and how dramatically the extensive dyking and dredging undertaken in the

Workers unload full sockeye nets on the Fraser, near Fort Langley, 1993.

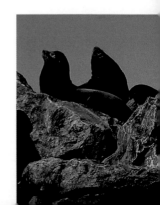

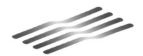

Fraser estuary have altered natural sedimentation patterns. If the dykes were not in place, much of Richmond on Lulu Island and the municipality of Delta, south of the river, would be under water at extreme high tide.

The Fraser Valley is the site of some of the richest farmland in the world, having been built out of some ten thousand years' worth of Fraser River silt. It is also the site of accelerating urban growth. Many more buildings than fields line the banks of this stretch of the river, growing larger and taller and more densely packed as the river proceeds toward Vancouver at the edge of the sea. The great majority of the 2,400,000 people who live along the Fraser Basin reside in the Lower Mainland. But urban sprawl did not always characterize the valley. This is an area that grew up on farms, forests and fisheries.

At the historic town of Yale, there is no sign of the concrete jungle. The village of Xwoxewla:lhp ("short willow trees") once stood in this area, and today there is a small town and an even smaller Sto:lo community. Just below the town, during winter's low water, prospectors still go out onto Hills Bar to pan for gold. It was here, in 1858, that one of the first group of Californians stopped for lunch on their way north in search of Fraser River gold. One of them, T. H. Hill, noticed gold flecks in the moss that covered the rocks and washed a pan of it, with good results. The bar named after him eventually yielded over $2 million in gold, becoming one of the richest bars on the Fraser. This and other strikes sparked a stampede of optimists up the river.

Once the Columbia River steamboat *Umatilla* had demonstrated that it was possible to get a paddle wheeler up the river beyond Hope, Yale entered its golden era as head of steamboat navigation, as it had been head of navigation for canoes for centuries. Passengers and freight going north disembarked at Yale and continued on the Cariboo Wagon Road, built in the early 1860s to carry gold-seekers upriver.

At its peak, Yale boasted a population of 50,000 people, a lot of hastily thrown-together shacks and saloons, and a reputation as a wanton party town. Today, while it is not exactly a ghost town, Yale is long past those glory days. Except for a few outboard-powered fishing boats, there is little water traffic in the 19-mile (32-km) stretch of river between Yale and Hope, which provides transition from the canyon to the valley.

This photograph looks upriver over the historic town of Yale, which marked the head of navigation in the Fraser River's steamboat days. Because Yale was a transfer point between boats and overland travel, it was flooded with gold-seekers in the 1850s and exploded into a party town crammed with lean-tos and tarpaper shacks.

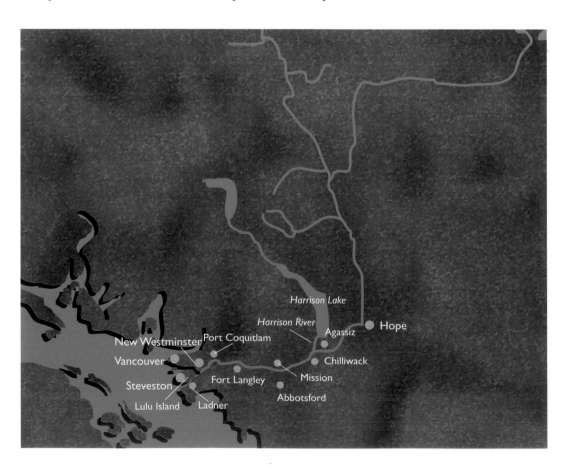

Harrison Lake

Harrison River

Hope

Agassiz

New Westminster — Port Coquitlam

Vancouver

Chilliwack

Steveston

Fort Langley

Mission

Lulu Island — Ladner

Abbotsford

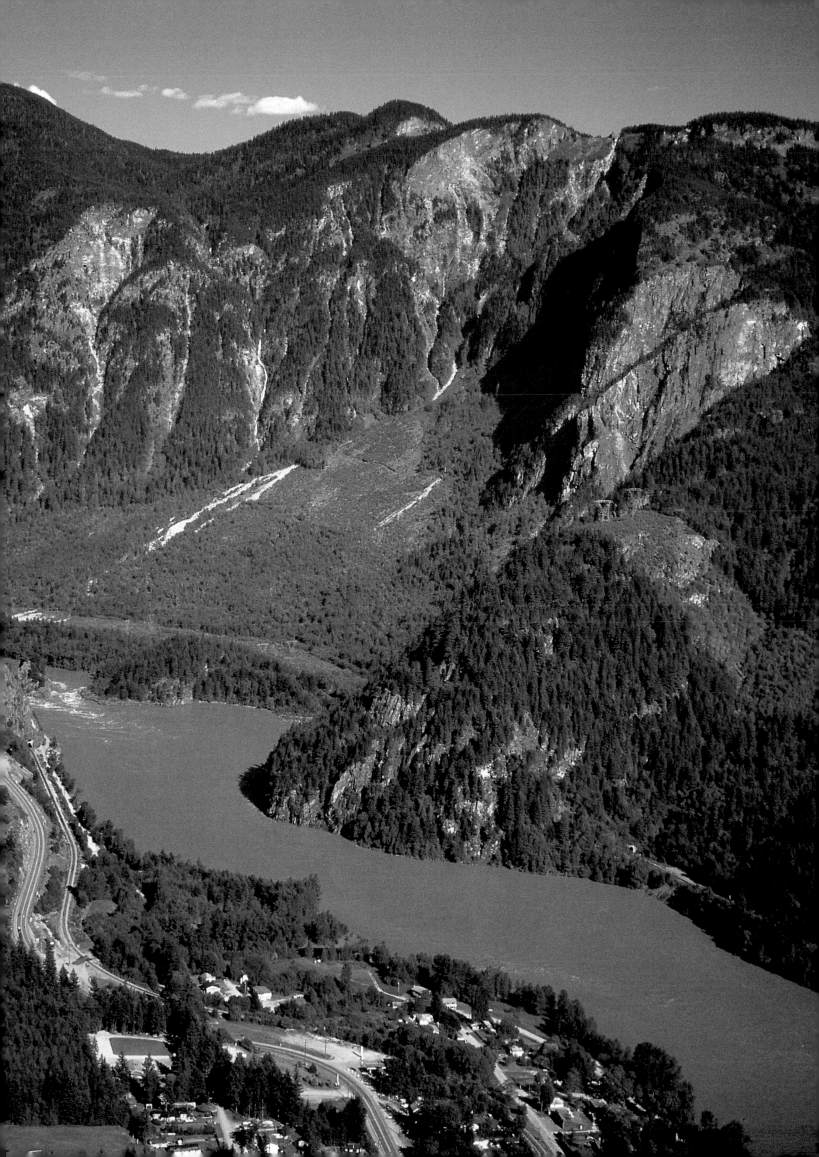

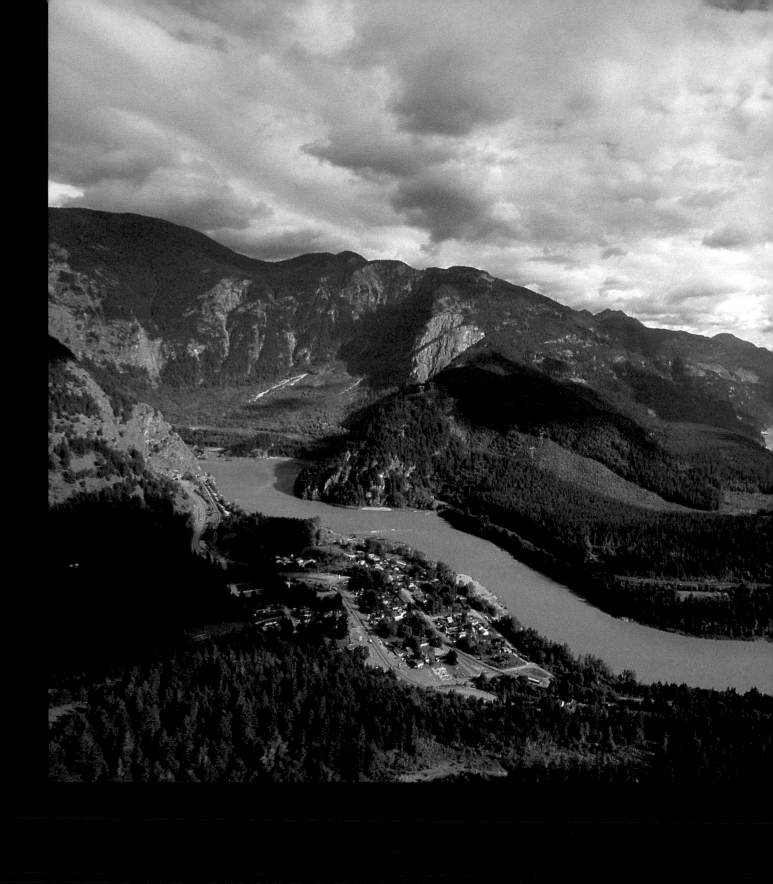

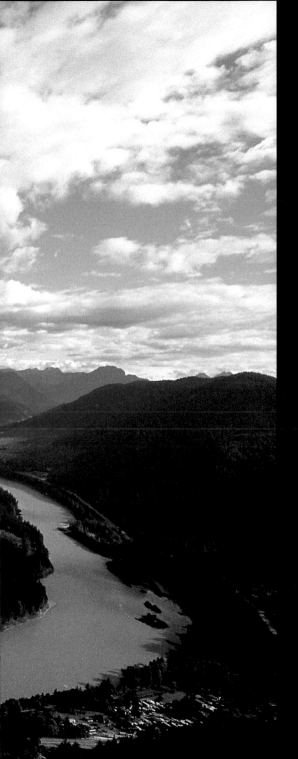

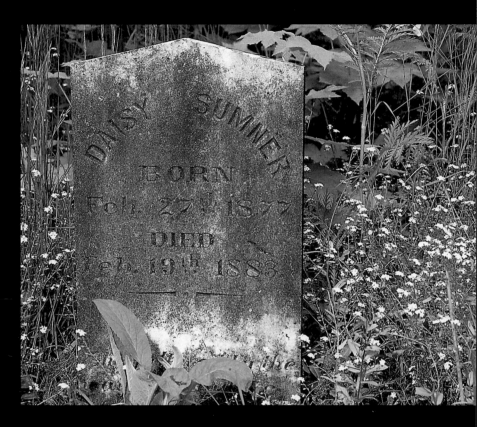

DAISY SUMNER

BORN
Feb. 27th 1877

DIED
Feb. 19th 1883

Left: Just around the big bend downriver from Yale is Hills Bar, from which more gold was taken than any other part of the Fraser's main stem. That is where the river, having churned out of the canyon and reached a more comfortable passageway, slows down to the point where heavy minerals such as gold can settle into the river bottom. Yale was a boom town in the gold rush days and again during railway construction, but today there is little sign of the town's colourful past. It goes quietly about its business between the highway and the river.

Above: The cemetery at Yale hints at lives lived and lost during the past century.

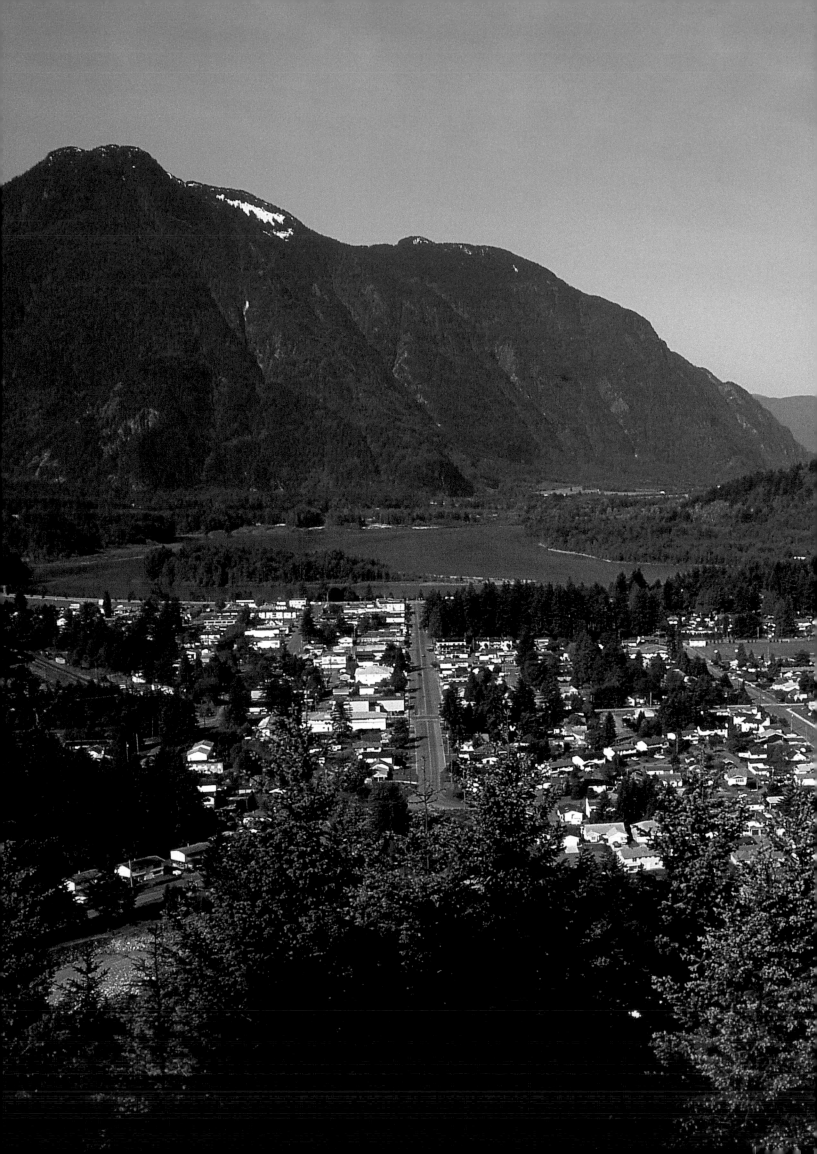

At the town of Hope, the Fraser swings dramatically from its southward course, turns to the west and flows through the Fraser Valley to the sea. Until this point, the river has been confined by the mountains, but now, at its first opportunity--an opening between the Coast Mountains and the Cascades--the river moves directly toward sea level.

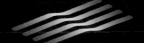

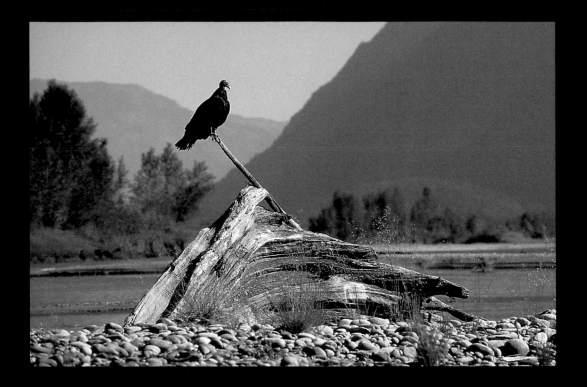

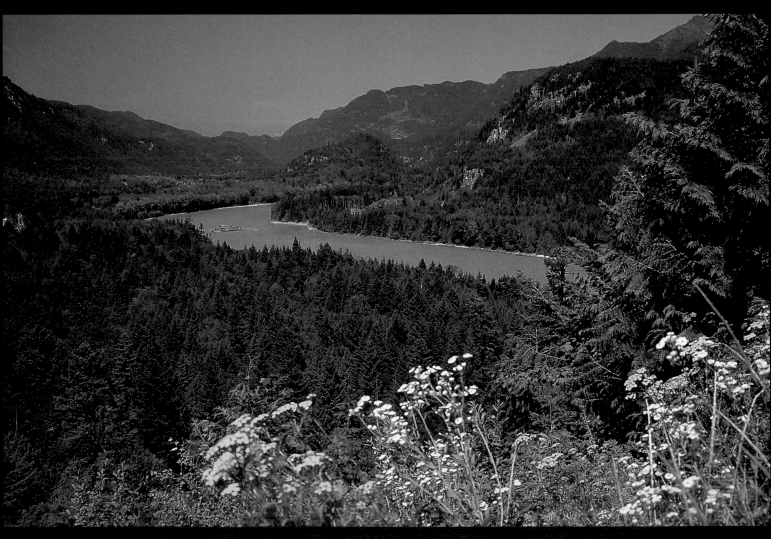

Top: A turkey vulture rests atop a chunk of driftwood on a Fraser River bar near Rosedale, a farming
community just downriver from Agassiz.
Above: The view north from Hope looks upriver, with the Cascade Mountains on the right and the southern
end of the Coast Mountains on the left.

From Hope to Mission, some 30 miles (50 km) downriver, commercial navigation is pretty much limited to small, specialized high-speed tugboats that guide booms of logs down the river from log dumps at Hope and Chilliwack. Most of this timber is taken from the high sides of the valley and trucked down to the river, as the valley floor was long ago logged off to create farmland. More log booms come down the Harrison River and join the sawmill-bound stream of logs in the Fraser main stem about 10 miles (16 km) above Mission. In these lower reaches, the Fraser continues to support the greatest concentration of shake and lumber mills in the province, many of them small operations with just a few employees.

Harrison Lake, near the head of the Fraser Valley, has long supported several logging operations. Every year about 2,000 boom sections, each a 50-foot (15-m) square of floating log bundles, are collected and moored to the shore in the outlet of the lake just west of Harrison Hot Springs, a resort town. There they await the short towing season, which can start only when the snowmelt in the surrounding mountains brings the spring freshet, usually in mid-April. Towing continues until late September, when low waters bring the bundled logs dangerously close to the salmon-spawning gravel bars of the Harrison River.

For towboaters moving logs from the Harrison into the Fraser River, the protruding boulder near Calamity Point at the downstream side of the confluence is a hazard. But to Allen Williams, a Sto:lo fisherman, it is an asset. One day Allen and John Antone and I stood together on the rock bluff over the confluence, watching the green Harrison and the brown Fraser surge against each other. At our backs the forested hill rose abruptly to the sugarloaf mountain known as the Harrison Nob, and in the turbulent waters below us, a seal knifed through the dividing line. "We set a net off there for Harrison fish," Allen told me. "In the fall the water is low, and there is an eddy in there that is good for dog salmon. We get the fall run of Harrison white springs there also." John spoke of the good deer hunting that he and the other people of Sq'ewlets (Scowlitz) have always had around this hill. There are no permanent residences here now. Band members live across the river in a village with road access, but the deep importance of the land on which we stand is in the very cadence of the men's talk.

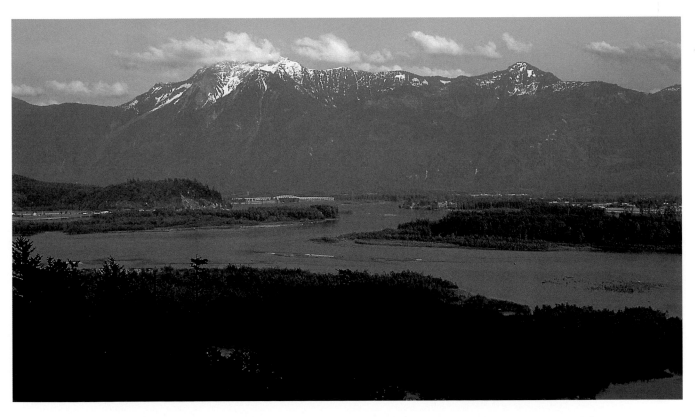

The upper Fraser Valley is crowded narrow by the steep Cascade Mountains, but soon gives way to the delta, where the river can spread out and move more languidly through its last miles.

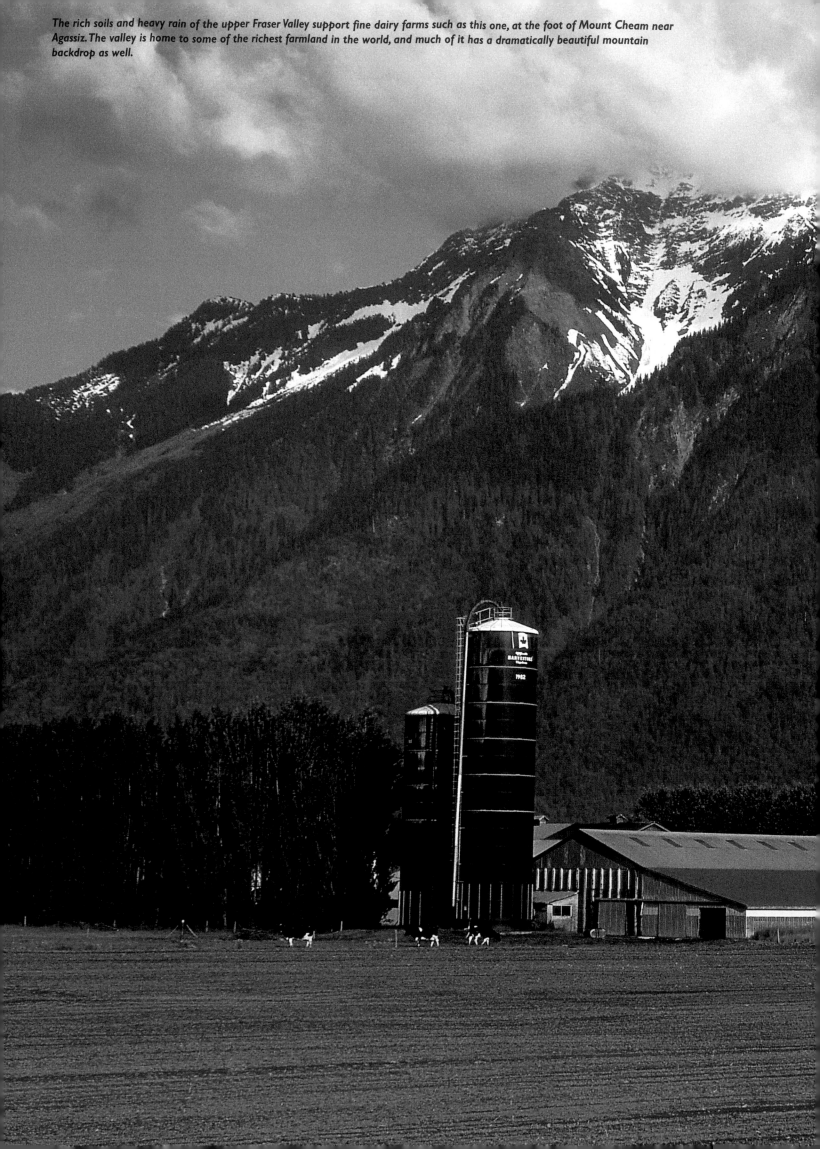

The rich soils and heavy rain of the upper Fraser Valley support fine dairy farms such as this one, at the foot of Mount Cheam near Agassiz. The valley is home to some of the richest farmland in the world, and much of it has a dramatically beautiful mountain backdrop as well.

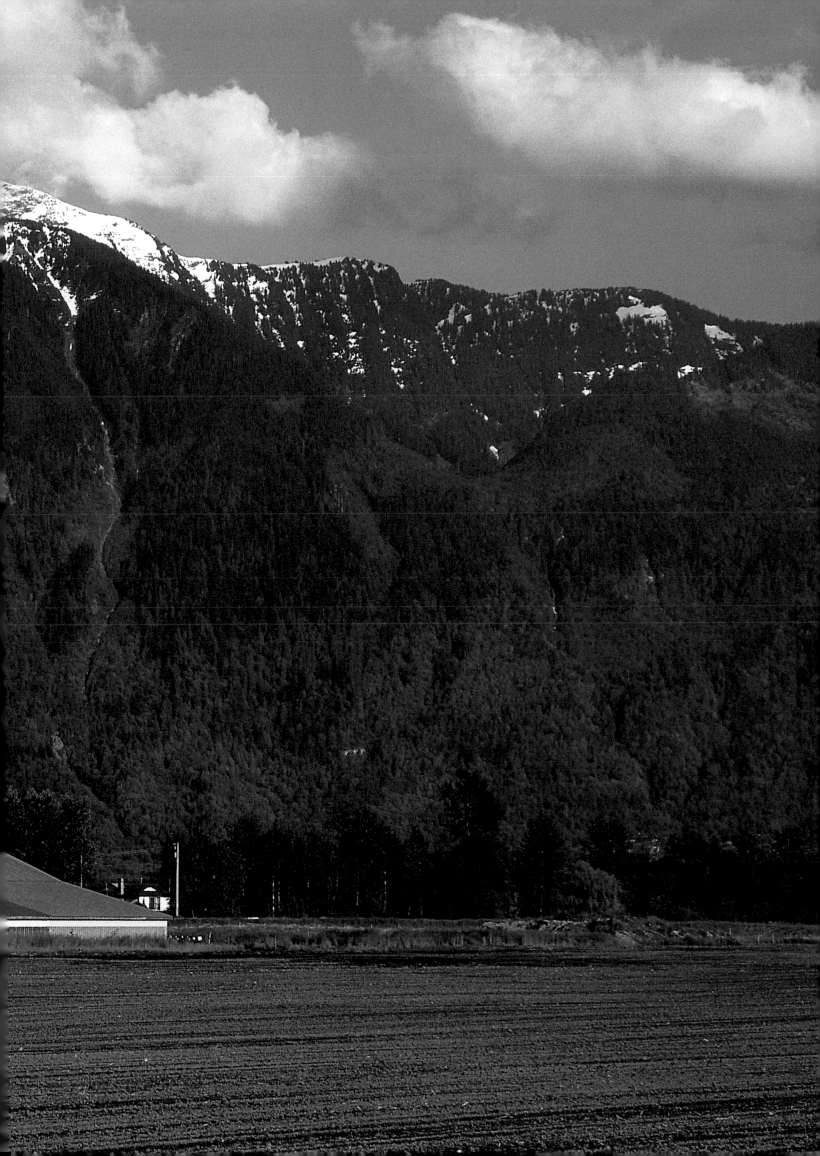

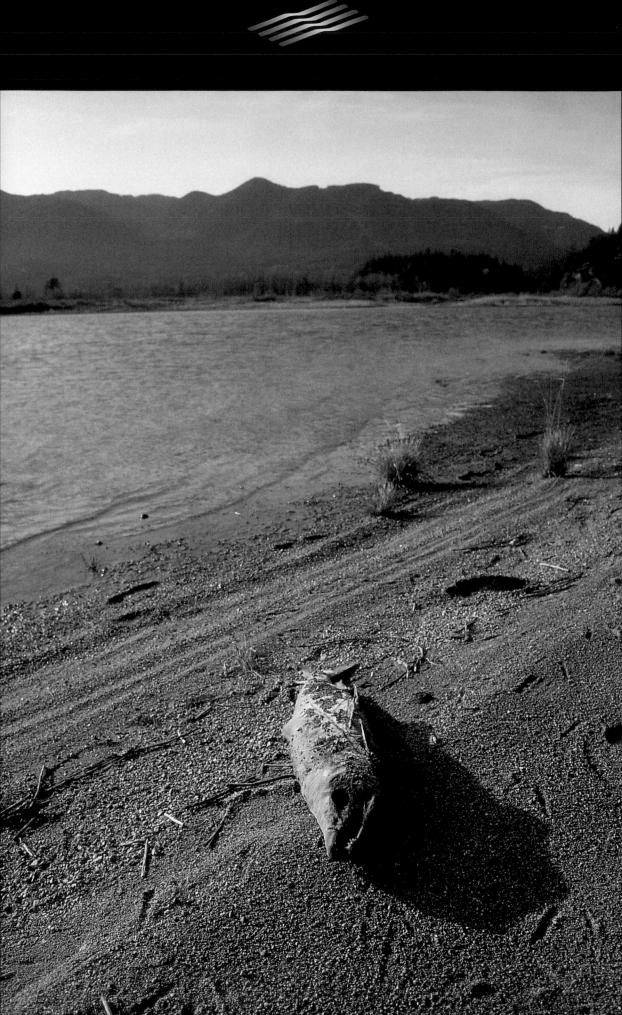

Seasons of Salmon

When I visited with Allen Williams and John Antone near the confluence of the Harrison and Fraser rivers, Dr. R. G. Matson, an archaeologist at the University of BC, was conducting an archaeological field school there, on the site of the ancient Sto:lo village of Scowlitz. There had been some question as to whether this was a winter or a summer village site, and Allen explained that good fish could be caught here practically year-round. "Once you get snow on the hills and it turns nice and cold in November and December," he said, "the steelhead come up to the Harrison and the dog salmon are still running in November. In late January and February the Fraser River springs can be caught just over here," and he pointed to a place out in the brown river waters. The springs keep coming until they are eclipsed by the summer sockeye runs. The oolichan would arrive in April, giving a springtime burst of fresh fish, but they have not come this far upriver for the past decade. The early sockeye, those that would be going way up through the Nechako to the Stuart, start coming in June. They are followed by the summer bounty as the pink and coho salmon join the spring, steelhead, sockeye and chum salmon in both the Fraser and Harrison rivers.

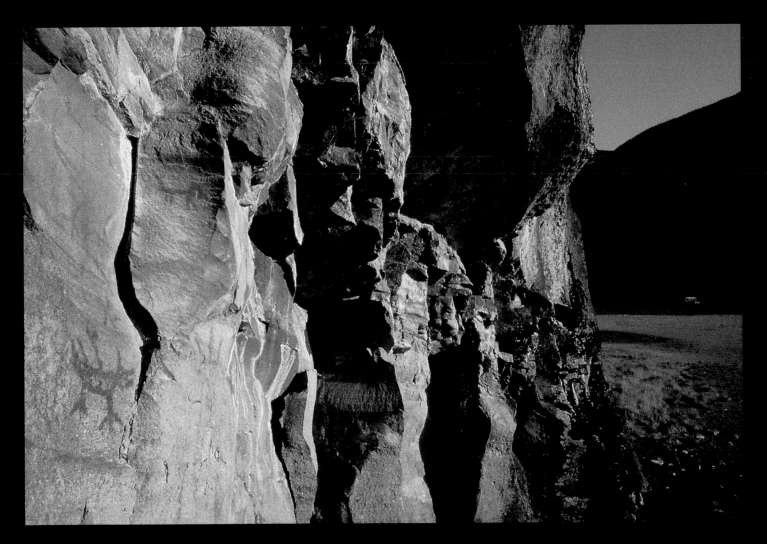

Pictographs on the rock face of the riverbank mark the importance of sacred First Nations sites along the Fraser.

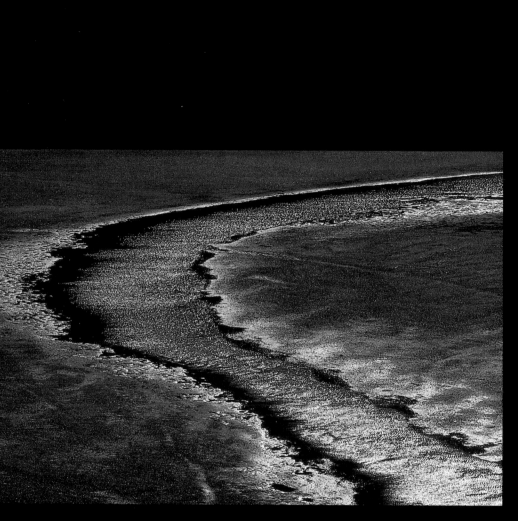

The waters of Morris Creek meander across the muddy shallows of the Harrison River during the low-water period of winter.

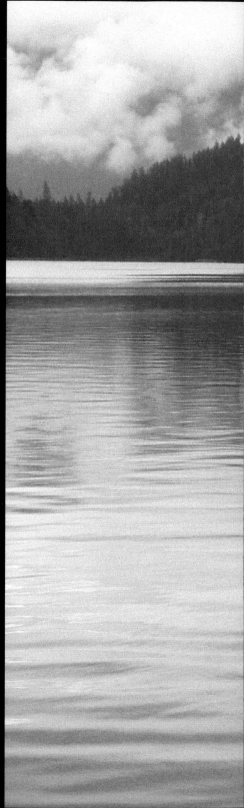

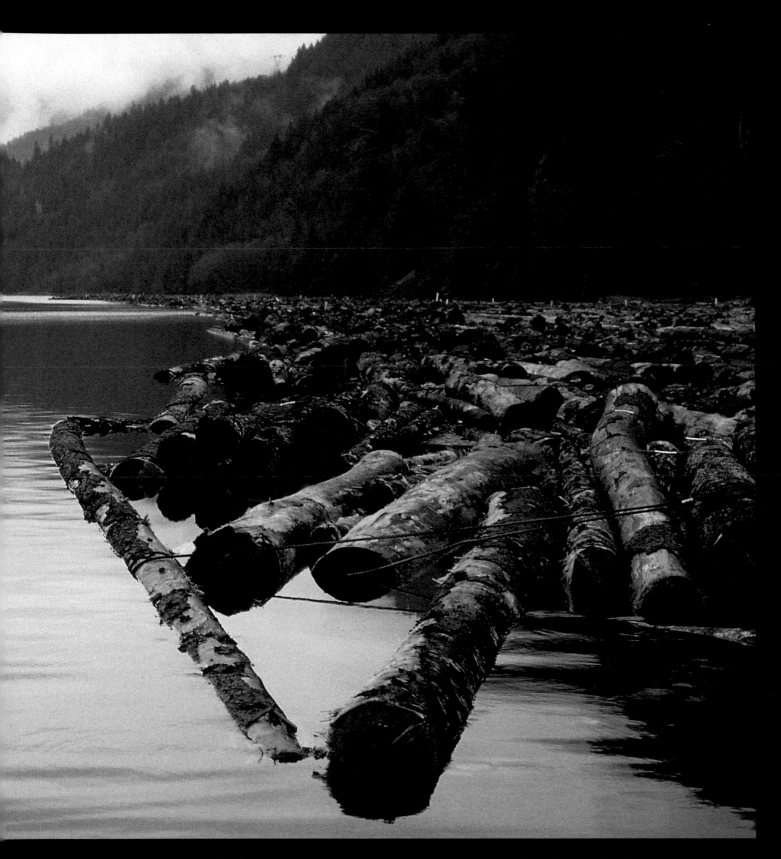

The Harrison River is an important route for towing logs down to the Fraser Valley and estuary. Small tugs gather the logs from camps around Harrison Lake and take them down the Harrison to the confluence with the Fraser. The downstream side of the confluence, Calamity Point, is treacherous for towboaters but an asset to local Sto:lo fishers. Towing is stopped during salmon spawning season, for fear of damage to the delicate gravels with their precious eggs.

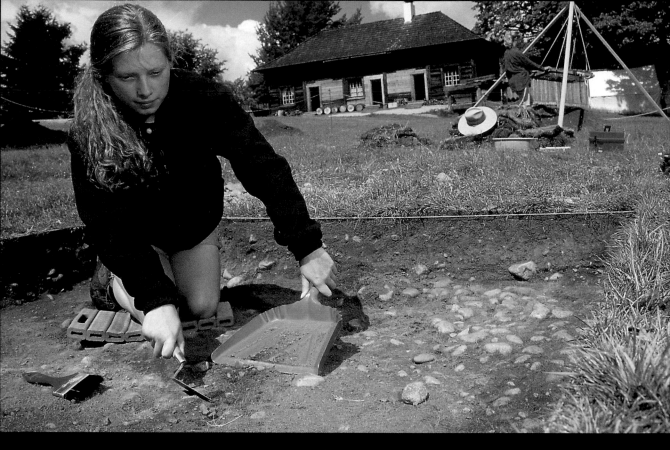

The Fraser River Basin has been home to human civilizations for some ten thousand years, and several village sites rich in history have been excavated. Archaeologists working at Fort Langley are among many who have found evidence that the Fraser's bounty has supported large, complex communities for millennia. By seven or eight thousand years ago, salmon-based cultures in this area had developed sophisticated technologies for working with wood, antler, stone and bone.

Reading the Scowlitz Site

The archaeologists who have worked at the Scowlitz site for some years speak and write with scientists' caution. Many painstaking hours, days, months and years of work remain before the site will have yielded its story. But even the minimal evidence points to the strength of the culture that has developed along-side the Fraser and Harrison rivers. In 1994 a 10-foot (3-m) burial mound, the largest of a series of mounds, was partially excavated. It contained the

remains of a middle-aged man in a grave that was built at least 1,300 years ago. Over the grave a cairn of rocks had been erected and that had been covered again with the pyramid-like mound made of some 20 tons (20.4 tonnes) of rock and nearly 400 cubic yards (300 m³) of soil. Among other artifacts in the grave were 7,000 beads sawn from the highly valued dentalia shells that come from deep waters off the coast and get traded on routes along rivers and lakes. The man's skeleton, the grave, the shells and other evidence show that this was a stable,

well-established society. Salmon bones found at this site, in the burnt soils near a "Coast Salish" type longhouse, tell the story: human beings have lived here for thousands of years thanks to the kind climate and the bounty of the Fraser River. The Sq'ewlets people continue to use this area extensively as a hunting and fishing site, but there is poor road access, and modern dependence on cars and roads rather than boats and rivers for transportation has discouraged year-round occupation.

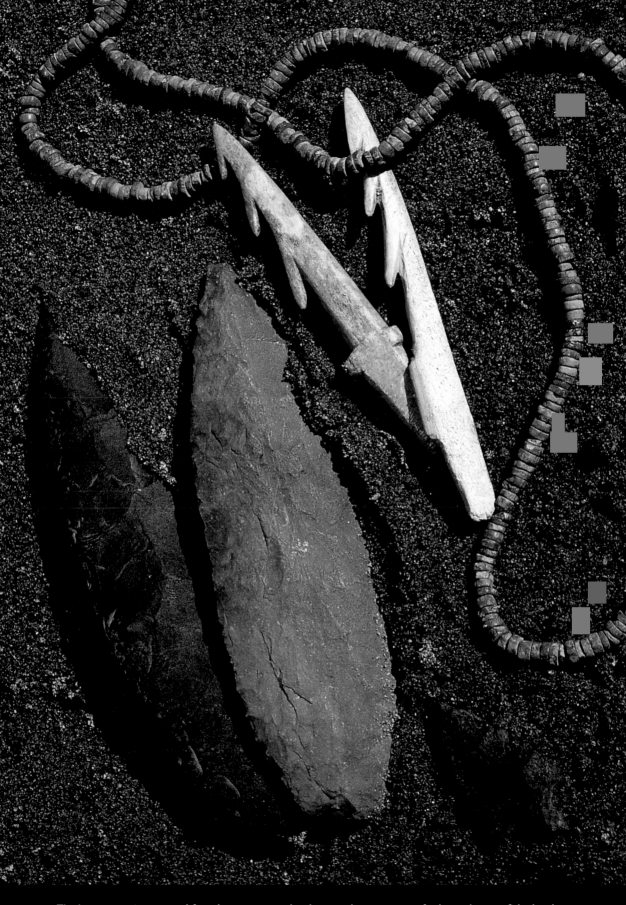

The harpoon points, carved from bone, were used to harvest the same runs of salmon that are fished today; the stone points and beads probably demonstrated wealth and status.

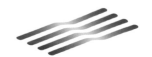

The heavy rains and moderating effects of the sea give the Fraser Valley luxuriant plant growth in remarkable contrast to the arid plateau vegetation at the north end of the canyon. At the mouth of the Harrison, salmonberries hang heavy from branches that earlier in the year were tiny succulent shoots, the first fresh green of spring, to be peeled and eaten. The knowledgeable gatherer can find numerous other treats along the shore and in under the forest canopy. Like the river, this land has suffered environmental indignities in recent decades, from clearcut logging to DDT sprayings to the draining of the great Sumas Lake in order to eradicate mosquitoes and create 32,000 acres (13,000 hectares) of farmland. But, also like the river, this land continues to provide for the Sto:lo and their neighbours.

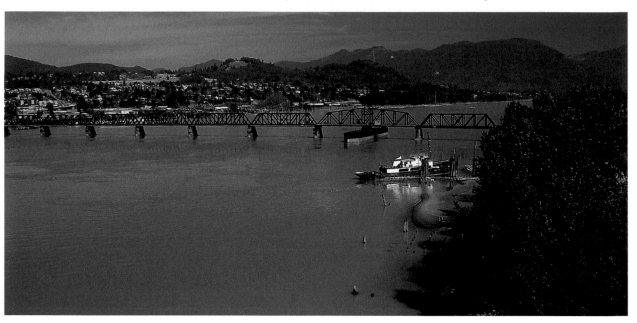

The railway bridge at Mission, well known among fishers and biologists, marks the upriver boundary of the commercial drift net fishery and is an important counting station for migrating salmon.

The iron railway bridge that crosses the Fraser at Mission marks the upstream boundary for the non-Native commercial salmon fishery. The bridge is also the place where a battery of sophisticated sonar equipment is used to count migrating salmon, so it enjoys considerable renown among fishers and biologists. It is common to hear someone on the dock at Campbell River speak of how many of the Chilko sockeye run had been counted "past the Mission bridge."

Sadly, another anadromous fish, the oolichan, which once passed under the bridge to spawn in the sandy bottom of the upper Fraser Valley, has not been seen up this far for the past ten years. The runs remain healthy in other BC rivers such as the Nass, the Klinaklini and the Dean. For aboriginal people living along these and other rivers from northern California to Alaska, oolichan has long been an important item in the diet and in the culture. The fish, about the size and shape of smelt, are taken in large numbers. On some rivers much of the catch is rendered for the rich oil, a trade item so important that it gave the name Grease Trail to the ancient trading route, along the Blackwater River to the sea, which Alexander Mackenzie followed in the eighteenth century. On the Fraser, a commercial fishery has been bringing in oolichan, but fishers all along the river say that oolichan stocks have declined dramatically since the 1970s. Each egg is anchored to the river bottom by enclosing a grain of sand in its outer membrane—a condition of hatching that may make oolichan particularly sensitive to water contamination. But there has been little long-term research on this important little fish.

The oolichans do get as far as Katzie, a Sto:lo village on the north side of the river, opposite Barnston Island 10 miles (16 km) below the Mission bridge. On the full moon in April, the arrival of the oolichans is heralded from Steveston on up the river by hundreds of seagulls dipping to the water surface and rising with the tiny silver darts in their beaks. Giant California sea lions also follow the fish up the river and, after gorging themselves, lie on the log booms basking in the sun.

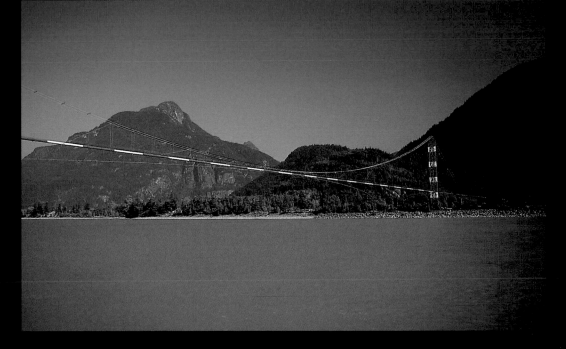

The Fraser Valley is a transportation corridor for rail lines, highways, powerlines and, here, a natural gas pipeline. It was less expensive and less damaging to the environment to run the pipeline over the river than under it, and the structure has been seismically upgraded.

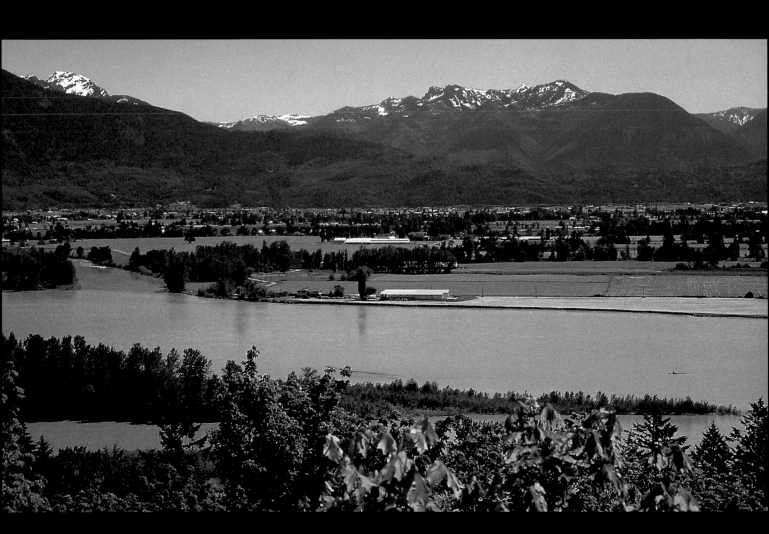

As greater Vancouver grows, urban development spreads up the Fraser, threatening priceless agricultural lands and putting more stress on the river. Where there is urban sprawl, there is growing pollution for the Fraser-- from vehicles, water treatment, sewage treatment, industry, large-scale agriculture and the toxic chemical cocktail of urban runoff.

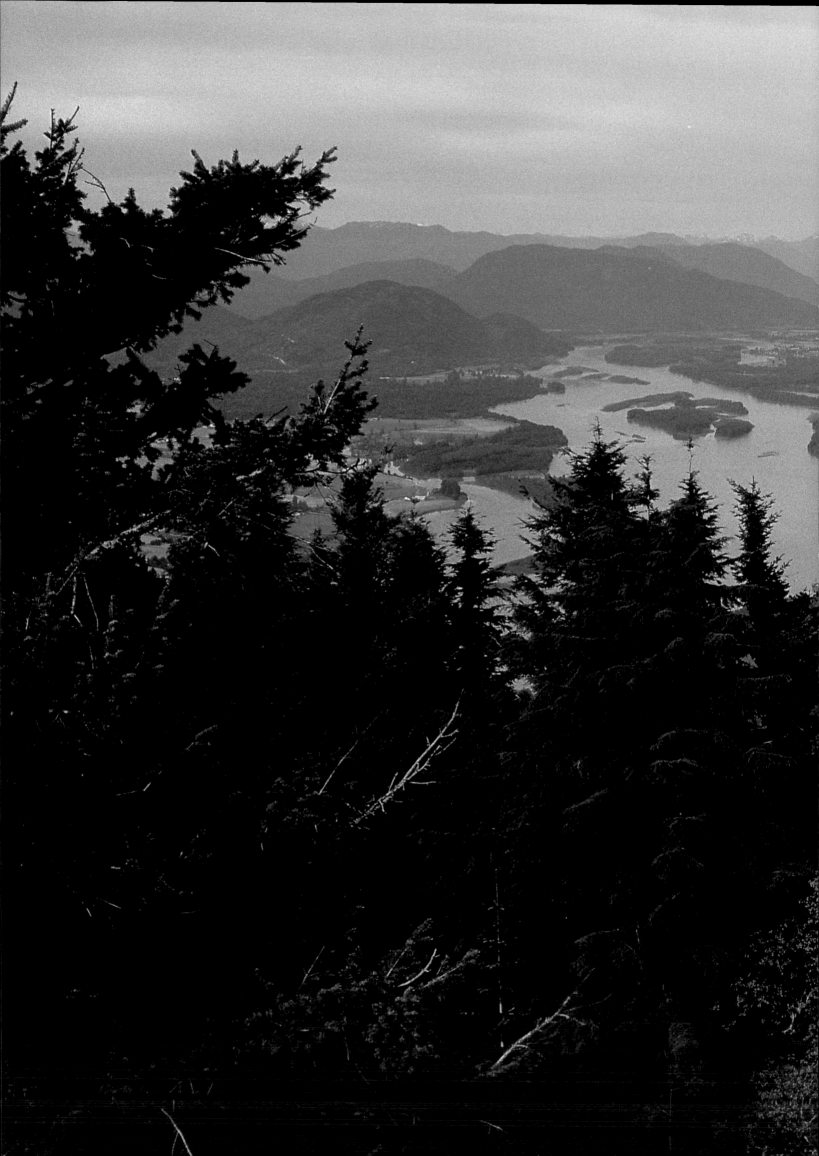

The Fraser begins to move more slowly once it enters the valley, and by the time it reaches Sumas Mountain, from which this photograph was taken, its coarser gravels have settled out of the current to form bars. Below Sumas, the bars are formed of sand; farther down they are made of mud. Much of the land on the south bank of the river (to the right of the river in this photograph) is fluvial.

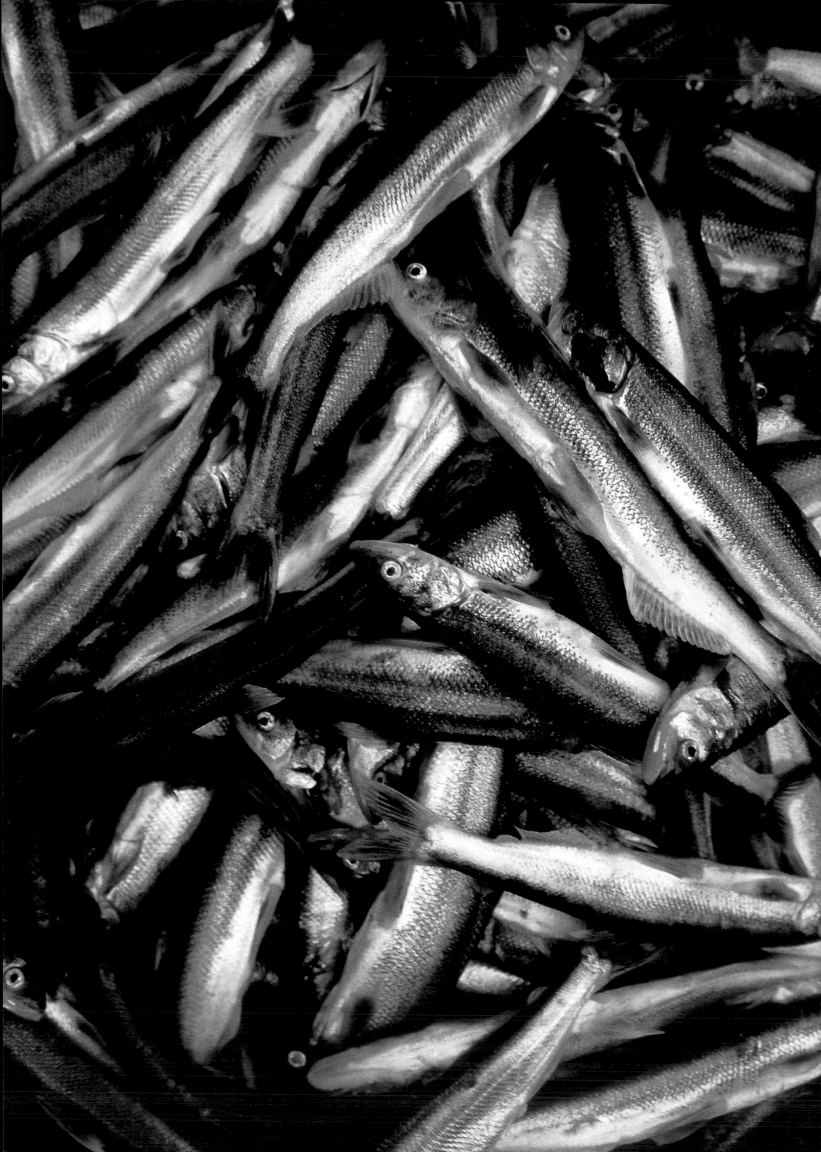

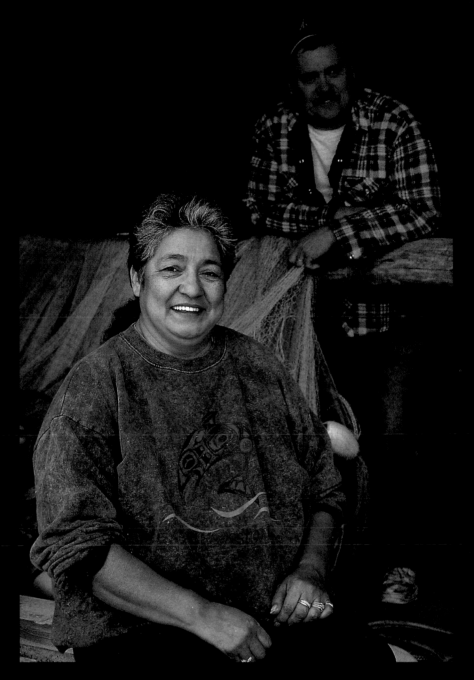

June and Jimmie Adams in their net loft at Katzie.

Spring Oolichans

Nowhere in the river do the oolichan runs come in the numbers that they once did, but at Katzie there are enough for Jimmie Adams, a Sto:lo fisher, to feed his family and to sell a little to others who look forward to the annual treat. The day I went out to fish oolichan with Jimmie, we got out on the river by 5:00 p.m, when the tide had backed up the river level by about three feet. Jimmie ran the boat upstream a little above the village and set his 1,200-foot (365-m) net across the river current. When the net was out and the boat was drifting

along with it, Jimmie glanced up at the mountains, north of the cottonwoods along the riverbank, to check that there was still plenty of current running downriver. "The strong current keeps the oolichans down on the bottom," he explained. "When there is a big freshet they hang right in along the shore." As far as Jimmie knows, the Sto:lo never made grease from oolichans. His family eats the fish fresh, smoked or frozen. The oolichan fishery is small, and even smaller since the decline in the runs, but it remains one of the important local rituals of springtime.

Jimmie has put in more than thirty

oolichan seasons, and the knowledge and practice of fishing oolichan on the Fraser River go back more generations than anyone knows. Once the season picks up, Jimmie can get more than 1,000 pounds (450 kg) of fish in one drift of his net. Occasionally he will end up with only a few pounds, especially if he brings in his net and finds that half the oolichans have had their heads or tails bitten off. Sea lions like oolichans too, and they know how to wait until a fisher has caught the fish for them.

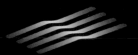

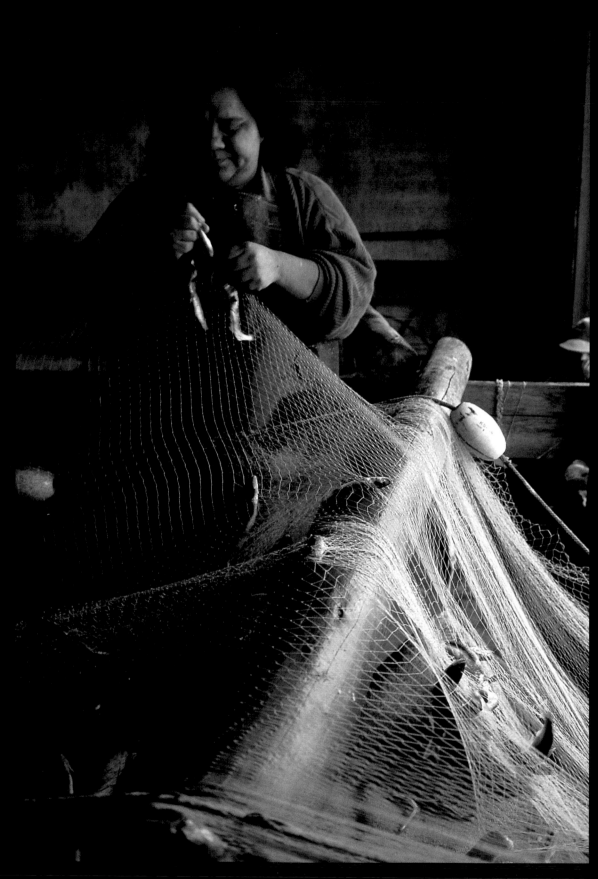

Helen Johnson picks oolichans from nets at Katzie, a Sto:lo village on the north side of the river, opposite Barnston Island. The Fraser oolichans no longer get as far as the Mission bridge, but they are still an important spring fishery here at Katzie.

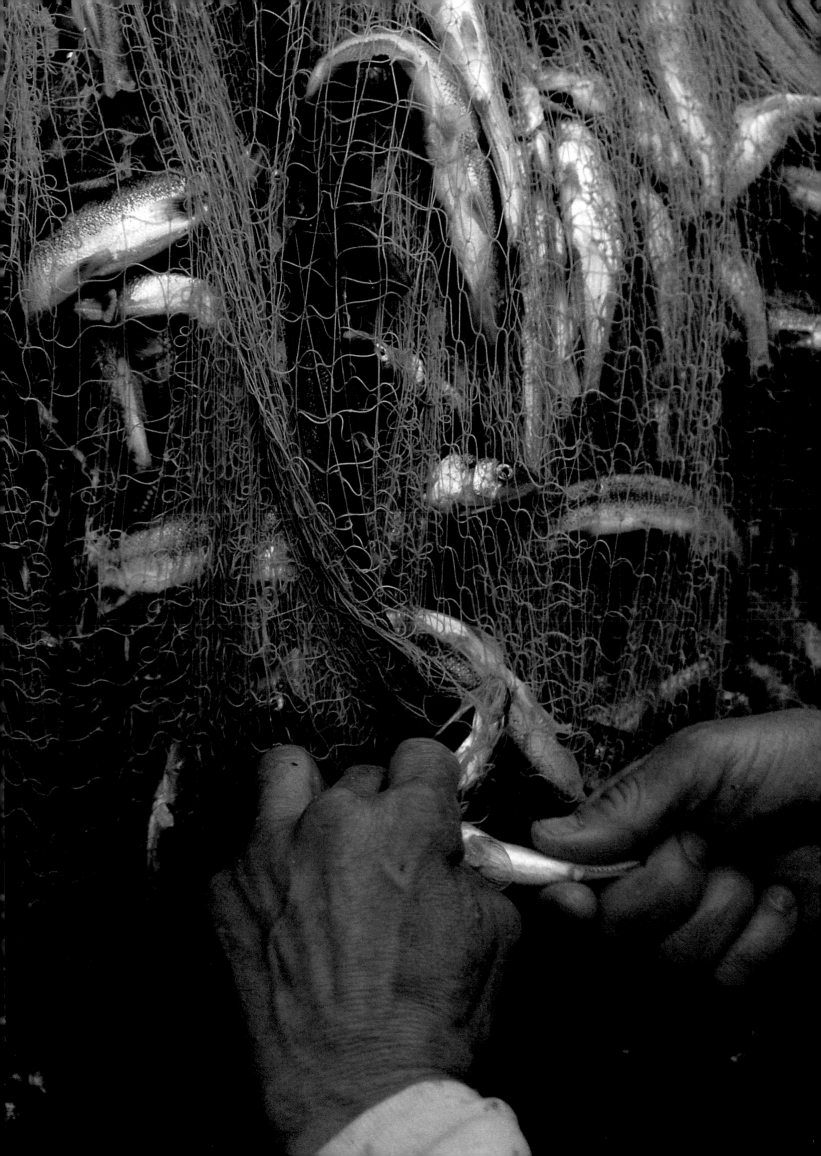

About 15 miles (25 km) below the Mission bridge is Fort Langley, founded in 1827, nineteen years after Simon Fraser's initial voyage down the river. The Hudson's Bay Company ship *Cadboro*, loaded with supplies to build the fort, was the first deep-sea (ocean-going) ship to enter the Fraser. On July 22, 1827, after spending several days finding a passage through the shallow silt-filled channel, the ship was able to proceed as far as the confluence of the Pitt and Fraser rivers, where she anchored for the night. The next day she proceeded upriver.

The fort was constructed under the command of James McMillan and his half-Abenaki superintendent François Annance, after whom Annacis Island is named. In an interesting foreshadowing of the future cultural diversity of British Columbia, the builders of this first non-Native habitation in the Fraser Valley were a mix of eastern First Nations, Kanakas from the Hawaiian Islands, and Scots and French from Europe.

The fur trade, Fort Langley's main activity, was also a foreshadowing—of the Fraser Valley's economic future. A few miles from the fort, a huge natural meadow was brought under cultivation, and the Hudson's Bay Company post became the supply centre for farm produce, not only for their own settlers but also for the Russian communities in what is today Alaska. Most of that meadow, alongside the present-day Highway 10, is still farmland, although it is increasingly threatened by the encroaching urban sprawl of greater Vancouver. The Agricultural Land Reserve, introduced by the provincial New Democratic Party government in the 1970s to protect fertile farmlands, has done much to protect the precious soil built up by the Fraser over the millennia. But the temptation of the windfall profits to be had when farmland is converted to commercial or residential land, is too great for some developers. Not long ago a sign was posted in the Fraser Valley, on some of the best farmland in Canada, that read: "For Sale, Affordable Industrial Land."

Fort Langley was established for the fur trade, but it was situated on the Fraser River. It was inevitable that salmon processing would start in the earliest days of the fort. At its original location—what is today known as Derby—and at the present site of Fort Langley a short distance upriver, the salmon business was a brisk one. The Qw'ontl'en (Kwantlen) and other Fraser River Sto:lo peoples caught the fish, and were hired to cut it for drying and salting.

It was at Fort Langley that on November 19, 1858, the colony of British Columbia was officially proclaimed by representatives of the Colonial Office in England. It rained on the ceremony, which was moved inside. There, about a hundred people watched Governor James Douglas administer the oath of office to Matthew Baillie Begbie as Chief Justice, who, having been sworn in, then administered the oath of office to Douglas as Governor. A good part of the reason for the declaration of British Columbia was to stop the United States from taking over the land. Officials had already been concerned with questions of defence where the Oregon Treaty of 1846 had established a compromise boundary, and in 1858 their fears had been intensified when gold was discovered in the Fraser's upper reaches and 20,000 American gold-seekers and hangers-on flooded into Canada.

That same year, Douglas decided to situate the capital at Fort Langley (today's Derby). But in January 1859, Colonel Richard Clement Moody of the Royal Engineers persuaded Douglas to change his mind, as the site would be hard to defend against an American invasion. Moody chose Mary Hill, which he named for his wife, just below the Pitt River at the junction of the Coquitlam and Fraser rivers. But he in turn was dissuaded by one of his officers, Captain Jack Grant, who favoured the present site of New Westminster, 7 miles (12 km) downriver from Fort Langley. That location received more tide, so big ships could reach it more easily, and Grant thought it could be better defended against attack from the south.

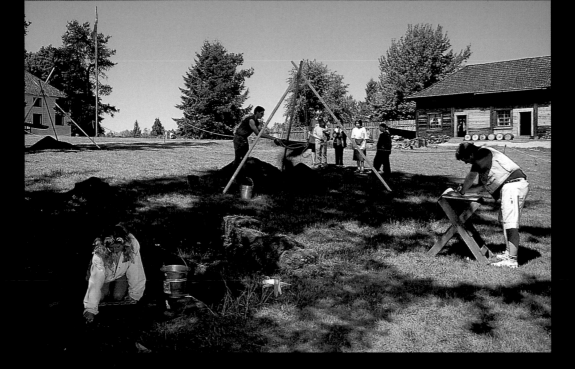

Archaeologist Doug Hudson has been conducting a dig to locate the base logs of historic buildings at Fort Langley to assist in reconstruction. The site is being restored to its condition in 1858, when the mainland colony of British Columbia was formed with the lowering of the Hudson Bay Company ensign and the raising of the Union Jack.

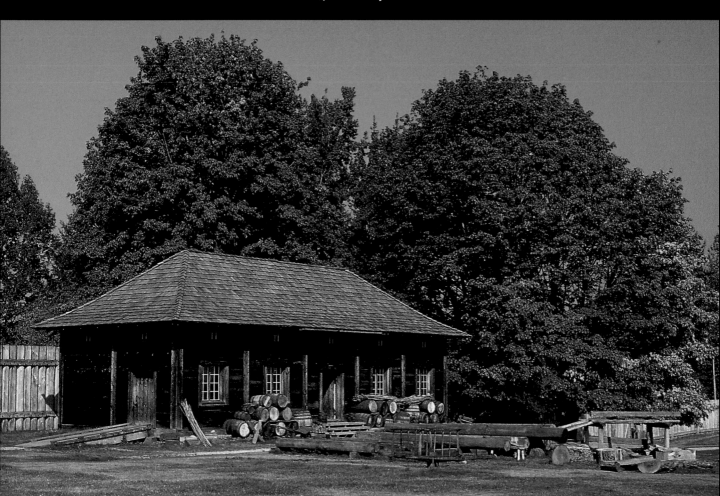

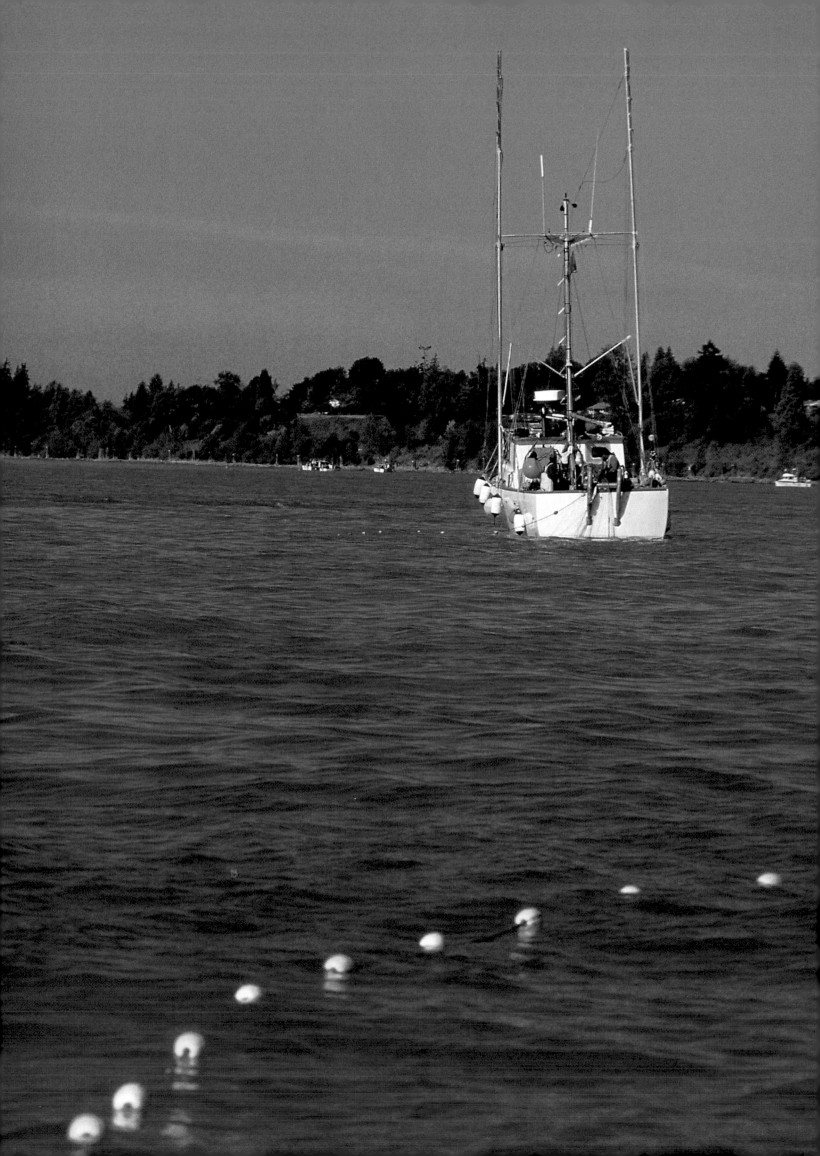

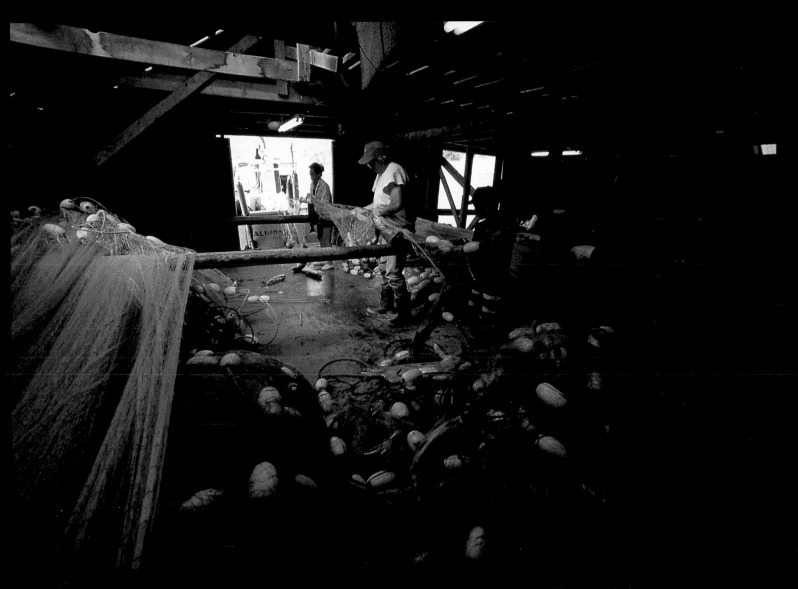

Gillnetting has been the method of commercial harvest of salmon on the lower Fraser River since the last century. Today the number of boats is such that fishing is often permitted for only a few hours at a time. Gillnetting gear presents problems: it catches nontargetted species, such as steelhead, by the gills. In 1996 an experimental fishery employing a drag seine for chum salmon along the shore was initiated by a group of Native and non-Native fishers. This method allows the live release of nontargetted species.

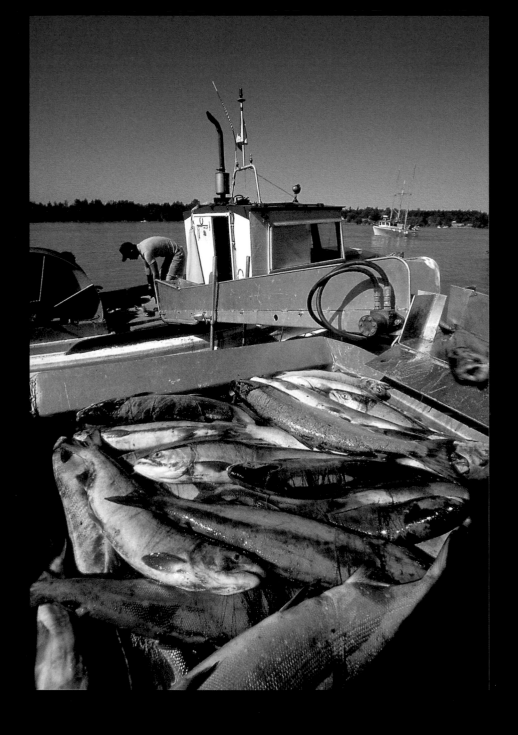
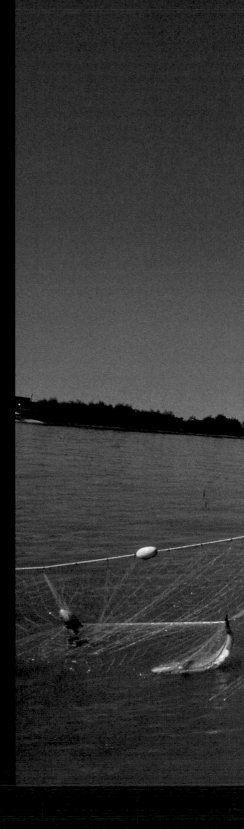

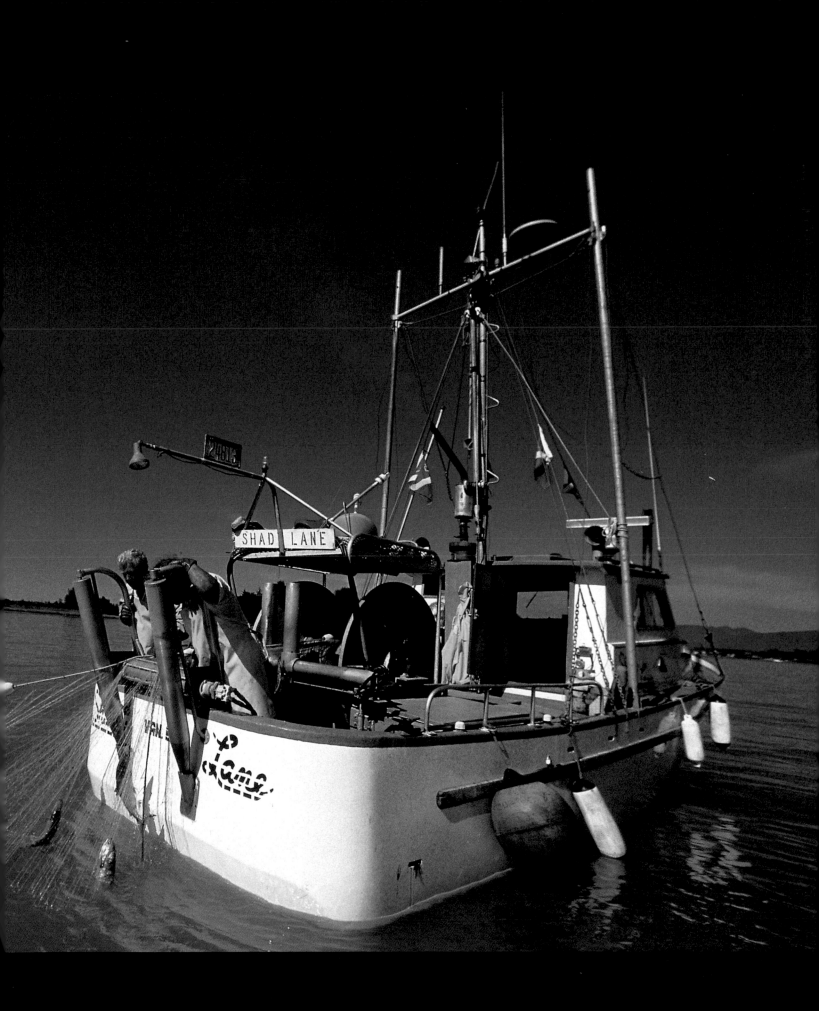

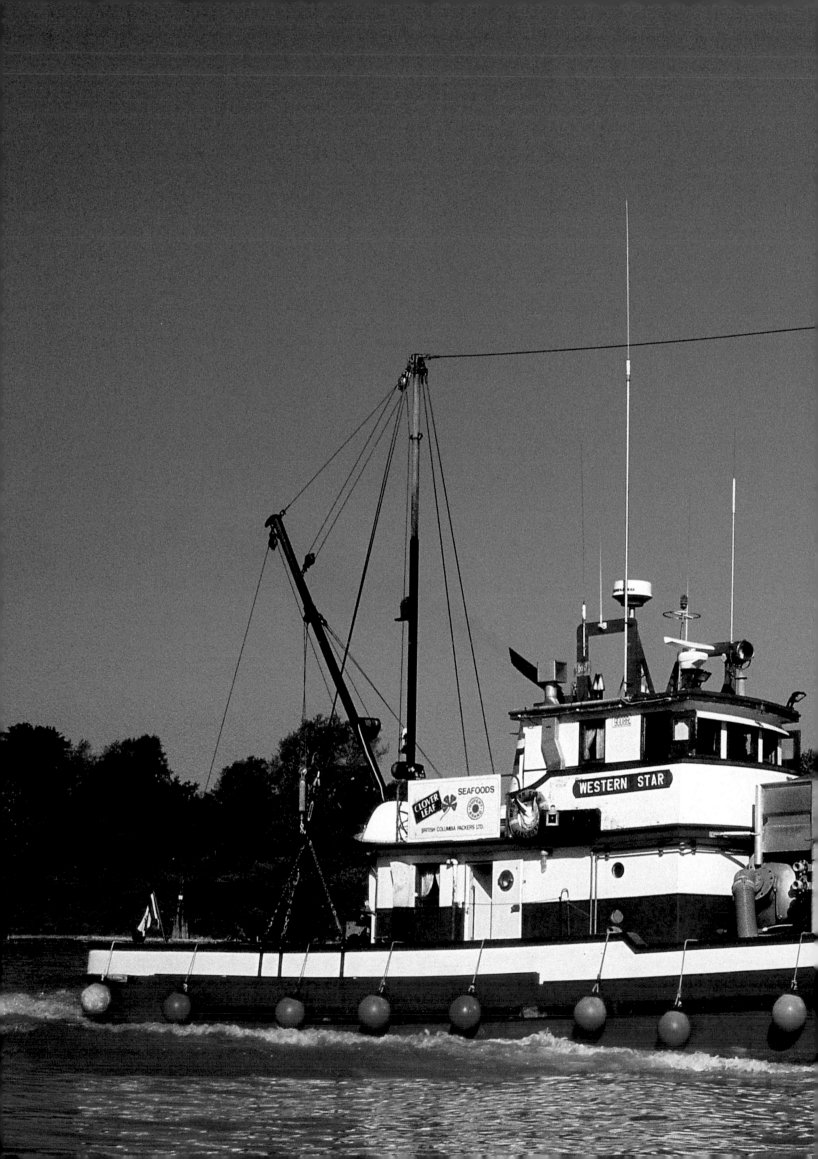

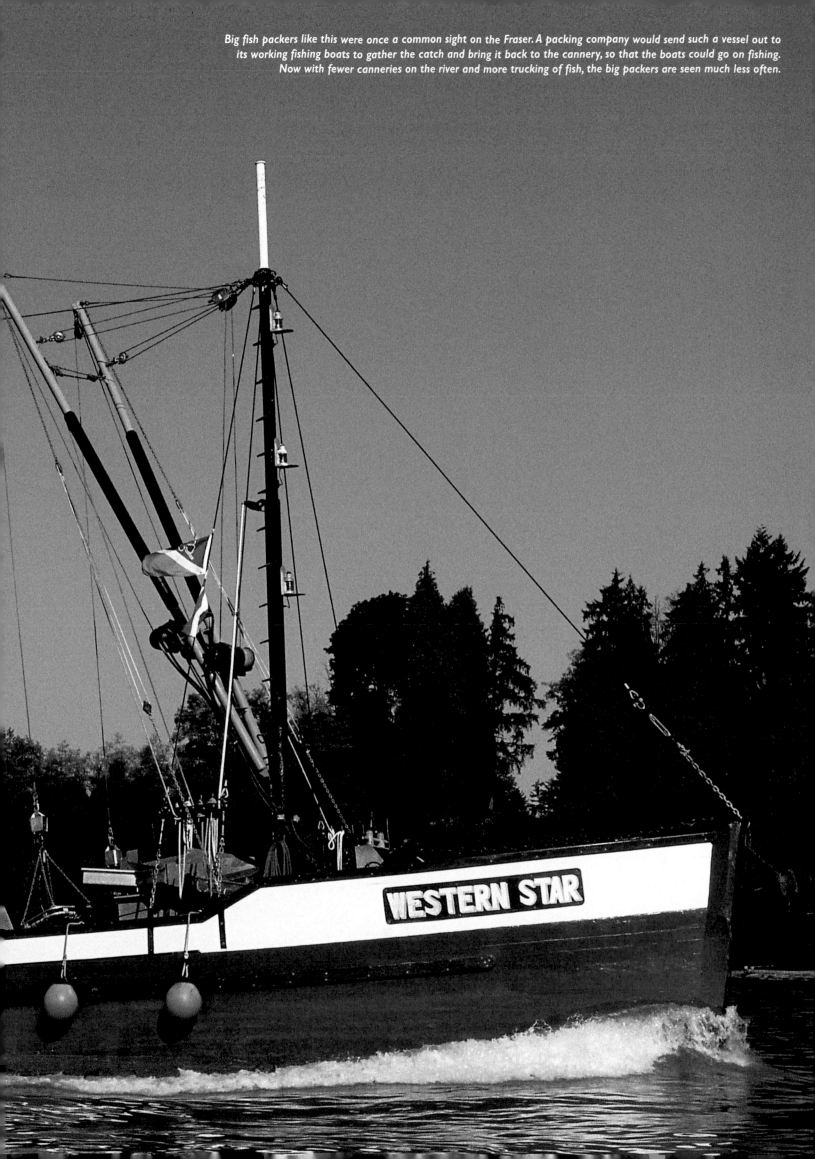

Big fish packers like this were once a common sight on the Fraser. A packing company would send such a vessel out to its working fishing boats to gather the catch and bring it back to the cannery, so that the boats could go on fishing. Now with fewer canneries on the river and more trucking of fish, the big packers are seen much less often.

In 1868 Victoria was chosen over New Westminster as capital city, following the amalgamation of the two colonies of British Columbia and Vancouver Island. Over time the threat of an American invasion receded, but New Westminster's relation to the river has endured. The opening of the Panama Canal in 1914 helped the port of New Westminster to prosper, and it continued to grow into the 1960s and '70s, when increased use of containers and bulk shipments demanded a different style of port, dominated by large paved areas and cranes. In the 1980s, the waterfront at New Westminster began the conversion from industrial to residential, and the sites that Moody identified as "most coveted as commercial" are now lined with apartments and condos fronted with a boardwalk on the river side. The quay that Moody mentioned has become a fine market and restaurant complex.

Unlike Vancouver, Burnaby, Richmond and Surrey, all of which are built along the banks of the Fraser, New Westminster is a town shaped by its river—literally. The streets elsewhere in Greater Vancouver are laid out on a north–south and east–west grid, but New Westminster streets are oriented to Front Street, which runs along the natural lay of the river. And through all the changes to the waterfront, the city has tended to its working river.

You can still see decades-old remnants of New Westminster's working waterfront. At one of them, Westminster Marine, log barges are moored for repairs and small tugs are lifted bodily from the water. Work in the log-filled river often results in bent propeller shafts, and bringing the hard steel of a shaft back into perfect alignment is a special challenge. Joseph Morell knows how to do it. His lathe is just a few feet from the brown waters of the Fraser, and he works just a few yards from where he came ashore in 1968. The day I met Joe, he was repairing a propeller shaft 5½" (14 cm) in diameter that was bent in three places. He had it mounted on a lathe and was alternately applying a torch to heat it and water to cool the high spots in order to ease the shaft into alignment. Joe has worked in this shop for some thirty years. "Have you been at this very lathe all that time?" I asked. "Well, no," he replied, pointing at a second lathe nearby. "Sometimes this one, sometimes that one."

Joe's shop is unusual—most of the waterfront has changed radically in recent decades. But plenty of riverfront space has been allowed for Westminster Tug's fleet of boats, which dock ships at the Fraser Surrey Dock just downriver on the south shore. A few hundred yards from the waterfront is the dock of Russ Cooper's Westminster Towing, which operates in association with the Cosulich family's Rivtow Marine, owners of the boats that tow up on the Harrison. Family continuity characterizes much of the Fraser towing business. People who live in riverside apartments or who sip cappuccino at New Westminster Quay can spend whole days watching the working boats of Russ Cooper and his crews, and the working boats of the Catherwood, McKenzie, Forrest and Stradiotti families.

New Westminster is the point at which the Fraser River splits into three "arms," or channels, as it makes its way around Annacis and Lulu islands (both of which are Fraser deltas) on its way to the sea. River traffic converges here, which is why it is such a good viewing spot. More than one towboat aficionado comes to New Westminster to take a room at the Inn at the Quay. Set out over the water just at the junction of the three arms, the Inn is one of the finest spots on the continent for watching a working river. The main arm brings the deep-sea ships up the river, and the North Arm is a towboater's channel.

For most towing companies, the main source of work on the river is yarding log booms from storage to mills. On a flood tide it is usual to see several 40- to 50-foot (12- to 15-m) tugs taking advantage of the inflow current to tow booms from the lower reaches of the North Arm of the Fraser, around Point Grey in Vancouver, upriver to the mills. In the same way, ebb tides are often used to assist downriver tows. Wood chips, an important by-product of the mills, are loaded on barges that also provide a good bit of work for the river tugs. Deep-sea freighters such as car carriers need assistance from tugs as well. At the Fraser Surrey Dock, the tugs help bring in the specially built carriers of forest products.

These deep-sea ships take on their Canadian pilots when first entering Canadian waters near Vancouver Island; if they are entering the Fraser River they take on a river pilot off the Sand Heads, the point where the silt banks drop off to deep water at the mouth of the river.

Where the Fraser Surrey Dock is now, there used to be a grain elevator with a spur of railway built down to it. And before that, there was a small group of Norwegian fishermen who made their living on the Fraser. They built a little pier out on the water, which created a back eddy, which began to collect sand. Then a man named Gunderson brought in a scow to sell fuel from, and in time the scow sank and added to the buildup of sand and silt. Before long there was a significant tail of sediment behind the pier, and with a little work infilling and building walls, a small island was created. Some say it was claimed by the fishermen, and others say it wasn't because they didn't want to pay the taxes. In the years following, the top end of the island was connected to the mainland, and Gunderson Slough and the little fishing community of Annieville became a home base for a group of Scandinavian fishing families. Much later, fill was added upriver from Annieville to create the modern docks. But Gunderson Slough still provides moorage for a fleet of salmon gill-netters and seiners, as well as a number of halibut and black cod longline fish boats with names like *Viking Spirit* and *Viking Joy* which honour their Norwegian ancestry. Some families have lived around the slough for four generations. The city of Surrey has crowded the shore side and the deep-sea dock crowds the river side, but people still mend nets and paint boats in Gunderson Slough.

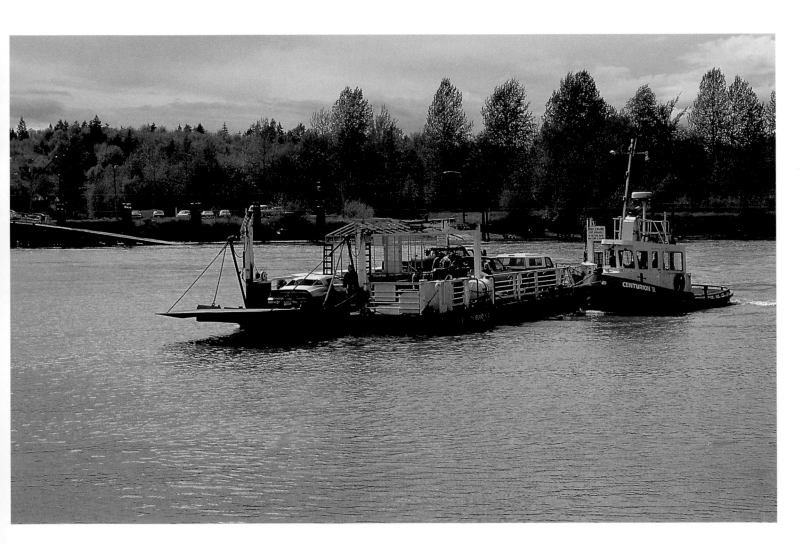

Barnston Island, located between Surrey and Maple Ridge, is served by a simple ferry—a ramp barge pushed by a tugboat, which is tied alongside.

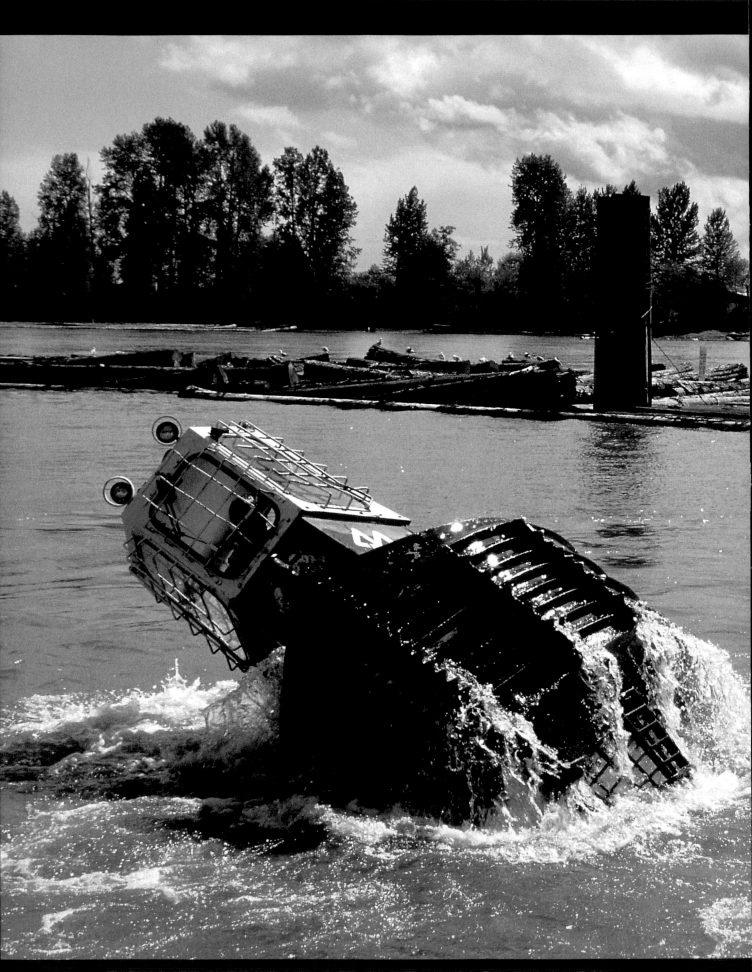

The Fraser is still lined with sawmills, and much of the river traffic serves them. Boom boats, also called log broncs, shepherd logs from the booms into the conveyors at the mills. A boom boat has "teeth" which keep the logs from slipping away, and it is built deep with powerful diesel engines set low so that they can manoeuvre quickly without capsizing.

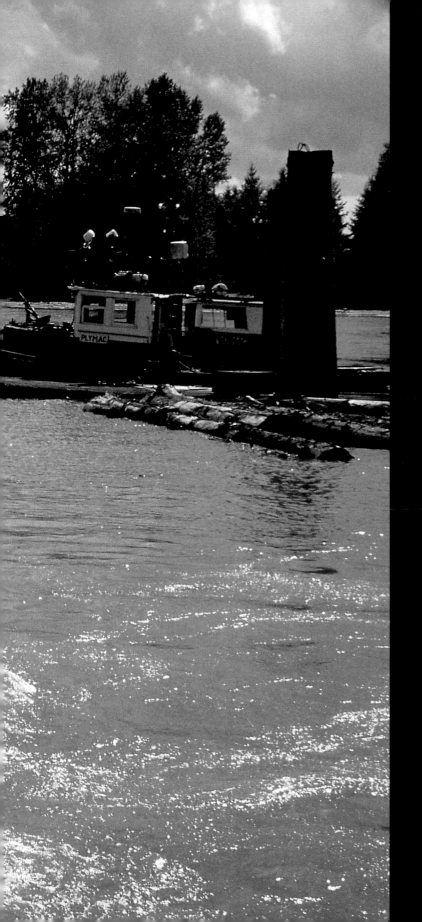

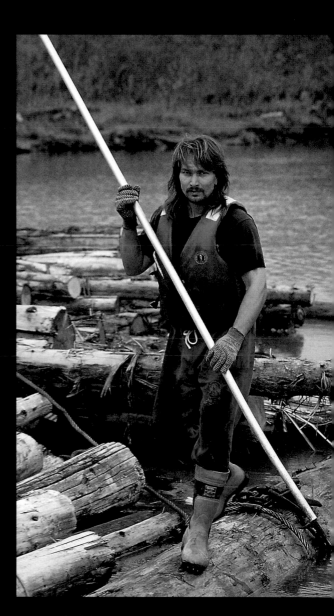

*Caulk-booted boom men like Randy Arden assist
the log-herding process with pike poles.*

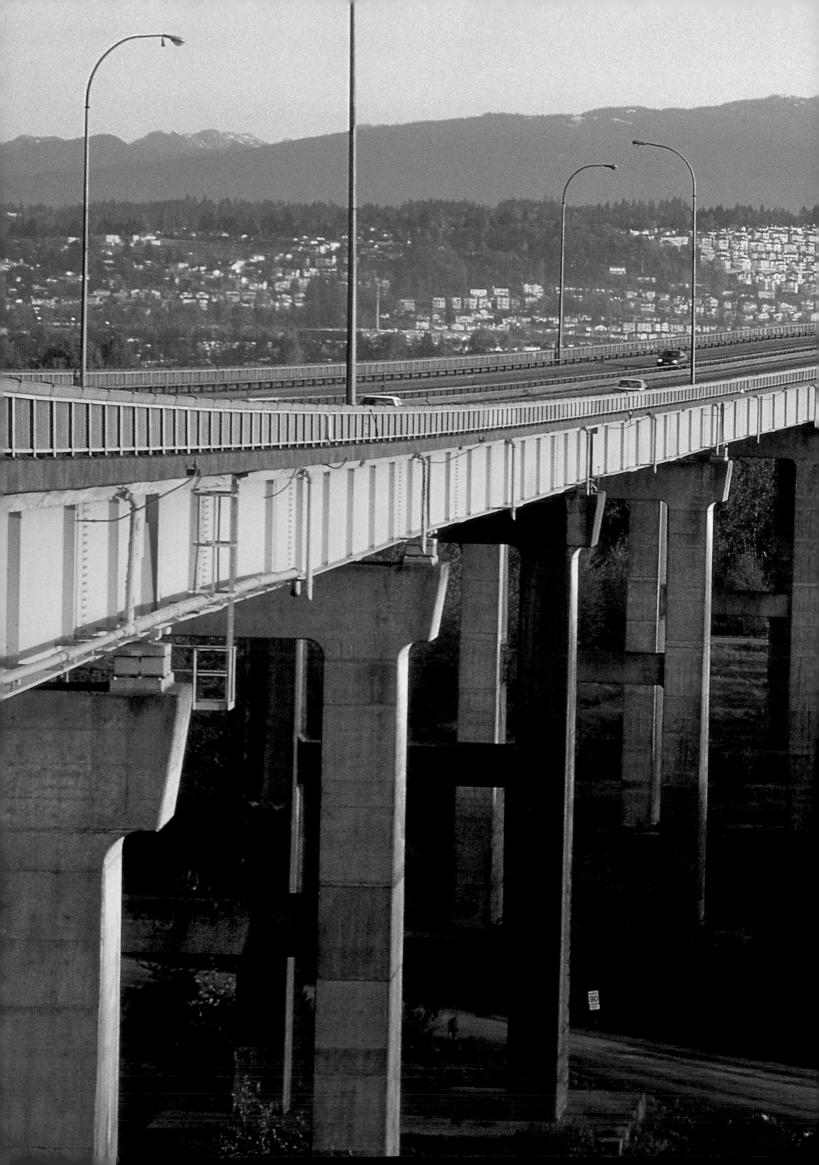

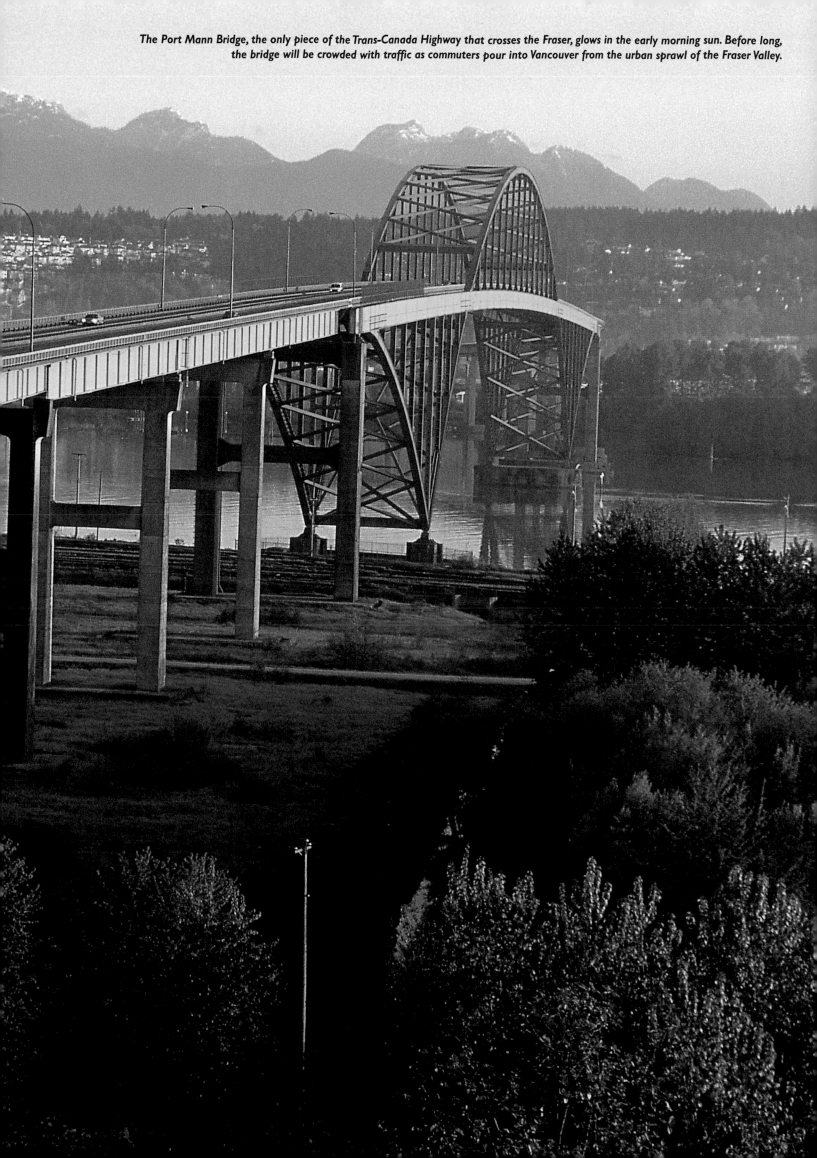

The Port Mann Bridge, the only piece of the Trans-Canada Highway that crosses the Fraser, glows in the early morning sun. Before long, the bridge will be crowded with traffic as commuters pour into Vancouver from the urban sprawl of the Fraser Valley.

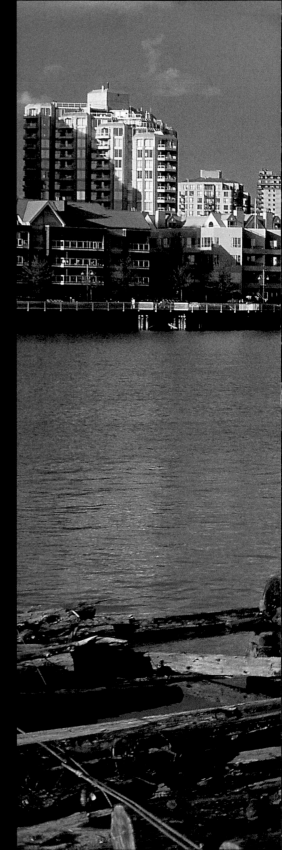

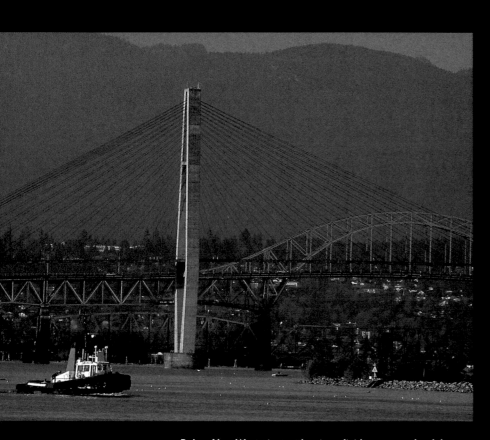

Below New Westminster the river divides among the deltas, so three bridges have been built here, one each for light rapid transit (closest bridge), railway and automobile traffic.

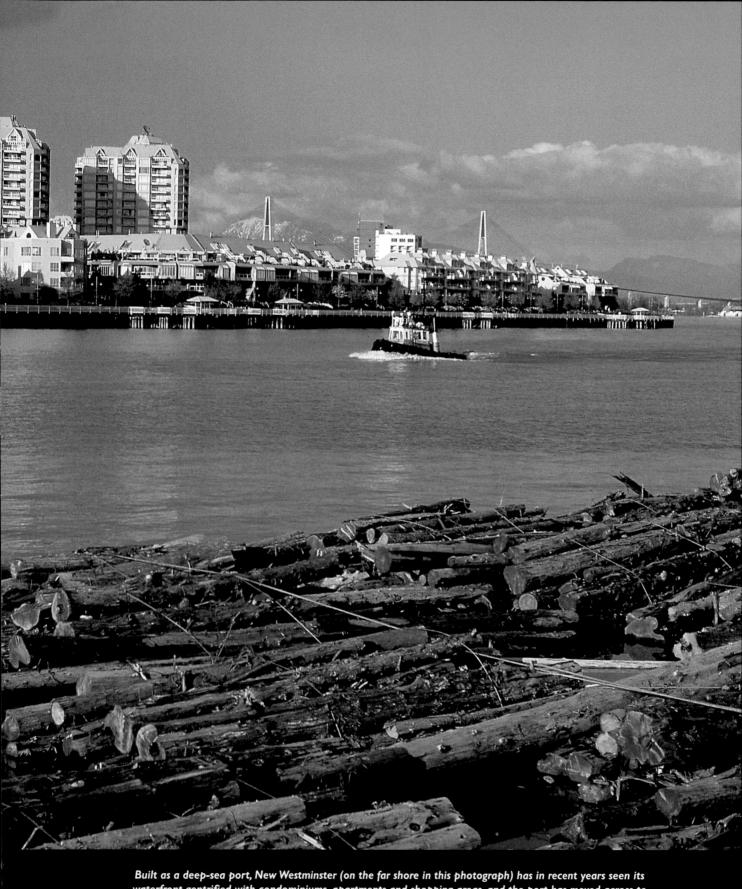

Built as a deep-sea port, New Westminster (on the far shore in this photograph) has in recent years seen its
waterfront gentrified with condominiums, apartments and shopping areas, and the port has moved across to
the south side of the river at the Fraser Surrey Dock. But New Westminster was always a river town, and it is
aware of its working river. This is still one of the best spots to watch towboats in action. The logs in the foreground are a typical sight along this part of the Fraser--booms from upriver and upcoast still make up much
of the river's commercial traffic.

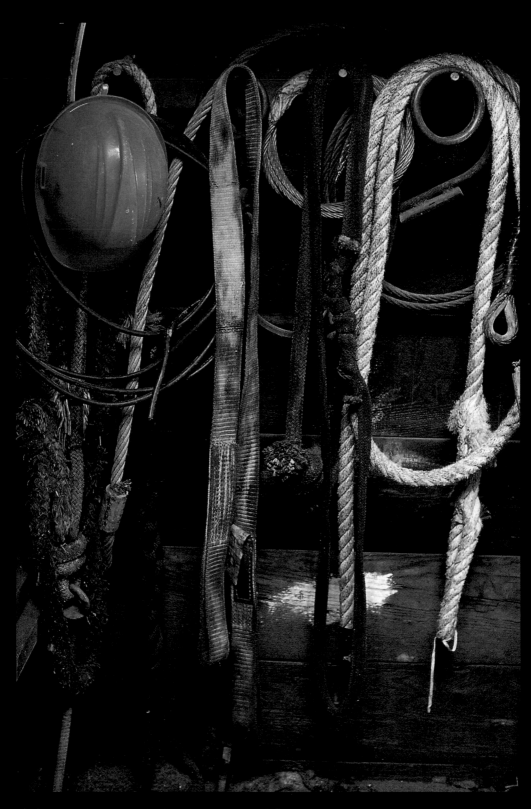

At Tom-Mac Shipyard on the Fraser's north arm, a skilled craftsman works on the massive timbers of the keel and forefoot of the Corregidor, a fifty-year-old seine boat. The tools of his trade are still simple.

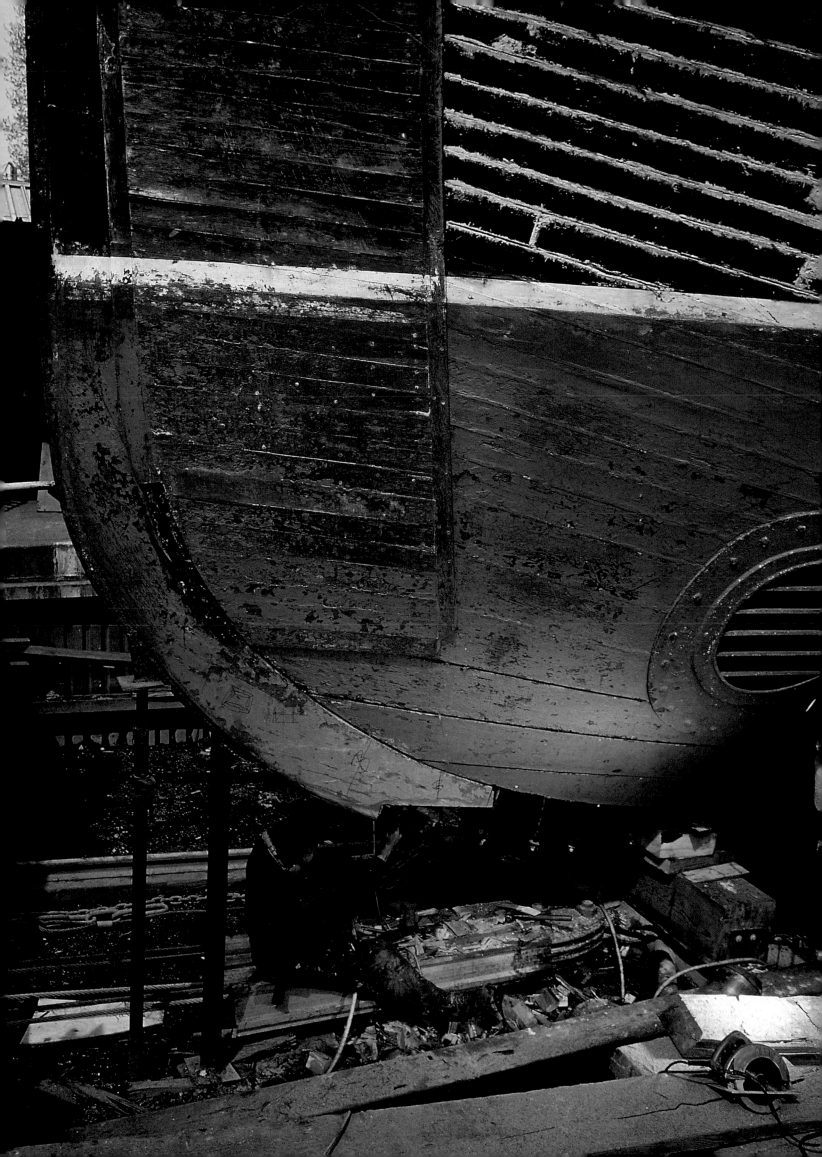

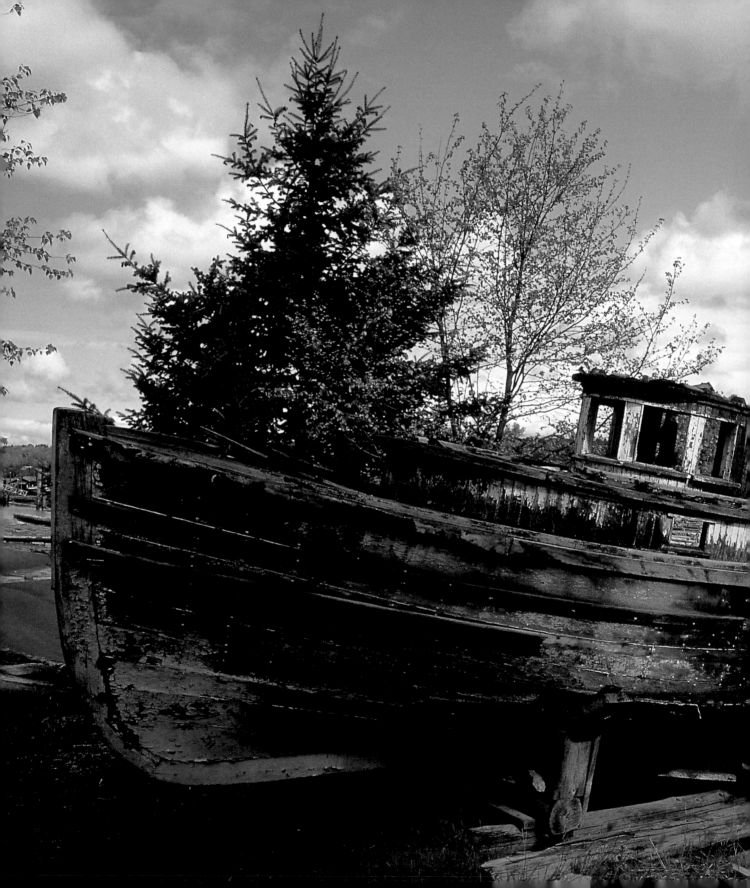

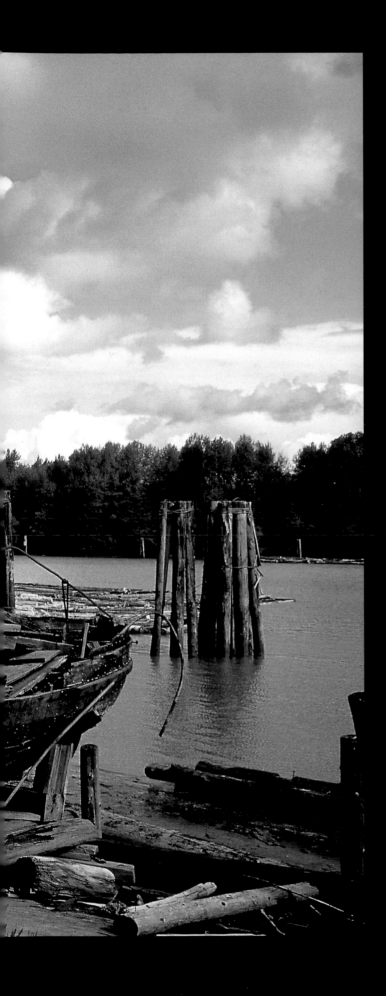

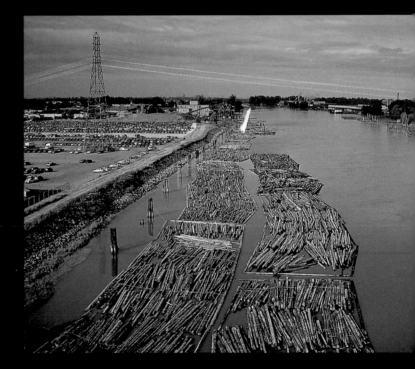

Beside the river a classic 1930s era gillnetter (left) is gradually disintegrating into the delta as her rotting planks become a part of the delta, while on the North Arm (above), new logs await transformation to lumber.

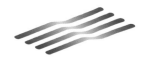

A few miles downriver from the Alex Fraser Bridge, the busy George Massey Tunnel takes highway commuters from Tsawwassen and White Rock under the main arm of the Fraser, to and from the Vancouver area. The four-lane tunnel was constructed by sinking six 2100-foot (650-m) concrete sections into the river, deep enough that there was still 40 feet (12 m) of water over them to allow passage for deep-sea ships. At this point in its life, the Fraser River moves through very flat land with no naturally elevated bridge approaches, so the tunnel was the most practical way to provide a river crossing that didn't impede shipping. Opened in 1959, the tunnel created a direct link between the United States border and downtown Vancouver. It also opened up still more farmland to development and brought the little fishing community of Ladner, previously serviced by a ferry from Lulu Island, closer to Vancouver.

On the Lulu Island side of the river, the old ferry docked at Woodward's Landing, named for an early settler, William Woodward, who built good-quality gillnet skiffs there and sold them to fishermen and canneries for about $45 each. The little ferry *Delta Princess* has been gone from Woodward's Landing since the tunnel opened, but today it is the site of the BC Ferry Corporation's repair facility, so the tradition persists.

And the Woodward name lives on, just below the George Massey Tunnel. Here there is a particularly good deep stretch of river that gillnet fishermen like because they can set their nets at the top end and drift down with the current, not worrying that their nets will be snagged on the bottom or twisted by cross-currents. Marked on marine charts as Woodward Reach, it is also known to gillnet fishers as the Finn Drift.

South of the tunnel are some small islands, and behind them more marshy islands and sandbars, which form a great grassy area of brackish shallow waters. This is a wonderful transition place for ocean-bound salmon fry in spring and for southbound birds in fall. It stretches south and west 2 miles (3 km) to the little fishing community of Ladner, where modern condos and floating homes crowd fishers' net lofts and piers from the dykes along the river.

Just downriver from Ladner, the slim ridge of Gilmore Island lies along the north shore, separating the main river channel from Finn Slough, a fishing community known to tourists as a pleasant jumble of small houses and a net shed on stilts and floats. Gus Jacobson likes to take his granddaughters with him when he goes down to the slough to work around his gillnet boats. They are the fifth generation of residents there, and he wants to show them how things are done. These waters, where Gus's granddaughters help him rack the nets and put fish in the hatch, are the same waters where he sneaked out with his dad's little rowboat to fish oolichans when he was eight years old. They are the same waters to which his own Finnish-born grandfather came in 1892. They were good and productive waters a century ago, and other Finns came to join the founder. By 1927 there were twenty-seven families in the community, some of whom had recently moved from a spot a few hundred yards downriver. They were being forced out by the threat of land tax on one side and river erosion on the other. But these were strong people, with that special mix of stamina and stubbornness that Finns call *sisa*. It was *sisa* that kept the community together through the depression and war years.

Today the families still need their *sisa*. After the last great Fraser flood of 1948, dykes were built higher and drainage was improved. In many ways, dykes are simply another form of dam, but rather than blocking a channel they block off river access to sloughs, back-waters and marshes. Firming up the line between land and water reduces the amount of rearing area for salmon fry, but it also removes habitat for amphibious animals like muskrat, beaver, otter and frogs. A dyked river becomes a faster river with the currents channelled around the land rather than spreading out over it, and the Fraser's rich silt that built the land is now carried past the land out into the Gulf of Georgia. But real estate developers profited from the dyking when they began to subdivide as much Lulu Island farmland as they could in the 1960s and '70s.

The introduction of the Agricultural Land Reserve did protect some land, but more recently, developers have been purchasing dyked riverfront properties from cannery owners. And in 1989, a Toronto developer bought Gilmore Island, the small island outside the dyked area that forms Finn Slough. He put up No Trespassing signs and had his lawyer order the residents to leave. The Finn Slough Heritage and Wetland Society, a coalition of current residents and some of the original community, who now live nearby, lobbied extensively and have managed to hold off development for the moment.

If we are to care for the Fraser River, we must understand the importance of its sensitive tidal and estuary lands, and we must realize how quickly those lands can be lost. Finn Slough is much loved for its picturesque beauty, but the most important treasures saved there are less visible. At low tide a trickle of water wends its way along the bottom mud and reveals the slough's most ancient and valuable resources, the marsh grasses. These grassy marshlands may yet turn out to be the Achilles heel of the great Fraser salmon stocks, even if all the upstream habitat is recovered, because the marsh plays a crucial role in the life cycle of the fish.

After they travel down the river from their spawning grounds in ribbon-like formations along either bank, the young salmon fry and smolts must pass a critical final period feeding and growing in the insect-rich brackish marsh waters before they are ready to strike out on the great ocean journey from which they will return as mature adults. As the grassy marshland disappears, fry and smolts are confined to ever-diminishing areas of intact habitat, where food supplies are overtaxed and the greater concentration of young salmon can disrupt the ecological balance of the food chain. Of an estimated 44,500 acres (18,000 hectares) of marshland originally in the whole Fraser estuary, less than 7,000 acres (2,800 hectares) remain. Some 300,000,000 salmon fry and smolts are now crowded together in this radically reduced space. Since these estuarine waters carry the full load of pollutants the river has absorbed throughout its length, ever-rising toxic concentrations are also a grave concern. How much higher can levels rise before irreversible damage is done? Every single anadromous fish on the Fraser spends part of its life in this small but crucial area, which means every run on the river is at risk when the estuary is not healthy.

A blue heron keeps an eye cocked for salmon fry among the delta grasses. These precious grasses are a crucial habitat for sea-bound salmon smolt, which in turn feed a number of larger fish, birds and mammals. Some three-quarters of the estuary's marshland has been removed, and while foreshore redevelopment is under way, serious damage to the ecosystem has already been done.

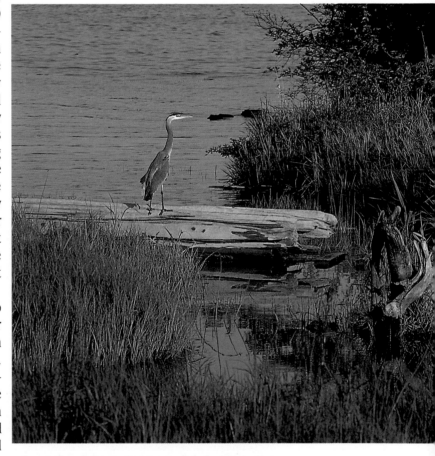

If the Fraser salmon runs are to be brought back to their former strength, or even survive at their present levels, each square yard of marshland will be essential. Some fine work has been done on fore-shore rehabilitation by various groups. The T. Buck Suzuki Foundation, in association with the United Fishermen and Allied Workers' Union, has cleaned drift, logs and garbage out of selected intertidal areas throughout the delta to improve fish habitat. But much more work needs to be done, and the pressure from developers who want to build on the foreshore continues to grow.

The George C. Reifel Migratory Bird Sanctuary, located on the small Westham Island south of Lulu Island, is an example of a successfully preserved marsh. Together with Boundary Bay, this area is an essential stop for birds migrating up and down the Pacific coast. The Fraser delta has the largest concentration of overwintering water and shore birds in the country.

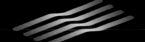

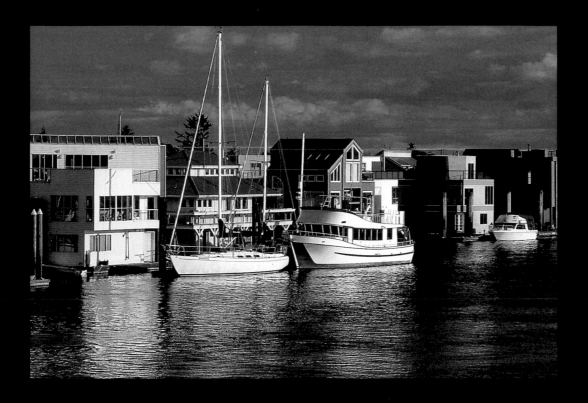

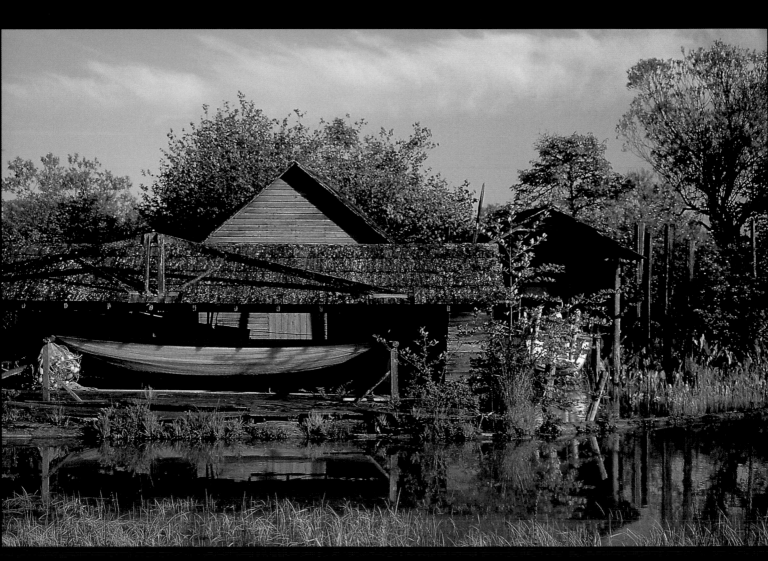

The face of the Fraser River estuary is gradually changing from picturesque backwaters like Finn Slough (lower left and right) to modern float home developments like these at Canoe Pass (top left).

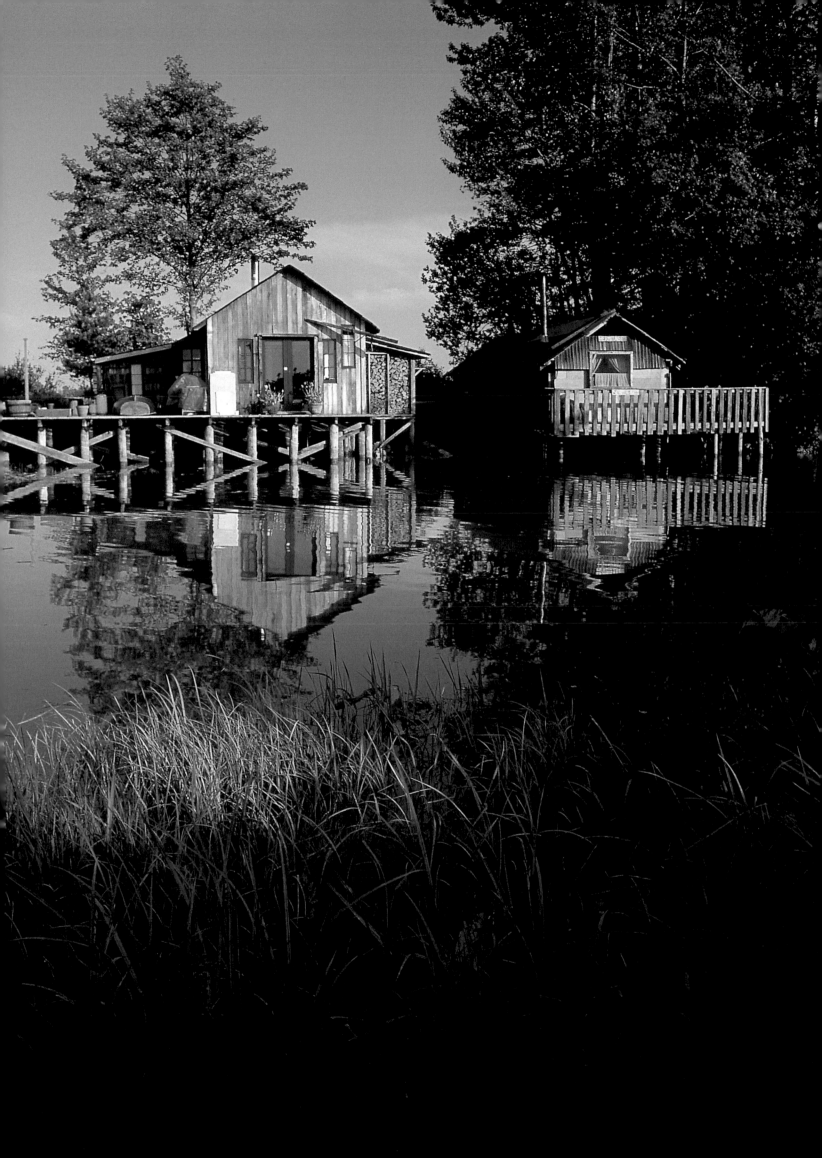

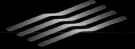

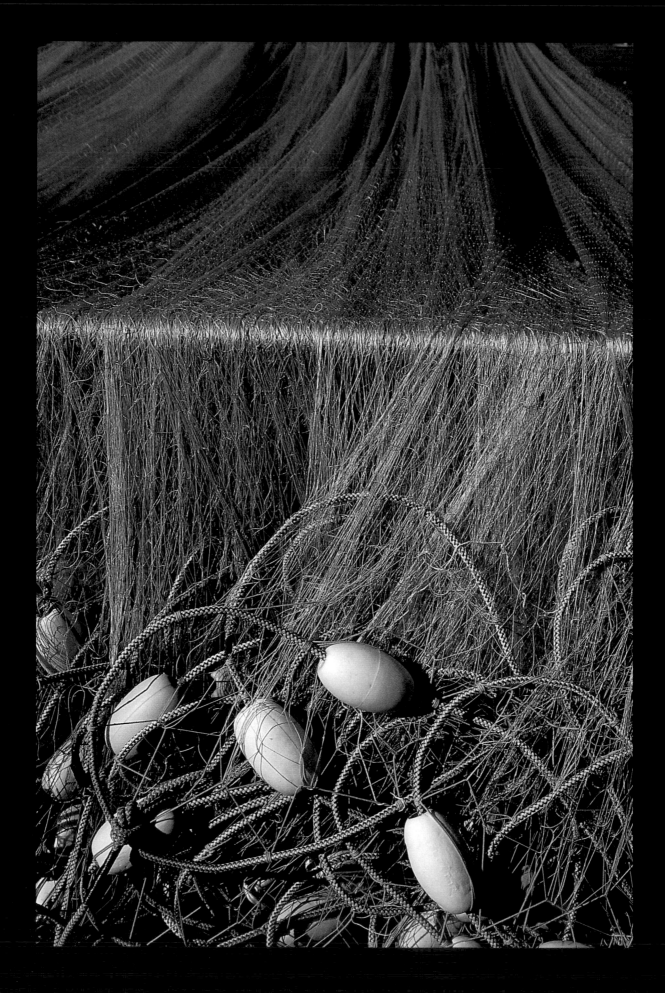

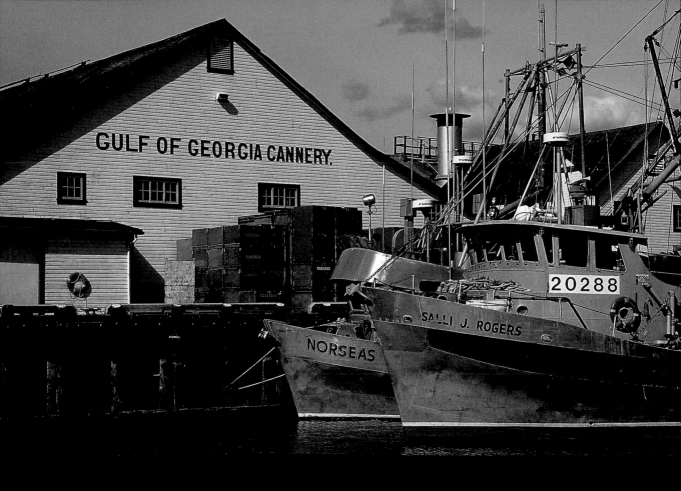

The New Cannery Row

After a concerted effort by Steveston citizens, including Mary Gazetes, retired BC Packers manager Jerry Miller, boat-builder Jim Kishi, and Harold Steves, a councilman and descendant of the founding Steves family, the Britannia Shipyard was converted to a heritage site in a public park. The central building, constructed in the traditional L-shape of a timber-framed cannery in 1889, is the oldest remaining cannery on the Steveston waterfront. In July 1889, the 200-foot (60-m) tea clipper *Titania* loaded Britannia's first direct shipment of canned salmon for the United Kingdom. But Britannia was destined to be one of the first commercial fishing casualties of irresponsible development. For some years after 1913, when railway builders blasted the side of a mountain into the Fraser River at Hells Gate, few sockeye could struggle upriver through the blockage. In a dramatic demonstration of how every part of the Fraser River is affected by every other part, the devastated salmon catch forced the Britannia Cannery out of business in 1919. It was converted to a shipyard, and continued as the working shipyard for the Anglo-British Columbia Packing Company until 1969.

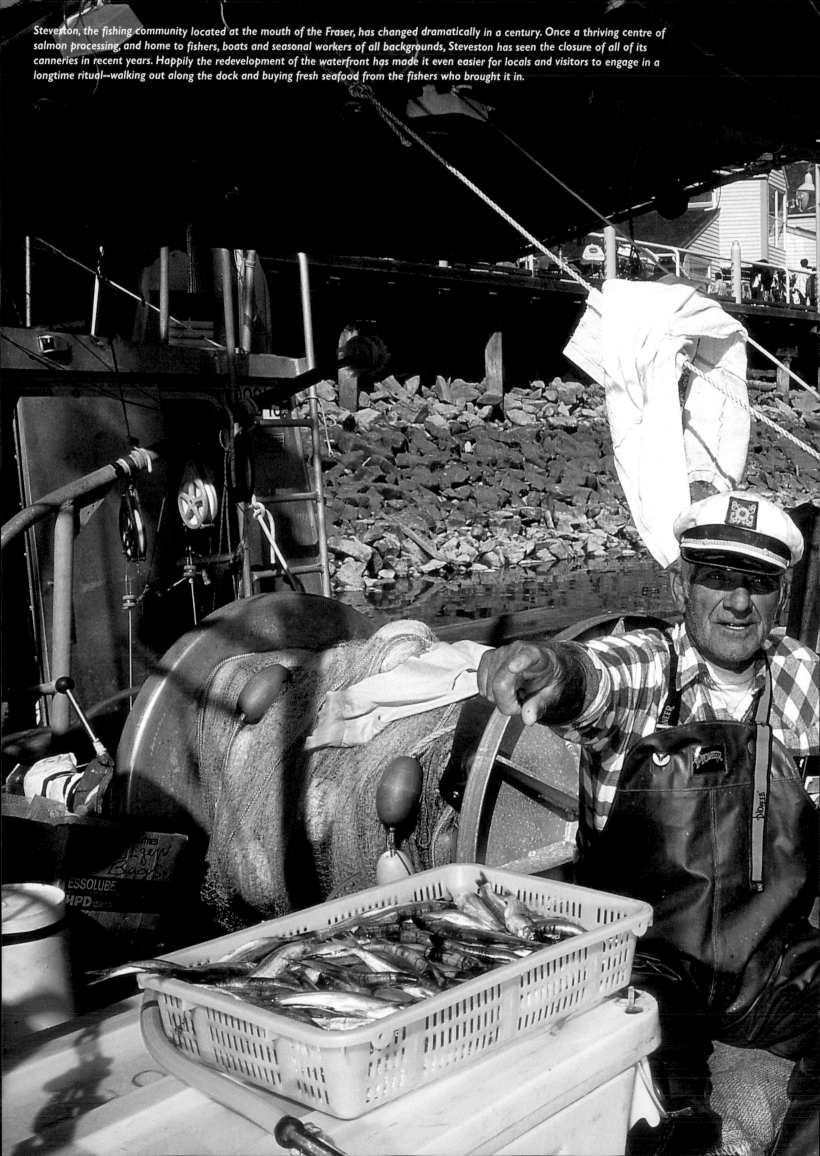

Steveston, the fishing community located at the mouth of the Fraser, has changed dramatically in a century. Once a thriving centre of salmon processing, and home to fishers, boats and seasonal workers of all backgrounds, Steveston has seen the closure of all of its canneries in recent years. Happily the redevelopment of the waterfront has made it even easier for locals and visitors to engage in a longtime ritual--walking out along the dock and buying fresh seafood from the fishers who brought it in.

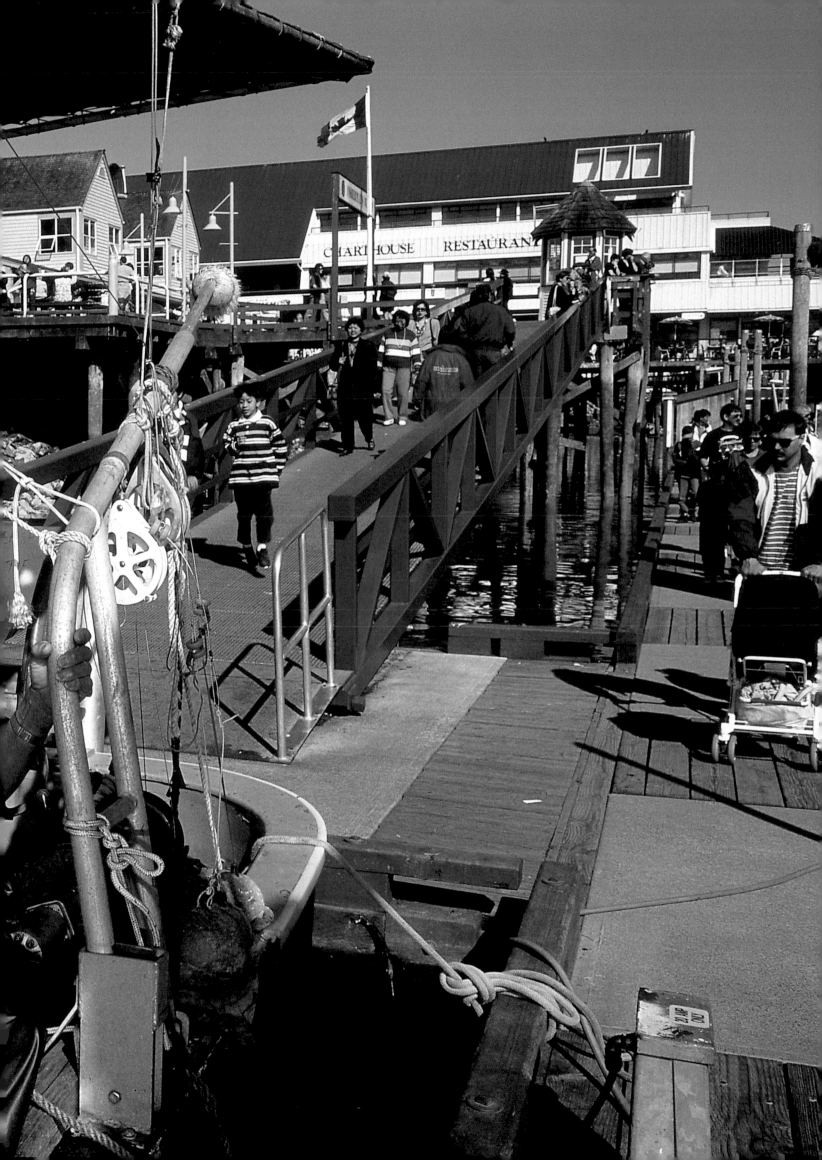

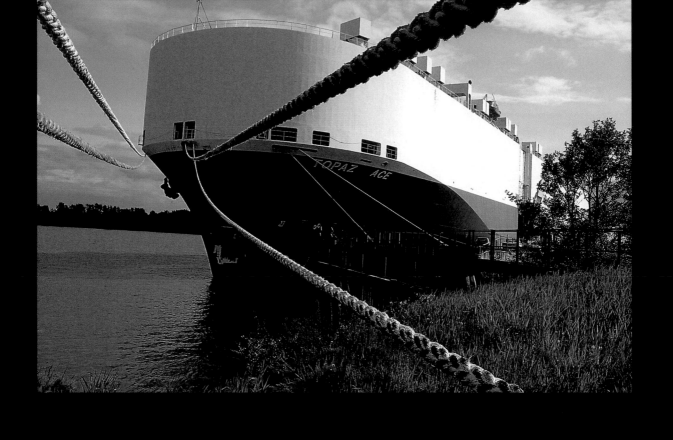

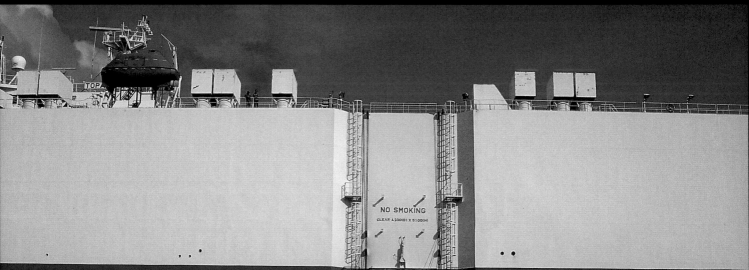

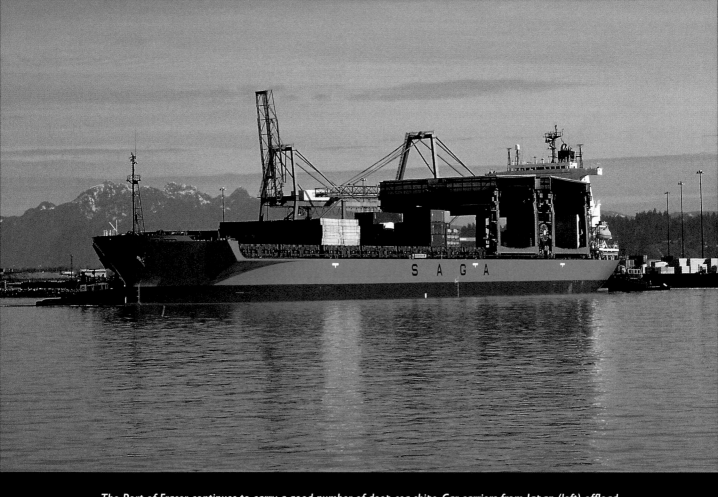

The Port of Fraser continues to carry a good number of deep-sea ships. Car carriers from Japan (left) offload vehicles manufactured in Asia, which will then be shipped by rail to dealers across Canada. Specially built forest product carriers (above) load kiln-dried lumber and pulp for transport through the Panama Canal to Europe, and across the Pacific to Asia.

Just across the Fraser's main arm from Westham Island, on the southwest corner of Lulu Island, is the town of Steveston, named for the Steves family who settled there in 1877. Located right at the mouth of the Fraser, Steveston started out as a family farmstead but by the turn of the century had grown into the capital of the British Columbia salmon fishery. A number of canneries were built at locations farther upriver, but Steveston's cannery row grew from three canneries in 1891 to a dozen by 1897.

I first came to Steveston as a deckhand on salmon and herring seiners in the 1960s. When it was time to come in after we'd been fishing up coast, we would go to Steveston first. We'd steer the boat east across the Gulf of Georgia and set course straight for Mount Baker, which would bring us down from the Inside Passage right to the lightship at the mouth of the Fraser. I bought my first pair of gumboots in Steveston, and drank (illegally) my first glass of beer in a bar.

The lightship isn't actually a ship and hadn't been one for many years when I first came to the river. It is a lighthouse set up on piles, on the very edge of Sturgeon Bank where the buildup of Fraser River sediments drops off to the deeper water of the Gulf. In an earthquake, they say, the whole thing would topple into the deep.

When we brought the boat in to Steveston, we would turn at the light-ship and follow the jetty, a long rock-and-pile breakwater that trains the river to follow a narrow course into the Gulf, scouring a deep shipping channel as it goes. Coming up along the jetty, we would see land at Garry Point, at the south-west tip of Lulu Island, then run up past the canneries and all the other boats to the plant for whom my skipper fished. Coming down across the Gulf I always thought of Steveston, at the mouth of the Fraser River, as the place where the fish turn left.

Now, a century later, the once-numerous Steveston canneries have closed. Declining salmon runs are only part of the reason. More and more fish are being frozen rather than canned. Corporate concentration has closed some canneries, and free trade policies have moved other processing plants to the US to take advantage of lower wages and benefits. And the dramatic increase in the value of real estate has had a huge impact on Steveston. Absentee owners have decided that developing waterfront property for suburban housing and shopping is more profitable than continuing an industrial tradition with a century of history.

For anyone who knew Steveston as the salmon capital of the world, it is sad and a little frightening to see the changes of the last decade. Until recently Steveston was a healthy fishing village, home to clusters of fish boats, busy canneries and all the little jettys and net lofts that had been worked by generations of fishermen. Small cannery houses where Japanese Canadian families lived, the old China House for contracted Chinese workers, cabins in which upcoast First Nations people camped while the men fished and the women worked in the canneries—all were part of Steveston for a century, and all have been destroyed.

Fortunately some people have had the vision to save parts of cannery row. At the west end, the classic buildings of the Gulf of Georgia Cannery are now a national park site. Toward the east end, the municipality of Richmond has restored the Britannia Heritage Shipyard as a living museum of boatbuilding skills. The 7½-acre (3-hectare) site is a public park with access to the waterfront, where several structures from the community's hundred-year history are preserved.

Ocean Going

The Fraser Surrey Dock, a massive infilled parking lot running parallel to the Fraser River along the south shore, within sight of the Alex Fraser Bridge, specializes in handling forest products. Other cargoes pass over the face of its pier, from containers of lentils to rolls of steel, but it is lumber, paper and pulp that make this a busy and important dock. A familiar sight here is the bright orange ships of Saga Carriers, five vessels built in the early 1990s to transport Canadian forest products to Europe and Asia. The ships were designed specially to take the utmost care of British Columbia's wood products. Each ship is 660 feet (200 m) long and each has ten holds with a total volume of 67,200 cubic yards (51,700 m³). The holds have special dehumidifiers to protect lumber and pulp from humid tropic climes, and the self-loading gantry cranes are equipped with a special West Coast feature—huge nylon awnings to keep rain off sensitive cargoes while loading.

A wooden gillnetter–troller combination boat from the 1960s rests in front of a much older derelict cannery building on the Steveston waterfront.

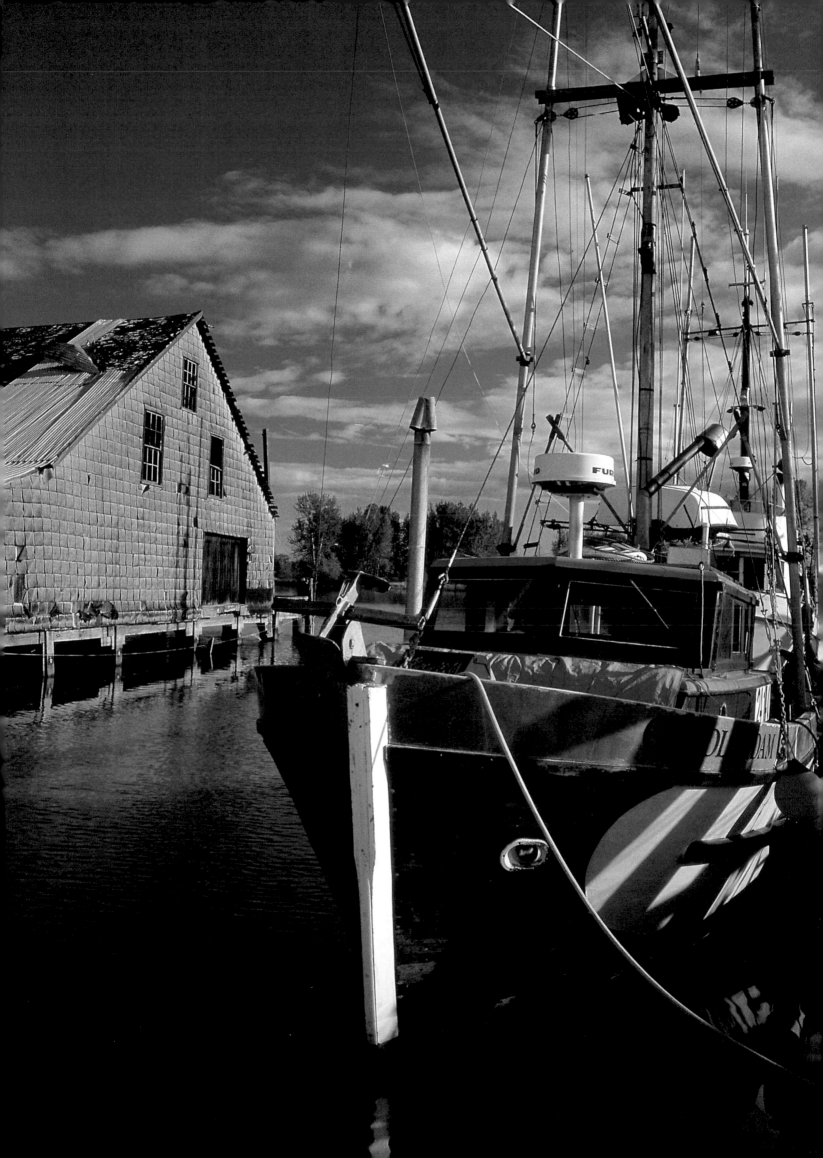

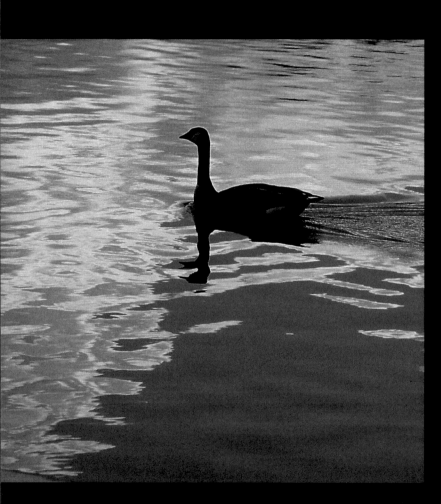

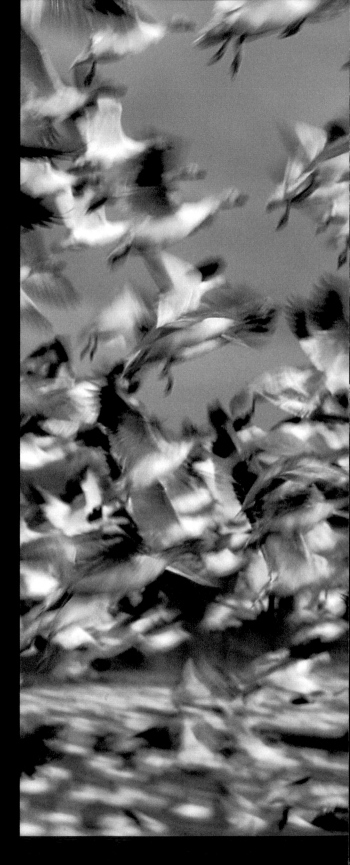

The Fraser estuary is an important stop on the Pacific coastal flyway for thousands of migrating birds. The snow geese at right were photographed in mid-November, during their brief rest stop on the shores of our river.

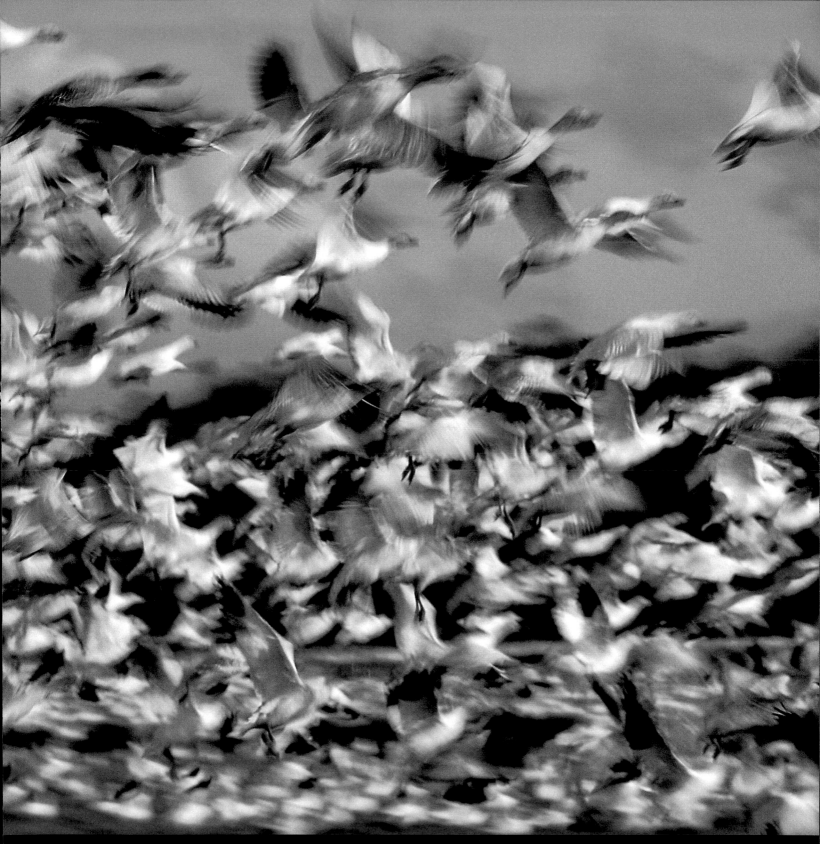

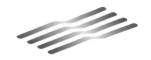

Garry Point, at the southwest tip of Lulu Island, was named by the captain of the *Cadboro* when it first entered the river in 1827. The lightship that stands there, at the "Sand Heads," marks as well as any piece of land the end of the Fraser River. But the greater part of the river's waters go on, curving along the training wall to spill out from the main arm past the lightship. South of Westham Island, other Fraser water meets the salt through Canoe Pass. North of Lulu Island and south of Sea Island, the quiet Middle Arm of the Fraser serves a busy floatplane base before joining the sea. Along the Musqueam flats and under the height of Point Grey, the North Arm follows its own jetty to the sea.

There, the Fraser's accumulated mass of water sweeps in a great regal plume out into the green of the Gulf of Georgia to brush its brown-gold along the Gulf Islands—most dramatically during spring freshet. On the ebb tide, it swings south into American waters along Point Roberts, before the flood tide pushes it north to curve around Point Grey, building the flats off Spanish Banks and colouring the waters as far north as Sechelt and Texada Island. The plume has proclaimed the river's reign over the Gulf for thousands of years. With a firm, even hand, it has transported nutrients from the interior of BC, together with the new crops of ocean-bound salmon smolts.

In recent decades, the river's regal status has been compromised. The plume has come to represent the same threat as a pollutant-spewing industrial smokestack, exhaling not into a breezy atmosphere but into a poorly ventilated room. The Gulf of Georgia's ability to cleanse itself through tidal flushing is finite, and the Fraser River continues to spew the accumulated sewage and industrial waste of its own 820-mile (1368-km) length, as well as the detritus of its tributaries. Through no fault of its own, the Fraser has become a polluter.

There is much more stress on the river along the Fraser Valley and the estuary than in other areas of BC, but the health of Fraser is being threatened along its entire length. Effluents from industry, especially mills and wood treatment plants, are legally dumped into the river even before we know what they are; and when a company finds a pollution law onerous, it can apply for permission not to comply. Fertilizers and pesticides used on farms and ranches contain chemicals that can harm groundwater. Livestock manure is overwhelming indigenous plants, agricultural lands and the water itself. Agricultural supernutrients washed into the river cause abnormal algae growths and rob the water of oxygen needed by fish.

Some of the worst problems in the Fraser Basin are caused by population growth. Sewage treatment has lagged behind the needs of our waterways, especially in the Fraser Valley and estuary. Domestic water use in the Basin as a whole increased by 10 percent between 1991 and 1994, accompanied by a proportionate increase in chemicals used to disinfect the water, much of which ends up in the river. Throughout the river system, public transit remains underdeveloped and people rely overwhelmingly on private cars and trucks for transportation. In Greater Vancouver, the number of passenger vehicles on the road has increased by 22 percent, and average trip time has increased as well. Besides damaging air quality, vehicle emissions produce greenhouse gases that can create dangerous climate change, and airborne pollutants disrupt the ecological balance of water surfaces, which carry natural nutrients, trace elements and the eggs of some fish. Vehicles are also a main culprit in street runoff, responsible for excess oil, maintenance fluids and road de-icing compounds. Add to these contaminants a domestic chemical cocktail of paints, medicines, solvents, adhesives, cleaning fluids and construction waste, and we've got a serious problem for all the waterways of the Fraser Basin.

When I was a boy, my father taught me that rivers should be treated as precious resources and endangered species. Now, I would like to be able to assure my own children that all is well, that people are beginning to understand and appreciate the river; but this is difficult when they are reading in the newspapers that in 1996, for the second year in a row, the Fraser was listed as one of the province's ten most endangered rivers. Despite some reprieves in the big battles against damming the Moran and the Nechako, and a gradually improving sensitivity to environmental issues in riverside communities, the proliferation of lesser problems has caused continued decline in the health of the system.

The good news is that, unlike the dams that have permanently deformed the neighbouring Columbia River, the problems that bedevil the Fraser are reversible, and can be remedied whenever the public decides they are important enough to demand action. Improvements in pulp mill waste management, using biological treatment and other methods to minimize and even eliminate effluent discharge have been proven elsewhere. Technology for cleaning up municipal sewage is available to any municipality whose taxpayers make it a priority. Some already have: large-scale upgrades to the Annacis Island wastewater treatment plant and Lulu Island treatment plant, serving greater Vancouver, are scheduled to be complete by 1998. The provincial government, which is technically responsible for the river, and the federal government, which is responsible for the salmon, are talking about working together to protect and rebuild fish stocks. All of this is happening, but with a painful slowness that leaves open the question whether or not solutions will arrive in time.

Those of us who have access to the Fraser are fortunate enough to know a great river that still retains much of its natural integrity. One summer evening as I neared the completion of this writing, I travelled by ferry across the Strait of Georgia. I looked west into the setting sun and saw that the flood tide had pushed the silt-laden plume of the Fraser miles to the north. As I watched, a porpoise broke the surface of the sea, its dorsal fin following the graceful arc of its dive. In the water that flowed from the porpoise's back, the red of the sunset glowed with a golden hue that came from glacial sediments laid down eons ago in the faraway upper reaches of the Fraser River, having finally washed into the living current and passed south through all those fabulous places so fresh in mind from my own travels. Having carried its life-giving sediments into the delta, the river was still reaching outward into the heart of the gulf, bestowing nutrients and supporting cycles of life beyond our ability to comprehend.

It was a glorious image that seemed to sum up all that I have found magnificent about the Fraser system in all the years I have known the river. And yet, just as my moment of exhilaration shooting the Iron Canyon rapids had been tempered by the little voice warning me not to swallow the water, this moment was tempered by a little voice asking how many more years that porpoise could go on performing its ballet in the Fraser outwash, before it drifts up on the beach, a victim of the abuses we persist in heaping on the river.

The answer is an old one and a simple one. It is up to us.

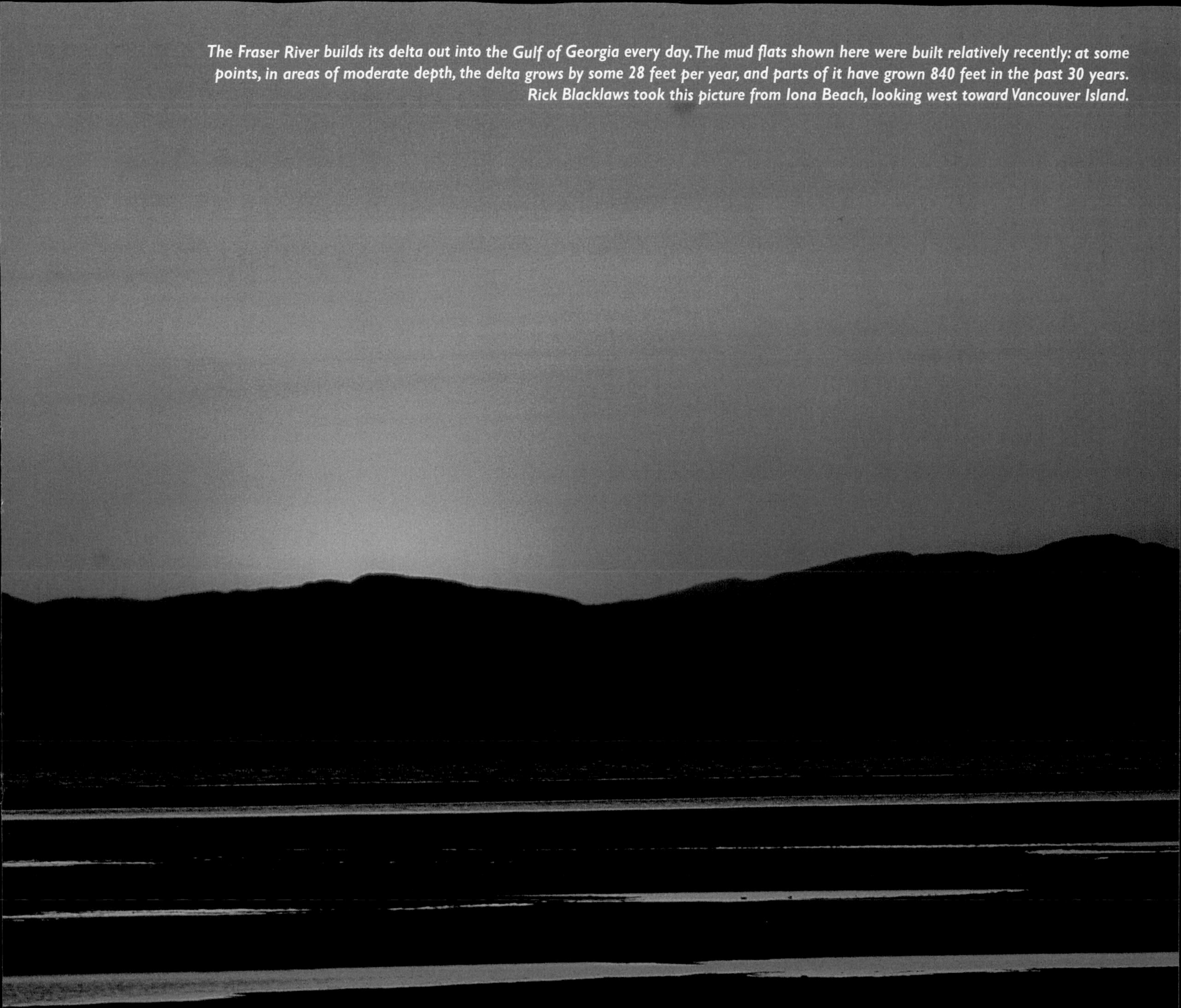

The Fraser River builds its delta out into the Gulf of Georgia every day. The mud flats shown here were built relatively recently: at some points, in areas of moderate depth, the delta grows by some 28 feet per year, and parts of it have grown 840 feet in the past 30 years. Rick Blacklaws took this picture from Iona Beach, looking west toward Vancouver Island.

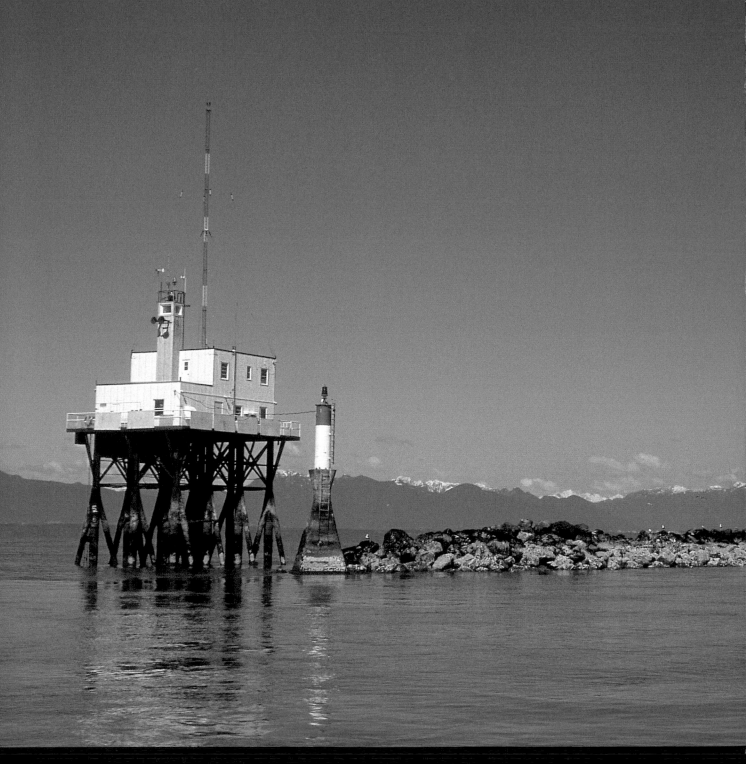

The lightship at the edge of Sturgeon Bank is not really a lightship but a light station built on sturdy piles. The light is automated now, but still flashes its warning to mariners to keep clear of the surrounding shallows as their boats approach the river's main navigation channel.

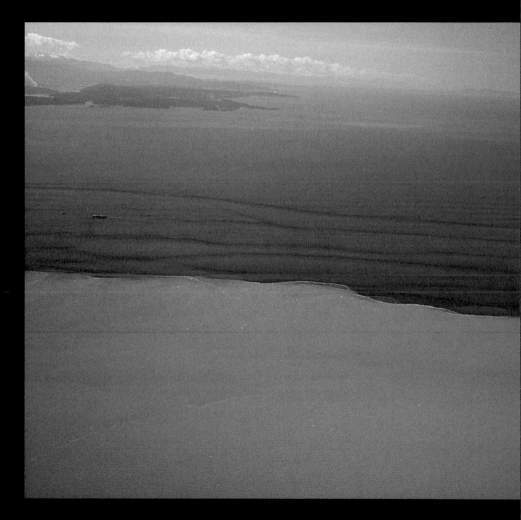

Out in the Gulf of Georgia, the tide marks the boundary between the Fraser's silt-brown waters and the blue-green of the sea. The powerful force of the Fraser pushes its golden plume well out into the seawater and brushes the edges of the Gulf Islands.

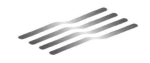

INDEX

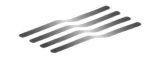

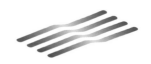

Published by
HARBOUR PUBLISHING
P.O. Box 219
Madeira Park, BC V0N 2H0 Canada

Published with the assistance of the Canada Council and the Government of British Columbia, Cultural Services Branch.

Cover, page design and composition by Roger Handling, Terra Firma Design
Photograph of Rick Blacklaws by Alan Haig-Brown; all other photographs by Rick Blacklaws.
Printed and bound in Canada

Canadian Cataloguing in Publication Data

Haig-Brown, Alan, 1941-   ʹ
    The Fraser River

    Includes index.
    ISBN 1-55017-147-X

    1. Fraser River (B.C.)—Description and travel. 2. Fraser River (B.C.)—Pictorial works. I. Blacklaws, Rick, 1953- II. Title.
    FC3845.F73H34 1996   917.1'304   C96-910514-2
    F1089.F7H34 1996

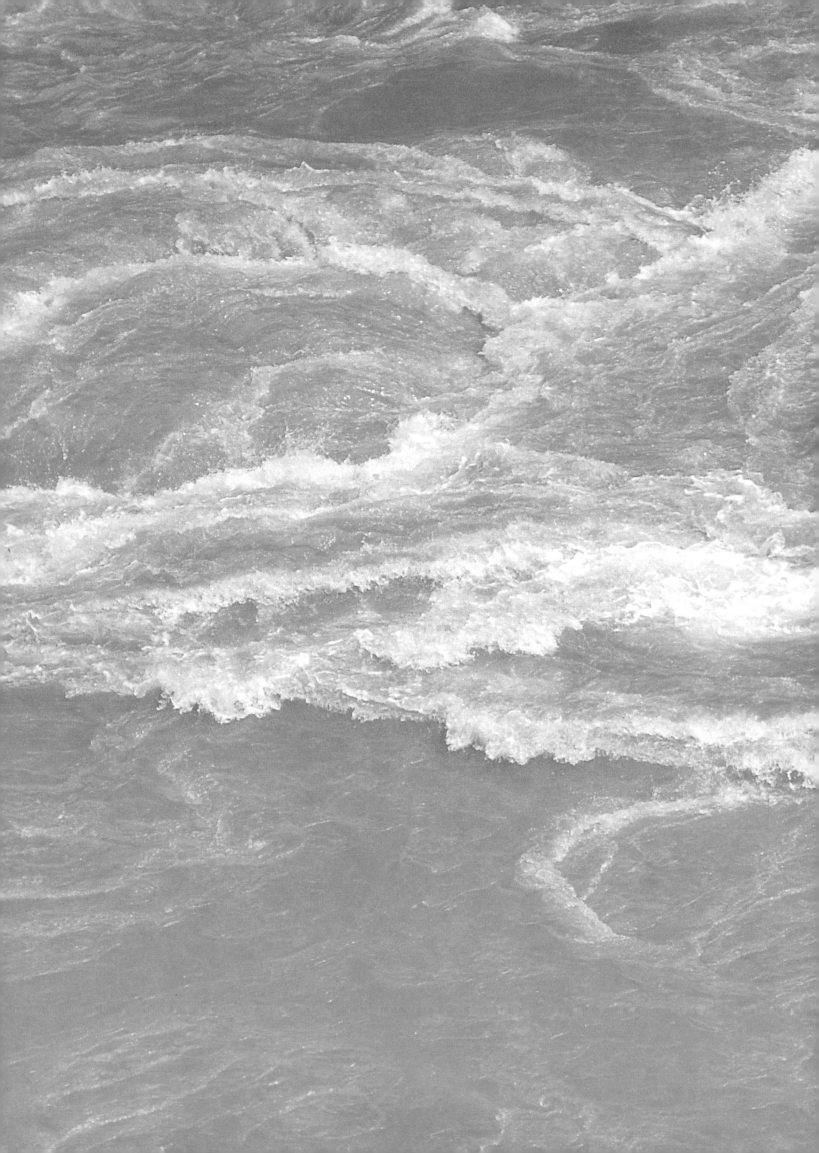